Everly Books
Publishing Press

MARSHALL FRANK

AMERIKASTAN

CONQUEST FROM WITHIN

JIHADIST PERIL IN THE UNITED STATES OF AMERICA

ALSO BY MARSHALL FRANK

NONFICTION

From Violins to Violence

Militant Islam In America

Criminal Injustice in America

Frankly Speaking

So You Want to Write a Book

The Way Things Oughta Be

FICTION

The Upside to Murder

The Latent

Call me Mommy

On My Father's Grave

Dire Straits

Beyond The Call

Messages: Short Stories For The Thoughtful

READERS ALSO LIKED

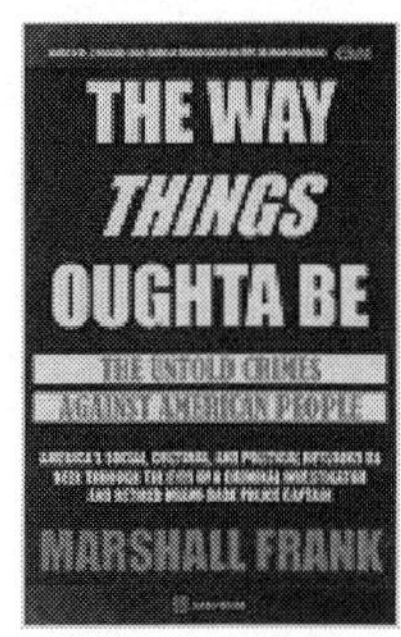

MARSHALL FRANK

AMERIKASTAN

CONQUEST FROM WITHIN

❖

JIHADIST PERIL IN THE UNNITED STATES OF AMERICA

❖

A MOSAIC

MARSHALL FRANK

EVERLY BOOKS
PUBLISHING PRESS

New York Boston London Paris Vancouver

MARSHALL FRANK

AMERIKASTAN – CONQUEST FROM WITHIN

Fist Edition
Printed In Canada

54 24 66 74 12 98 15 01 14

by

3232 W38th Ave Vancouver BC V6N 2X6 Canada
www. EverlyBooks. com

BIBLIOTHÈQUE ET ARCHIVES CANADA / LIBRARY AND ARCHIVES CANADA
CATALOGUING AND PUBLICATIONS

ISBN-10: 0-9949809-5-7
ISBN-13: 978-0-9949809-5-3

PUBLISHER'S NOTE

Book design by C. S. Douglas - Everly Books Publishing

To the children

■ EARNEST RENAN (FRENCH THINKER)

"Muslims are the first victims of Islam. Many times I have observed in my travels that fanaticism comes from a small number of dangerous men who maintain others in the practice of this religion by terror. To liberate the Muslim from his religion is the best service that one can render him".

■ JOHN QUINCY ADAMS (6th U.S.PRESIDENT)

"THE ESSENCE OF MOHAMMED'S DOCTRINE WAS VIOLENCE AND LUST: TO EXALT THE BRUTAL OVER THE SPIRITUAL PART OF HUMAN NATURE".

■ SAMUEL LANGHORNE CLEMENS a.k.a. MARK TWAIN

"That is a simple rule, and easy to remember. When I, a thoughtful and unblessed Presbyterian, examine the Koran, I know that beyond any question every Mohammedan is insane; not in all things, but in religious matters."

■ SIR WINSTON CHURCHILL (BRITISH PRIME MINISTER)

The River War 1899

"How dreadful are the curses which Mohammedanism lays on its votaries! Besides the fanatical frenzy, which is as dangerous in a man as hydrophobia in a dog, there is this fearful fatalistic apathy. Improvident habits, slovenly systems of agriculture, sluggish methods of commerce, and insecurity of property exist wherever the followers of the Prophet rule or live. A degraded sensualism deprives this life of its grace and refinement; the next of its dignity and sanctity. The fact that in Mohammedan law every woman must belong to some man as his absolute property – either as a child, a wife, or a concubine – must delay the final extinction of slavery until the faith of Islam has ceased to be a great power among men."

■ WILL DURANT (U.S. HISTORIAN)

"The Islamic conquest of India is probably the bloodiest story in history. It is a discouraging tale, for its evident moral is that civilization is a precious good, whose delicate complex of order and freedom, culture and peace, can at any moment be overthrown by barbarians **invading from without or multiplying within."**

■ MARK THOMAS WAYNE (PHILOSOPHER, WRITER)

"The militant Muslim beheads, while the moderate holds the Qur'an."

CONTENTS

ACKNOWLEDGMENTS

This book would never have been necessary if not for the bumbling political scene in all four corners of the United States. Whether it stems from a mentality of greed, ignorance or subversive ideology, our country's leaders have aided and abetted those who would manage the demise of the American way of life in future years, knowingly or unwittingly.

Therefore, I suppose I should acknowledge the bumblers and, at worst, the undying tenacity of Jihadists for making this possible.

Thankfully, there are hundreds of conscious journalists and experts (and a few politicians) who can see through the mist, who have been working hard at trying to inform the American people of the darkness that looms ahead, citing data, facts, trends and clarity. Many are named sporadically throughout this work. It is from them—and a competitive media—that a lay writer like me can drink from the well of knowledge.

Credit is due to two fine editors, Jaimie Engle and Francis J. Clifford for ensuring this body of work was fine-tuned and prepared for publication.

As well, I greatly appreciate the support of Everly Books and publisher, Chris S. Douglas, also an editor and author, for navigating this book into the marketplace.

As always, my primary allegiance belongs to a woman who patiently stands by my side, supports my efforts, criticizes, praises and provides undying love. She is the most perfect human being on planet Earth, my wife, Suzanne.

PREFACE

This was no labor of love. I did not want to write this book.

It took almost two years, stopping-and-going, rethinking, rewriting, welcoming distractions, finding other things to do while ceding to gross procrastination. It was a painful task indeed. I also figured I'd be seen by readers and critics as a conspiracy theorist nut-ball, a total whacko and perhaps – with some validity. In the long run, I had no choice but to share and convey what I had deduced because the global threat and the threat to America from diehard Jihadists and other enemy subversives has become very clear to me but unfortunately, not to others. It is more than a vision. It is so real I can feel it, taste it, smell it and see it clearly, like being afforded a glimpse of a looming catastrophe before it unfolds. And when it does, many lives—by the billions—will perish, physically, emotionally and spiritually.

I felt compelled to reveal what I see, because so many do not or could not. I had to reveal the truth because it is literally vital – in the truest sense of the word. If I knew these things, and did nothing, I would have let my country down. I would have denied my fellow Americans a point of view they needed to know.

Clichéd as it may sound, I truly love my country. Imperfect as it may be, considering our long history of wars, discrimination, bitter infighting and corruption, it is still the greatest land in the history of mankind, because we have what so many cherish around the world: Freedom. I am not only talking about the Bill of Rights freedoms, but also the freedom of self-destiny, the freedom to excel, to be who we wish to be because we are unharnessed by any fascist or hostile government.

Generations have passed since America was at war to save our culture. Most youngsters have no clue what life was like for our grandparents, our soldiers, and the victims who suffered catastrophe after catastrophe throughout Europe and Asia while America scrimped on food coupons, gas restrictions and basic commodities. Nor do they care. The only thing that matters is the *Today* mentality. We are spoiled, our kids are spoiled, and so are their kids. So many people fail to understand how horrifying life could be if we allowed our country to slip away into a state of fascism where freedoms we know today will become nothing more than a blip in the history books. Some people still remember.

When my pianist partner, Jay Barnhart, and I play music at retirement homes and senior centers (I play violin), we conclude our one-hour programs with a theme to Americana, a medley of old and new songs that represent the bedrock of national love; *Battle Hymn of the Republic, Ashokan Farewell, When Johnny Comes Marching Home, Dixie, O Susanna, Yankee Doodle Dandy, God Bless America* and *America the Beautiful.* Often, without prompting, half the geriatric audiences who can stand, will stand, eyes blurred and fixed into the distance, hands over their hearts, singing along, heads raised, loving their nation. *Oh Beautiful, for spacious skies*...a small gentleman steps forward wearing a blue Garrison cap with "WWII Veteran" sewn on its side...*for amber waves of grain*... I see his weathered lips moving, quivering... *for purple mountain majesties*...then, a tiny unsteady woman with straggly white hair rises from her wheelchair... *above the fruited plain*...suddenly the room bursts with a fragile chorus... *America, America, God shed his grace on thee*... Jay and I play at full volume, while I turn my head away to control my emotions... *And crown thy good with brotherhood*... two of the male attendants, one black, one white, step forward, their eyes welling... *From sea to shining sea.* Then, quiet.

Unique moments.

That's love for America. The way it was.

Sadly, time is passing and so are too many heroes and patriots of the greatest generation. But we can be just as great, and just as patriotic, if we venture to learn truth about those who are preparing to destroy the American dream and all the freedom that have come with it. They are a clear and present enemy, and they are at our doorstep, not only figuratively, but literally. Sadly, with rare exception, we don't even know it. The modern generation is oblivious to the reality that is staring us in the face.

If we listen only to media and to our top level government officials, we hear about "terrorism" as the greatest threat. We fail to consider that terror is but one tactic being deployed in an overall war that also includes propaganda, psychology, deceit, religion and infiltration of our cultural, economic and political infrastructure.

This body of work will take the reader through the muck by assembling fact after fact and circumstance upon circumstance to the only plausible conclusion, that we are presently losing a war that will enslave or even eradicate our children and grandchildren for time ad infinitum.

Tough words, yes.

The book will cite articles and publications within some pages, along with known historical facts, but the reader will not be presented with a glut of footnotes and glossaries. This is not a text book, nor a work of genius. I'm an ordinary guy who has a fairly extensive background in major crime investigations which has afforded me skills in assembling court cases based on evidence, be they forensic or circumstantial. Plenty of murderers have been convicted based on non-forensic evidence when the circumstances were so compelling only one logical verdict could be reached. This book is a semblance of opinions and conclusions formed by connecting dots and jigsaw puzzles together, by highlighting the events of recent times which, by themselves, do not tell a story. But when the pieces are assembled, the conclusion is undeniable. If readers are doubtful of any assertions within, they are welcome to research and challenge.

I ask readers, though it may be near impossible, to set aside their party allegiances when turning these pages. The content is not about

Republican or Democrat, or conservative versus liberal. If our enemies continue on the victory path, political parties in America won't matter any more because they won't even exist.

We are literally at the crossroads. We must change our course in order to change the course of our enemies, and the only way to do that, is to first acknowledge the existential threat. If we don't change the course, our children are destined to wake up one morning and see that their entire world has been turned upside down.

Our enemies have clearly stated their goals, but we've ignored them. They have stated their strategies, and we've ignored them. We know their plan for tactics, but we do little else than to swat cockroaches without focusing on the nest. The enemy has gained access to our deepest, darkest secrets, gorged with intelligence gathering while preparing for ultimate victory. And we still do nothing.

It's not too late. But we must become knowledgeable, and we must act, or else time will run out. Then, there will be no turning back.

Peace.

— Marshall Frank

AMERIKASTAN

ONE
A STATE OF WAR

The United States is at war. That's not a cliché. It is a fact.

We're not talking about metaphor wars, like the "war on crime" or the "war on women" or other idiotic misuses of the term. This is a solemn fight against an enemy who is warring against the United States with intent to destroy our way of life.

This is not about Afghanistan, Iraq, Libya or any other conflict involving guns, airplanes and generals. It is not a war where we are tallying dead soldiers like we count home runs and auto accidents. It's much deadlier than that. It's a war that can, and will, terminate American freedom and democracy forever. It's a matter of life and death for our nation, and for our descendants.

This author's journey through this project can barely touch on the complexities because they are so far reaching. We can debate individual issues one at a time and argue from the left and from the right. But that gets us nowhere, because we're not seeing the whole picture. We should see it as a mosaic. A myriad of colored tiles may each represent an undefined blip in the overall image, and do not form a picture until they are assembled and then, Voila! Clarity. Once the reader absorbs the entire mosaic, it all comes into focus and we can face the undeniable truth.

The story of America at war today can only be seen through a mosaic that connects dots and merges all the elements into one huge tactical picture. That's when the clouds part and the full universe becomes clear to the reader. This particular war has been waged directly against America for thirty-seven years. We are losing.

To comprehend what we face, we must think outside the proverbial box. It is more complicated than any conventional conflict we have ever known. It is a war to which our government, our media and the majority of our citizens are, for the most part, remain oblivious. Those who are far-sighted and have a keen sense of awareness are trying desperately to awaken the populous, but so many are lonely voices in the wilderness. Nothing could be going better ... *for the enemy!*

We have been privy to a plethora of warnings from a wide array of authors, scholars, experts, authorities and journalists, some of whom are brave converts (apostates) from the Islamic faith and others who are actually practicing Muslims who consider themselves more as secular, thus distancing themselves from fundamentalists. They have been specific, fact-based and heaped with warnings that support the fact that we are under stealth siege today and have been for thirty-plus years.

Yet, we ignore the threat. So many decent people seem to live and work in a daze, oblivious to the sinking ship. Naïve Americans choose to turn a blind eye labeling knowledgeable scholars and experts as partisan politicos, blathering about Republicans versus Democrats or vice versa. The stupidity is mind boggling, especially when the facts are right under our noses.

For starters, here are a few experts and scholars for readers to access for credible data and general knowledge concerning the history and makeup of radical Islam:

- David Horowitz
- Robert Spencer
- Frank Gaffney
- Nonie Darwish
- Ayaan Hirsi Ali
- Steve Emerson
- Daniel Pipes
- Clare Lopez
- Paul Sperry
- Brigitte Gabriel
- Wafa Sultan
- Walid Shoebat
- Tarek Fatah
- Andrew McCarthy
- Tawfik Hamid
- Lt. Gen. Michael T. Flynn

If we lose this war, we lose America. Our great-grandchildren will see the transformation of lifestyles, cultures, freedoms and legal systems that do not even resemble what we know today. And as the future passes, names like George Washington, Oprah, Tiger, Beyonce, Pavarotti, Martin Luther King Jr., Nancy Pelosi, Thomas Edison and Mickey Mouse will be forever removed from history books as irrelevant, as if they never existed at all. They will be replaced by the teachings of Mohammed and the Ayatollah Khomeini and the glory of Islamic history. Average grade school kids will never have heard of Mark Twain, Thomas Jefferson, or even Ronald Reagan. Cultural icons like Elvis, Sinatra, Stevie Wonder, Michael Jordan, Streisand and Lady Gaga will vanish like a burst bubble, unheard of by generations beyond the 22nd century. Libraries and hard drives will be seized and cleaned out, replaced by new ideology and skewed accounts of history. And there will be no bibles.

These kinds of things have been imposed in other predominantly Islamist nations and – when opportunity prevails – they will do it again only on a much larger scale because they will have conquered the unconquerable.

The War On Terror:

There is no such thing as a "war on terror."

When one stops to think about the phrasing of that term, it's utterly asinine. What makes this war so different than other wars is the element of stealth. The enemy's most dangerous weapon is not terror, but deception.

The enemy has no specific borders, no national government and no uniform. Within our country, the enemy hides behind a cloak of legitimacy, using religion as a shield and our own First Amendment freedoms (speech, religion, etc.) as tools with which to accomplish their mission.

In places like Afghanistan and Iraq, we engaged in conventional wars only to realize a negative outcome. Afghanistan is slipping back to the control of the Taliban while Jihadists in the form of the Islamic State of Iraq and Syria (ISIS) have seized control of Iraq. Thousands of our own brave soldiers and others from allied nations lost their lives, not to mention many thousands more of mostly Muslim people indigenous to their native land. I am sad to conclude that the conflicts in these two countries were an utter waste in human loss and suffering, plus a devastation to our economy and our international image. While we were chasing after combatants, we were actually looking in the wrong direction as the enemy proceeded quietly, stealthily, patiently toward their ultimate goal of conquest – right through our own back door.

It's like the old shell game—look here, look there, but don't look where it really is. And we—our government—fell for it.

The Islamist movement is stronger than ever, not just in Egypt, Syria, and Libya. We're talking about the entire United States, Canada, and Europe. Government leaders from all parties are too cowardly to name the enemy, so they say we are in a war against "terror." That's a safe term, invented to avoid offending Muslims. But nothing could be more absurd. To declare "terror" as an enemy obfuscates the truth. Government representatives and journalists who use that term are supporting, however inadvertently, the sworn enemy of the United States. By failing to truthfully identify the very people who are trying to destroy America, they are aiding and abetting our enemies in a time of war.

"Terror" is a tool. It is a tactic. It is one of many and varied devices used by our enemies. A war against "terror" is like saying we were at war against bullets and tanks in World War II. But in World War II, we had the courage to identify the enemy, and we won. We will never win a war unless we are willing to identify who we are fighting. That's War Education 101.

Identifying The Enemy:

The enemy of the United States and of free societies everywhere is not limited to the domain of al Qaeda. The enemy is radical Islam and the proponents of the fascist ideology that it stands for. This is nothing new. People who have studied the issue have known this for a long time. Even our government representatives know this, though too many are unwilling to act upon it with meaningful legislation.

Americans were fighting radical Islam as far back as Colonial times, when the pirates (Islamists) from the Barbary Coast of North African (hence "Barbarians") ravaged our ships in commerce routes to Europe, and forced our leaders to pay ransom in lieu of robbery and murder. These same Islamist pirates also terrorized the southern coast of Europe, raiding towns and villages, capturing women and children converting them into slaves and concubines, and indoctrinating children into the laws of Islam.

It wasn't until President Thomas Jefferson finally had enough of the bullying and ceased capitulating. He changed the game plan, putting a stop to senseless seizures of ships, goods and hostages. The only "negotiations" the enemy understood came from the end of a gun. He waged all-out war against the barbarians defeating them at Tripoli. Remember the famous segment from the Marine Corps Hymn; "...to the shores of Tripoli?"

It is worthy to note that in the years prior to waging war, while in a quandary on how to deal with the savages of North Africa, Thomas Jefferson and John Adams visited London in 1785 to negotiate with Tripoli's barbarian envoy, Ambassador Sidi Haji Abdrahaman. Jefferson inquired why the pirates continually waged war against nations who had done them no harm. Jefferson wrote in his diary how the Islamist responded:

"It is written in their Quran, that all nations which had not acknowledged the Prophet were sinners, whom it was the right and duty of the faithful to plunder and enslave; and that every Muslim man who was slain in this warfare was sure to go to paradise."

So, what has changed?

Radical Islam has been terrorizing and conquering nations since the early part of the seventh century, following the death of Mohammed. They tried to conquer Europe through France, but were defeated at Tours in 732 A.D. They tried to conquer Europe through Vienna, Austria, in 1683, but were defeated. They did conquer all of Turkey when it was the Ottoman Empire, but lost that after World War I.

They do not, have not, and will not ever give up. It is an endless struggle that has been waged for 1400 years, nations defending themselves against the conquest of Islam. The warriors have no fear of death, or do they fear the death of loved ones, if it can be justified as dying in the cause of Jihad, that is, conquest in the name of Allah.

Today, it's a whole new ball game. Their warriors live far and wide throughout a high-tech world of Twitter, Skype, iPads, and Facebook. Millions continue with the same mindsets as barbaric throwbacks to the seventh century while many more live among us wearing suits and ties. They exist in places like Saudi Arabia, Syria, Iran, Egypt, Turkey, England, France, Norway, Canada and the United States. Radical Islamists are rooted in almost every nation on planet Earth, though the big prize, the ultimate target, sits between the Pacific and Atlantic Oceans, known as North America.

Radical Islam may not be a country, like Germany or Japan, but it is a firm ideology that spans scores of countries with strict sets of laws called Sharia and written doctrines that govern social and legal behavior, known as the Quran and the Hadith. From there, the goals and mandates were unwaveringly established to follow Mohammed's command in 632 A.D. to spread Islam throughout the world, and to conquer all those who are infidels, that is, unbelievers (non-Muslims).

Radical Islam has a detailed set of plans. In truth, they are brilliant. And, they are effective. That is not an opinion. It is a fact supported by the documented trends around the world, plus thousands of events, violent and non-violent, and by the manifesto of the Jihadists themselves. This has been revealed, spoken and written by many experts and scholars, some of whom are Muslim, who you will learn about as you read further in this book.

Some skeptics, apologists and indignant readers will likely attach labels to this author as being a right wing, fanatical, racist, Islamophobic, xenophobic bigot. So here are a few comments as a caveat to allay those concerns:

The author of this book is aware that all Muslims are not extremists or terrorists. The world of Islam is not all radical or militant. I believe the majority of Muslims in the world are humble people who wish to live peacefully in coexistence with all people on planet Earth like the rest of us.

Now that we've covered that base, readers should know it is *not* the majority of Muslims that we should be concerned with. It is a very significant minority, much the same as the Nazi Brown Shirts were the minority in early 1930's Germany. What ultimately happened is that the boisterous and aggressive minority took control of the passive majority. The old squeaky wheel got the grease while the populous stood by as survivors. No one would have believed how barbarous the Nazi movement would become. Today, it is the significant and power-driven minority who are creating all the havoc in the world while the passive majority stands by in silence. That radical minority is growing rapidly not only on a global level, but here at home as well. So rapid, in fact, that if left to mere birth rates alone, it will only be a matter of a half century before Europe and the American continents will be living under various forms of Sharia Law.

It is up to us, today, to make a difference for the future of America. If we wait for the next generation to act, or to react, it will be too late.

Defining "Radical" Islam:

We often hear the adjective "radical" or "militant" attached to Islam when we are talking about the extreme fundamentalists who strive to conquer the world. This raises the politically correct antithetic term, "moderate," when referring to Muslims who are not of the conquering mentality. We have been comfortably lulled into a false mindset that "radical" is only synonymous with terrorism and "moderate" is synonymous with nothing other than a religious leaning, as a non-practicing Jew or Catholic might be identified.

Fact: The most radical of all Muslims in America do not chop off heads or strap bombs to their bodies. They walk the halls of our government and educational institutions as welcomed guests wearing modern garb and speaking perfect English. They are masked among our children and our government representatives pretending to be what they are not.

So, how is "radical" truly defined?

In a word: *JIHAD*!

Jihad literally means struggle! But struggle for what?

Jihad is the fuel of radical Islamic ideology. It propels fanatics in the global cause to expand Islam so that it eventually dominates all societies of the world.

Most Americans are brainwashed into believing that Jihad is only about terrorism. The news media teaches us that "terrorists" are synonymous with "Jihadists." That is not true. If we watch CNN or Fox News and read only the *New York Times* and the *Huffington Post*, we're taught that our main concerns are with ISIS, al Qaeda and their Taliban associates. (Yes, *taught*. Editorialists often slant thinking—right or left.) We must remember that news media sources are owned by multi-millionaires with political agendas of their own.

Al Qaeda and now ISIS are the hard focus of media and politicians when it comes to the so-called "war on terror," as if to suggest there is only a small group or fanatics whom we should worry about. President Obama constantly tells us that we are not at war with Islam, and that our lone enemy is al Qaeda or ISIL that according to him, is a dwindling threat. In February of 2015, he told a CNN reporter that 99.9 percent of Muslims reject radical Islam. That statement is obviously not true and unsupported by many study groups, including the Pew Research Center as well as many authorities on the subject, some of whom are listed earlier in this chapter. So what is with the untrue propaganda?

Again, this is reminiscent of the shell game whereby the manipulator leads you to look in the wrong direction.

Such focus – whether deliberate or not – prevents Americans from knowing the whole truth as it relates to Jihad and radical Islamic inroads. The media and the government are not doing their job of informing the people, or are they engaging the stealth enemy. Rather, they perform at the bidding of moguls who live on yachts and Mediterranean villas, awash in the euphoria of money and power. The operatives of al Qaeda are nothing more than chessboard pawns in the network of global Jihad.

The make-up of al Qaeda is like the units of hit men in a Mafia organization. The Mafia is actually run by top leaders and business people, but there exists a few needed killers in the overall scheme of things. They are an effective force serving a purpose, but they are not the leaders of the overall mission. They do the dirty work, while the top soldiers and bosses go about carrying out their sordid white and blue collar crimes.

For every one violent Jihadist in the world, there are thousands more Jihadists who are non-violent. The majority of Jihadists present an appearance of moderation, so that we ignoramuses will love and accept them into the American womb. Stealth Jihadists are earnestly driven by religious duty toward the same objective: The Islamization of the Western World. These are the people who live among us pretending to be "peaceful" citizens and immigrants seeking a better life in America. All the while, they are part of the netherworld that is dedicated to the overthrow of freedom and democracy as we know it.

Our government leaders would do well to focus on the enemy's obsession with global domination, not the tactics toward achieving that goal.

Muslim clerics, writers and educators will write articles or go on television and radio claiming that the term "Jihad" simply means "struggle." In a literal sense, that is true. According to The Center for The Study of Political Islam, Jihad means war against Kafirs (unbelievers) to establish Islam." To Jihadists it means Holy War. The literal definition doesn't matter. What matters is how it is interpreted and acted upon by the nearly two hundred million Jihadi-minded Islamists on the planet and by the Prophet Mohammed himself.

For Muslims who live in the remote regions of countries like Indonesia, Sudan and China, Jihad may be defined as the struggle for self improvement. That may even be true among some Muslims in America. But to radical Muslims and Muslim immigrants who are imposing the most profound effect upon daily life in the Western World today, Jihad is a universal Islamic struggle defined as "Holy War." It is an on-going fanatic's war in response to the Prophet Mohammed's dying mandate, to obey Allah's commandment to spread Islam everywhere and conquer the world of non-believers (non-Muslims). According to the Jihadist, it is the duty of every Muslim to engage in this movement.

Duty!

This mandate is found in several of the historical and holy texts from which Jihadists are impelled. The word appears seventy-two times in fifty-six Hadiths. Here is one example: (Bukhari translation)

Narrated by Abu Huraira. *"The Prophet was asked, 'Which is the best deed?' He said, 'To believe in Allah and his Apostle.' He was then asked, 'Which is the next?' And he said, 'To participate in Jihad, in Allah's cause.'" (Book 26, Hadith 594)*

The Quran is replete with passages that command the killing or domination of non-Muslims. Here are a few of those:

"2.191 And kill them wherever you find them, and drive them out from whence they drove you out, and persecution is severer than slaughter, and do not fight with them at the Sacred Mosque until they fight with you in it, but if they do fight you, then slay them; such is the recompense of the unbelievers."

"2.216 Warfare is ordained for you, though it is hateful unto you; but it may happen that ye hate a thing which is good for you, and it may happen that ye love a thing which is bad for you. Allah knoweth, ye know not."

"4.89 They desire that you should disbelieve as they have disbelieved, so that you might be (all) alike; therefore take not from among them friends until they fly (their homes) in Allah's way; but if they turn back, then seize them and kill them wherever you find them, and take not from among them a friend or a helper."

"8.12 When your Lord revealed to the angels: I am with you, therefore make firm those who believe. I will cast terror into the hearts of those who disbelieve.

Therefore strike off their heads and strike off every fingertip of them."

"9.5 So when the sacred months have passed away, then slay the idolaters wherever you find them, and take them captives and besiege them and lie in wait for them in every ambush, then if they repent and

keep up prayer and pay the poor-rate, leave their way free to them; surely Allah is Forgiving, Merciful."

The purveyors of Jihad are hugely powerful and dangerous. They have invoked the longest running and bloodiest war in the history of mankind. From the time Mohammed died in 632 A.D., to this very day, the Holy War has been waging for 1,384 years leaving behind multi-millions of dead bodies, human misery and forced conversions. Following Mohammed's death, Islamic armies embarked on warring missions plundering over southern Asia, the near and mid-east, virtually all of North Africa and into a nation we now call Spain, for no other reason than to conquer and impose Islam on all human beings of the planet. It is a religious duty. It took only eighty years in the 7th and 8th centuries to sweep across North Africa and Europe to overpower these territories.

How could that have been accomplished? All they had were horses, camels and swords and no system of communication.

Answer: *Terror*.

It is the same tactic creating havoc in the 20th and 21st centuries. The random killing of innocent people posed an on-going threat to others that they will also be killed or subjugated if they did not convert to Islam. Sound familiar? And for every successful act of terror, people everywhere live in a state of apprehension, altering lifestyles to brace for the next attacks. All this, while we cowardly cede changes to cultures and laws, basically as bribes, to prevent further attacks.

The first order of business by conquering Islamists, once they successfully held a nation captive, was the subjugation of women and the indoctrination of children. It would only take one generation for a newly conquered society to be wholly submissive to Islam. Serious resisters would be efficiently eliminated, either through death or disappearance.

Twenty years later, "peace" would prevail. The word "Islam" translates to "submission to Allah."

Terrorism is effective. It works.

It would have spread further, but the zealous, non-relenting Islamic forces were finally defeated in France at the Battle of Tours in 732 A.D. Had the plunderers won their battle in France, all of Europe would likely have succumbed to Islam and changed the history books for all time.

The Jihad-driven battles for global conquest have never ended. Emphasis on *never!* All that has changed is modern technology, communication systems, tactics and the rise of petro-wealth in the Middle East. The Jihad mentality is the same as it was in the arid deserts of seventh-century Arabia. The war continues to rage and no amount of peace-table negotiations or appeals to human decency will ever change the will of Allah. That would be like training a hungry crocodile to cohabitate peacefully in a duck pond.

In order to truly understand the radical Islamic mentality, it is essential that readers study the life of Mohammed, the Koran, the Hadith (words and teachings of Mohammed), Sharia law and the history of Islamic conquest.

Objectives have not changed since the day Mohammed died.

Who Are The Jihadists?:

Now that we have delineated the difference between a "peaceful or moderate" Muslim and the oft used adjective, "radical," what does that mean to us? If Jihadists or radical Muslims only comprise a minority in the Islamic world, why should we worry so much?

Answer: Because the numbers are colossal.

According to every scholar and expert on the history and spread of radical Islam, including many listed earlier in this chapter, fundamentalist Muslim Jihadists comprise somewhere between twelve and twenty percent of the world's Islamic population. These are the people who believe it is their godly duty to assist in the march toward global Islamization. Remember, a Jihadist can be a doting mother who sends her sons out on a suicide mission, or a married Muslim couple who simply send their money to Jihad organizations.

For the most part, there are people who have been indoctrinated to justify hate. Supremacy, hatred and Jihad are taught in Islamic madrassas (schools) and mosques all around the world. They will propagandize young children and other minions by telling them how infidels hate them so much, and it is their duty to hate back to eliminate any resistance to Islam. They hate America. They hate western lifestyles. They hate Jews, Christians and all infidels, because they were indoctrinated with hatred from childhood. They teach the same to their children from the time they understand language. Those children grow up virtually hypnotized into a hate mentality. They grow up becoming our sworn enemy. In some places in the Middle-East, little boys from the age of five are taught how to handle a gun and play games that feign the shooting of Jews and beheadings of Christians. For that, they receive approval of their fathers.

The math is simple. According to most statistical records, there are 1.5 billion Muslims on planet Earth today. If we take the lowest estimate that twelve percent of Muslims are Jihad-radicalized (stealth or otherwise), that equates to some 180 million Islamists subscribing to the Jihad mission. These are the people who are programmed to kill us or see us conquered. These are the not only the people who commit acts of terror, they are the ones -- all around the world – who danced and celebrated the killing of three thousand *infidels* on 9/11. If we use the high estimate of twenty percent, it is well over a quarter billion.

A quarter billion Jihadists represent a daunting enemy, twenty to thirty times larger than we have ever faced. Hitler, Mussolini and Hirohito combined never had it so good.

Yes, there are millions of good and decent Muslims. But the other side of that coin is that the enemy lives among us, blending in until their moments of Jihadi violence arrive. They have no uniform. They do not wear a sign on their heads flashing "Jihadist." They speak English, Dutch, Chinese, Spanish or French or whatever language they must in order to blend in. To be a Jihadist, one does not have to wear suicide bombs, join al Qaeda, behead people or even own a gun. Jihadists come in all sizes, colors, sexes, nationalities and educational backgrounds. They are rooted in over one hundred countries of the world. Their network is vast and almost incomprehensible. They come from all walks of life, including taxi drivers, Imams, military officers, college students, college professors, journalists, lawyers, physicians, bankers, retailers and legal/illegal immigrants who overstay their visas. Some are even sweet old ladies wearing hijabs who proudly send off their children strapped with bombs so they can randomly kill innocent people in the name of Allah. Some provide housing, comfort, support, money and "donations" that are funneled toward one radical group or another with Jihad in mind. Giving aid and comfort to a terrorist by feeding, supplying or housing Jihadists can be considered an act worthy of Allah's praise, because it all contributes to the widening domination of Islam.

Jihadists are the soldiers of radical Islam, but they are like no soldiers you've ever imagined.

Consider this analogy: You and your family love M&M candies. A stranger from another culture smiles and hands you a gift, a jar of one-hundred M&M candies, with a grim warning; "Eighty-eight percent of these candies are pure and good. Twelve percent contain deadly poison. Will you risk accepting the jar?"

Will you embrace the majority knowing that death awaits you from the minority?

Moderate Muslims:

There is only one Quran. Contrary to the poly-authored Bible, it is the product of one man. To be a good Muslim, one must adhere and believe in everything the Quran teaches, because it is the word of God as transmitted to the prophet Mohammed via the angel, Gabriel. Therefore, to take the literal words of the Quran, there is no such thing as a "moderate" or "extremist" in the Muslim world. You are either a Muslim or you are not.

Yet there are many variations of Muslim life throughout the planet, and it would appear that millions wish to live alone, in peace, and not be corralled into Jihadist thinking. In other words, they don't care about world conquest. It's tough enough to make a living, support a family and be true to your religion without thinking about war. That's better left to the "extremists" to carry out the conquering will of Allah. There are plenty of those.

Some folks point out that the Bible contains many dreadful precepts that are equally as horrifying as those in the Quran. The Old Testament, for instance, declares that anyone who works on the Sabbath should be killed. Slavery is considered acceptable. God ordered many hundreds and thousands of people to be killed for one reason or another. The old Bible is replete with stories about the subjugation of women.

The Quran is replete with ghastly references to the inferiority and subjugation of woman, the hatred of Jews and the terrible punishments that await those who do not accept Islam as their religion.

The difference is that the human race, in general, has moved on from adhering to most of the outrageous teachings in the Old Testament and basically ignores such things as slavery, women's subjugation, stoning and killings or those who violate God's law. Jews and Christians have moved into the 21st century through reformation and modernization.

The 180-250 million Muslims in the world who support the Jihadist movement *have not* moved on. They are mired in 632 A.D. The rigid teachings of Mohammed, his model as a perfect human being and the imposition of strict Sharia law is as essential to fundamentalist Islamic life today as it was in the seventh century. In Islam, there has been no reformation as there was with Christianity. In some countries, the mere mention of "reform" in Islam is considered blasphemous and subject to extreme punishment.

In strict Islamic countries today, harsh precepts are rigorously followed. Homosexuals are condemned to death by hanging in Iran. A woman who is raped in Saudi Arabia or Afghanistan must produce four witnesses to verify her claim or be stoned to death for adultery. There are cities where public beheadings are routinely performed on Friday afternoons. Women in some countries are the virtual property of a dominant male, whether a husband, father, brother or uncle, and may do nothing without his permission. Little girls can be married off as children and marriages consummated when they are age nine, because it follows the teachings of Mohammed. Except in extreme circumstances, a woman cannot obtain a divorce from a Muslim man. But a Muslim man can divorce a woman by announcing "I divorce you" three times. If a Muslim decides to leave the religion to be a Christian or an atheist, it's an automatic death sentence.

These are just a few of the extreme examples of Sharia law that will ultimately be imposed on lands around the world if the Jihadists have their way. American life will disappear along with the Bill of Rights. Forget about Freedom of Speech and Freedom of Religion. The Constitution will be eliminated, replaced with the Quran. There will be no history books lauding the achievements of Benjamin Franklin or Martin Luther King Jr. There will be no Las Vegas, no gambling, no alcohol, no Broadway shows, no opera or rock music, no professional baseball or football, no school dances, no marriages to anyone unless he or she is a Muslim. People who are not Muslims will have to pay special tax for not converting to Islam, a Dhimmitude.

Fortunately, not all Muslims adhere to radical ideology. A small number of reform Muslims in America have displayed courage to openly denounce Islamic extremism, and I suspect, there would be more if they were not in dire fear for their safety or the safety of their families. Speaking out against Islam can have severe repercussions from peers.

One such enlightened person is Dr. Zuhdi Jasser, a Phoenix physician who calls himself a reform Muslim, yet he supports the existence of Israel and does not hesitate to publicly criticize Jihadists or Islamic extremists, especially in the United States. Dr. Jasser identifies as a loyal American having served as an officer in the US Navy, and is often called upon by more conservative news outlets to present his opposing views to the hard-core, mainstream Islamic doctrines that support organizations like the Council on American/Islamic Relations (CAIR) that has been exposed by the FBI as an agent of radicalism in the United States, terrorism abroad, or both.

How Doctor Jasser rationalizes his "moderate" leanings with the strict application of Quranic teachings is a question not yet resolved by this author. However, his voice is a welcome light within a dark tunnel through which we will be traveling in the years to come. Most people generally respect the religion of others, providing they reciprocate with that same respect.

Indian-born author, Tarek Fatah, is a Canadian Muslim intellectual who has avidly been warning the west of the advance of Islamic extremism, denouncing the Muslim Brotherhood as the enemy of the free world and, in particular, excoriating the administration of President Barack Obama for employing Islamic radicals in his administration and helping to advance the cause of western Islamization. Readers of this book should also read, *Chasing A Mirage: The Tragic Illusion Of An Islamic State,* authored by Tarek Fatah.

There have been other Muslims and ex-Muslims who have spoken out in condemnation of the Jihad movement, risking their lives and those of their families. Many more would undoubtedly come forward if it were not for the fear of retribution. Women in particular can be subject to severe punishments if and when they break from the rigors of radical Islam, as denoted by honor killings all over the world. A world-wide movement to modernize Islam might be possible if it were not for the heavy hammer of Islamic extremists.

Meanwhile, if and when radical Islam ever achieves its goals, it will be the Muslims who will survive and then suffer the least, whether moderate or extreme. The non-Muslims such as this author and most of you will face one of three ultimate consequences – conversion, paying a tax for remaining non-Muslim (Dhimmitude), or death.

That's the edict of Islamic history.

Morocco, Arabia, Iran, India, Turkey, Algiers, Egypt, Spain and many more. Check them out.

Who's in Charge?:

Every conflict has a leader. It can be on the battlefield, in the White House, the Mafia or on the football field. There is always someone at the top who runs everything. That's our orientation. We Americans have difficulty thinking outside that box.

With each leader, there are those who enforce the leader's mandates such as the "Don" of the Mafia family, cabinet heads, generals, quarterbacks, dictators, and others. Many Americans think al Qaeda chief, Osama Bin Laden was the big boss, the ultimate leader. Not true. He was just one of the generals carrying out a mission, answering to a higher authority, like the Muslim Brotherhood, to which he belonged before moving on to al Qaeda.

So who is in charge of global Jihad? With radical Islam, the true leader is physically dead, yet he is alive in the minds and hearts of Jihadist Muslims. His name is Mohammed. But he left behind a long list of instructions, found in the Quran and in the Hadith, which have guided Islamic life for fourteen centuries wherever Muslims live throughout the world. Mohammed is the ultimate leader. He reports only to Allah, the supreme commander.

Mohammed's life is considered perfect and a model for all Muslims to follow. But where are his top generals? Who is running global Jihad today? Who is calling the shots?

Answer: The Muslim Brotherhood.

The Muslim Brotherhood is an organization of fundamentalist leaders around the world who espouse the goal – and the duty – to establish an Islamic caliphate in the Western World and to destroy American democracy. It exists for no other reason. The organization was originally founded in Egypt in 1928 after the fall of the Ottoman Empire, and has since expanded with hundreds of interlocking, sub-organizations in over one hundred countries, with special designs on conquering Europe and North America.

Proponents of the Brotherhood will present a facade of being "moderate," though that's a proven fallacy according to the FBI, and scores of authorities on the subject. Experts abound in America and throughout the world, *except* inside our very government sworn to protect us and our constitution. The absence of knowledge of the sinister goals of the Muslim Brotherhood by our government leaders is astounding. Worse than that, it is dangerous.

One blatant example surfaced in 2011 when Director of National Intelligence, James Clapper, an appointed mouthpiece for President Barack Obama, told the House Intelligence Committee that The Muslim Brotherhood was a "heterogeneous group, largely secular." That outrageous statement, which is known by any authority on the Brotherhood to be untrue, is utterly worrisome coming from a leader of our intelligence community. Other countries, including those in the Middle-East have declared the Muslim Brotherhood a terror organization. Egypt has outlawed them. One can only wonder where Mr. Clapper's loyalty lies, or if his I.Q. is somewhere under fifty, unless his mission (to be cynical) is to mislead. In any event, Clapper must be the person whom the president wanted in that position for those very reasons.

Anyone who has studied the bane of international Jihad in modern times knows better. Yet we have many in our government who will deny the fact that stealth Jihad is actively engaged in this country today, and that it is led directly, or indirectly, by the Muslim Brotherhood. The reason for this ignorance is rooted in money (petro-dollars), power, (electorate numbers) and complicity.

Think of the Muslim Brotherhood as the grand puppeteer, so to speak, who pulls strings of global Jihad by forming scores of sub-organizations to carry out its mission. They vary in substance, depending on purpose and target population. One good example is the Muslim Students of America (MSA) that is financed by and born of the Brotherhood in order to infiltrate America's institutions of higher learning, to intimidate and secure capitulation to demands for Islamic needs as dictated through Sharia law. These include special prayer rooms, foot baths, segregated gymnasium hours for Muslim women only, etc. Members of the MSA are noted for their rabble-rousing and distracting behavior when guest speakers appear to support Israel or expose the radical side of Islam. They are also dedicated to luring converts and supporters among the impressionable youth of America.

Another Brotherhood-formed organization is CAIR (aforementioned) which some people call the ACLU of Islam in North America. These are the legal foot soldiers of the Muslim Brotherhood, i.e., Jihad, whose job it is to manipulate the United States Constitution in seeking redress against anyone who allegedly demeans, insults, or decries Islam and ensures that the term "Islamophobia" is attached to anyone who speaks out against terrorism and Jihad, to make sure that political correctness is a part of the media's mantra, and who lobbies powerful politicians to advance the inroads of Sharia.

Neophytes and apologists for the Muslim Brotherhood should read their explicit motto. It is brief but all-encompassing. All Brothers are required to adhere. It has not been changed since its inception in 1928.

Allah is our objective
The Prophet is our leader
Quran is our law
Jihad is our way
Dying in the way of Allah is our highest hope

We should not have a problem with the first two bullet points. The next three are frightening. Let's examine the last three and see why we should be concerned:

"Quran is our law." This is an edict requiring all Muslims of the organization to adhere to no other law but the law of the Quran, which then supersedes the Constitution and all other laws of federal, state and local governments. While Muslim followers obey our statutes for the time being in order to promote the overall agenda, these people have no respect for any laws other than what is prescribed in the Quran. If and when Islam takes control, the Quran will nullify the Constitution.

Consider this final vow of the Muslim Brotherhood motto: "Jihad is our way." Four words tell it all. The Muslims who recited these vows are promising to do whatever is called upon them to expand the influence and ultimate takeover of Islam over all other governments and religions. It is all about conquest, no different than the conquest of North Africa and Spain in the 7th and 8th centuries. No different than the Ayatollah's ascension into Iran in 1979, effectively returning that country to an Islamist state. No different than murdering innocent people in airplanes, trains and buses all over the world as the perpetrators scream "Allah Akbar."

"Dying in the way of Allah is our highest hope." Each member of this organization puts the Jihad mission far ahead of their own personal lives, even if it means dying for God to achieve it. This is the ultimate in brainwashing, effectively convincing intelligent human beings to kill themselves if needed in order to reap the rewards of heaven by engaging in Jihad.

This motto is recited at most meetings of the MSA.

The following pages will better explain the details that comprise the motivation and strategies of the Muslim Brotherhood. However, before moving on, it would be appropriate to reveal an important paragraph extrapolated from a written document authored by the hierarchy of the Brotherhood in 1987 outlining the strategic goals for expanding Islam in North America. This is, in part, the standing decree from the Muslim Brotherhood. Pay close attention to the wording:

"The process of settlement is a 'Civilization-Jihadist process' with all the word means. The Ikhwan (Brothers) must understand that their work in America is a kind of grand Jihad in eliminating and destroying the western civilization from within and sabotaging its miserable house by their hands so that God's religion is made victorious over all other religions...It is a Muslims destiny to perform Jihad and work wherever he is and wherever he lands until the final hour comes."

From Within!

TWO
UNDERSTANDING THE MUSLIM BROTHERHOOD

The Muslim Brotherhood was founded in 1928 in Egypt by Hassan al-Banna and a core group of followers as an Islamist religious, political and social movement. Its purpose, following the collapse of the Ottoman Empire, was to revitalize Islam as a global power and ultimately expand Islamic law in the four corners of the globe. Since then, it has grown into a huge force whose ideology has not wavered nor has its intent to Islamize the entire planet. Here is a pair of quotes from its leader:

"Jihad is an obligation from Allah on every Muslim and cannot be ignored nor evaded."

"It is the nature of Islam to dominate, not to be dominated, to impose its law (Sharia) on all nations and to extend its power to the entire planet."

Secular, peaceful and tolerant?

At a Senate subcommittee on terrorism in 2003, when discussing al Qaeda, Hamas and Palestinian Islamic Jihad, the Chief Counter-Terrorism Advisor on the US National Security Council, Richard Clarke, testified, "The common link here is the extremist Muslim Brotherhood. All of these organizations are descendants of the membership and ideology of the Muslim brothers."

Mullahs and representatives of the Muslim Brotherhood partnered with Adolf Hitler prior and during World War II in order to help facilitate the "final solution," i.e., eradicate Jews from the planet. This is common knowledge, easily verified in history books and Google.

Considered too extreme within a "moderate" Islamic state, the Muslim Brotherhood was outlawed by Egypt's President, Hosni Mubarak until 2011, when uprisings altered the political system there. That's when our president, Barack Obama, called for the removal of Mubarak, music to the ears of the Brotherhood.

It was the minions of the Muslim Brotherhood who engaged in the assassination of Egyptian President Anwar Sadat in 1981, in retaliation for daring to sign a peace treaty with Israel.

The Muslim Brotherhood had remained a relatively inert organization with minimal power and of little concern to western civilization until five important milestones of the last one hundred years took place.

1 – The glut of Mid-Eastern oil
2 – Establishment of Israel
3 –The Islamic Revolution - Iran
4 – The 9/11 Attack in America
5 – The Rise of the Holy War

Mid-Eastern Oil:

This is the well from which the Jihadists drink. It is the endless pool of funding through which they can achieve their goals without limitation. The Muslim Brotherhood, along with oil-rich nations like Iraq, Iran, Saudi Arabia and Libya, are awash with money flow, providing support to thousands or millions of Jihad-minded Islamists throughout the world. Add to that, Zakat donations to charity that all Muslims are required to make. How much of charity money is funneled to Jihad and terror groups would be almost impossible to know or calculate. If the Holy Land Foundation investigation, which sent five Islamists to prisons for funneling charity money to Hamas, is any example, the funding from donations must closely rival oil revenue. If a half-billion, or one-third of the Muslims in the world, each send an average of $200 a year that gets funneled to Jihad, that equates to $100 trillion.

Not too shabby.

Of the top twenty oil producing nations in the world, ten of them are predominantly Muslim nations of the Middle East or North Africa. Of them, the greatest oil-rich powers are Saudi Arabia and Iran. Unfortunately, these countries are not our friends and are often at the root of international terrorism and financiers of global Jihad, both stealth and violent. Yet, America continues to be held economically captive by our enemies, which – given our choices over the last forty years – is no one's fault but our own government and vicariously, the American electorate.

We are the dummies who have allowed this to happen.

These are the fundamentalist Islamic states – among others – who strive to bury us, who are sworn to the destruction of Israel and who are invading the infrastructures of Europe and the United States for the long-range purpose of establishing Islam as the only religion and Sharia as the only acceptable law. To them, it doesn't matter if this takes a hundred years. The motto of the Muslim Brotherhood is as etched into the tenets of 21st century Islam as the Ten Commandments were etched into the Old Testament Bible. It is unwavering.

It wasn't until the end of World War II, and further, following the Vietnam War, that the oil-rich Islamic states began to flex their muscles. Oil gushers meant trillions of dollars and with such a self-perpetuating monsoon of wealth came power and influence. The financing of global terror networks, Islamic colonization and the funneling of billions into western society was seeded from Middle-East oil rigs, greedy corporations and stupid power-struck politicians. We're talking about *very* stupid politicians, because they only cared about short range benefits of power and money, and not the future of their American grandchildren. As Islamic wealth and power grew, so did the world of diplomatic ass-kissers, all of whom wanted a piece of the proverbial pie or deals for oil.

Every United States president since Jimmy Carter has been decrying our dependency on foreign oil, vigorously campaigning with promises to end it, yet the situation has not improved. With that, America has become more beholden to nations that mostly hate us. Sheiks, Mullahs and barons can only laugh behind closed doors at our pathetic impotence. The Achilles Heel of western civilization can be identified by one human frailty – greed.

Carter established the Department of Energy for the very purpose of weaning off foreign dependency. When he was elected, the United States imported 26 percent of oil from overseas. Today, that figure is about the same, according to the Energy Information Administration. Among the top five nations from whom we import is Saudi Arabia.

If it were not for the discovery and exportation of crude oil from countries like Saudi Arabia, Kuwait, Iraq, Iran and the United Arab Emirates, they would not have the influence over the United Nations or would they be positioned as a major political stranglehold in the world today. Neither would they have the resources by which to wage a Holy War against the West. For the most part, they would be living peacefully in their own cities and villages, a non-threat to western life.

In a sense, we have ourselves—or our politicos on both sides of the aisle—to blame for much of the turmoil that we experience today.

The Establishment of Israel:

The history of the Jews is replete with stories about suffering, slavery, bigotry, mass death, and attempted annihilations. What most people don't know is why such an historic chasm has existed between Jews and Muslims. Why do fundamentalist Muslims hate Jews so much, when there is so little hate, in return, by Jews toward Muslims, or toward any other people of the world?

The Jewish conflict with Islam is dated from the life of the Prophet, Mohammed, the perfect man whom all Muslims should emulate. After twelve years of failed attempts to peacefully convert people to Islam in Mecca, Mohammed moved to Medina and took up the sword, or translated, terrorism. Over the next ten years, conversions came by the thousands. Mohammed, who taught many of the tenets from the Old Testament, tried to present himself as the long-awaited Messiah for whom the Jewish people had yearned throughout their entire history. The Jewish tribes rejected Mohammed as Messiah and by doing so, rejected Islam.

People should remember that the Jewish rejection of Islam is what fanned the flames of hatred that has burned for 1,400 years. It's part of the Quran and the Hadith, and is fundamental to the teachings of young Islamic children in extremist nations around the world.

From the Quran:

"2:65 *And certainly you have known those among you who exceeded the limits Sabbath so We said to them: Be apes, despised and hated."*

"5:51 O you who believe, do not take the Jews and the Christians for friends; they are the friends of each other; and whoever among you takes them for a friend, then surely he is one of them. Surely, Allah does not guide the unjust people."

From the Hadith: (Narrated by Abu Huraira)

Book #52, Hadith #176: "You (Muslims) will fight the Jews till some of them will hide behind stones. The stones will say, 'O Abdullah, (i.e. slave of Allah) there is a Jew hiding behind me, so kill him.'"

Though Jewish hatred among fundamentalist Islamists has prevailed for fourteen centuries, no single event did more to unite hatred around the world than the establishment of the state of Israel in 1948. Hundreds of books have been written about the many wars and positions of both sides, Arab and Israeli, but the one stipulation that has never changed among Israel's enemies is that they will never recognize Israel's right to exist. The only exception to that was the peace treaty brokered by President Jimmy Carter in 1978 between Jordan, Egypt and Israel. That has been in effect for more than thirty-five years although the treaty was on shaky ground when the Muslim Brotherhood seized control of power in 2011. In 2013, the people of Egypt rose up against the Muslim Brotherhood and deposed the new regime. That was a sigh of relief to Israel, though the conflicts still rage as this book is written. (It should be noted that the treaty would be better described as a bribe because the flood of foreign aid from the US to those countries served as the incentive) Imams, educators, Arab politicians and other leaders in the Islamic world, particularly in the Middle East, use this edict as a global wedge to separate the Jewish people from themselves, as though they were truly apes and pigs. Palestinian children are taught from early life that Jews are the swine of the Earth. Not only do they refuse to recognize Israel's right to exist, they do not even depict Israel on the maps of Palestinian text books.

While the Arab world tries to imply that the Middle East unrest would end if Israel were eliminated, that's highly unlikely. Jews have been hated and discriminated against long before the state of Israel was formed, and will continue to be hated until they are wiped off the planet. Not all Muslims subscribe to that hatred. But the fundamentalists—the *Jihadists*—consider the elimination of Jewry as a basic duty of all Muslims. Nothing provided a more cohesive purpose than Israel's statehood in 1948. Since then, the State of Israel has defended itself against seven recognized wars with Arab nations and two Palestinian Intifadas, not to mention on-going lesser conflicts at borders. Since 2001, more than 15,000 rockets have been fired into Israeli communities from Gaza mostly from Hamas and Hezbollah, killing fifty and injuring nearly two thousand innocents. In total, sixty-five years of on-going attacks have been perpetrated on Israel leaving many thousands of dead bodies along the way.

Could anyone imagine Americans living under those conditions?

The Islamic Revolution – Iran:

On February 1, 1979, after several years of unrest in the nation of Iran, the Ayatollah Khomeini returned from exile and stepped off a plane in Tehran to assume the role of supreme leader of that nation. It changed the course of history in the Middle East and awakened the fundamentalist Islamic world into believing Islam could, once again, be a conquering ideology. When the Ayatollah arrived, the deposed shah had already left the country into exile, never to return.

This was a pivotal event in the march toward global Islamism.

The deposed shah, Mohammad Pahlavi, had ruled Iran since 1941 as a friend and ally of the United States. Many considered him to be corrupt. Corrupt or not, he had tried to modernize Iran into a westernized-style culture, while still maintaining Islam as the state religion. While many warning signs were prevalent, no one, not even the highest level of brainpower within the Carter Administration, was able to foresee what was coming.

The return of a strict fundamentalist theocracy to Iran was seen by the entire Islamic world as a victory over the United States and western nations in general. It was the spark that emboldened fundamentalist Islamists into believing they could eventually conquer the mightiest nations of the world. We now face the current on-going war on a global scale, and in our homeland.

Nine months later after the Ayatollah arrived, Iranian students and militants seized the American embassy in Tehran, took sixty-six Americans hostage, paraded them blindfolded before international cameras while taunting and humiliating them. The radical Islamists in Iran and around the Middle East were not only ecstatic, they were euphorically enlightened with new-found power and influence. They had denigrated and disgraced the greatest power of the world for all to witness, the United States of America, land of the free and home of the brave.

Fourteen of the hostages were ultimately released, while the remaining fifty-two were held for 444 days. Negotiations were basically non-negotiable. The Carter White House authorized one inept rescue attempt that ended in an embarrassing incident where one helicopter crashed in the desert, leaving eight Americans dead.

The hostages were finally released on January 20, 1981, the day of Ronald Reagan's inauguration. What was our response to this act of aggression?

Nothing.

The image of the almighty United States across the world had been reduced to a laughing stock. "Hate America" chants echoed throughout the Middle-East. The sleeping giant that Imperial Japan had awakened on December 7, 1941, remained asleep in 1979. We were tested, and we failed.

The 9/11 Attacks on America:

September 11, 2001. Four planes, nineteen terrorists from al Qaeda and nearly three- thousand people were killed in the worst attack on American soil in history.

It was the second attack, not the first, with the same goal. In 1993, Islamists concocted a plan in which a truck bomb was detonated in the sub-floor of the north tower of the World Trade Center. It was intended to knock the north tower into the south tower, causing both to collapse, and killing thousands of people. But, it failed, killing only seven people and causing millions of dollars in damage. But the Islamists were determined and eight years later they succeeded.

But why did it happen? What was the real motive behind the terror attacks by radical Islam? Just to kill people at random? Hatred? What was radical Islam supposed to gain by attacking America in this way?

They gained exactly what they wanted. It was a brilliant, well executed plan and it achieved the desired results. We must never lose sight of the long-range goals of the Muslim Brotherhood, i.e., conquering *from within.* Everything is not always as it appears.

The long-range results of the 9/11 attacks:

1) President Bush and his staff made numerous statements to the media disclaiming Islam as any danger to be concerned about, stating it was only a handful of terrorists who were responsible and insisting that Islam is a religion of peace. This initiated the era of "political correctness" with which we are saddled to this day. It could not have gone better for the Islamists. Everything President Bush declared publicly was music to the ears of Islamists.
2) The misnomer, "War On Terror," was born and remains ongoing to this day. It is a war that cannot be won because we do not identify the enemy for fear of offending Muslims. Again, we played into the hands of the Islamists.
3) The United States deployed armed forces into two wars around the globe at a cost to our economy exceeding one-

trillion dollars. That's not to mention the deaths of over six thousand American soldiers and disabling many thousands more, plus costing the taxpayer enormous debts in health care and other entitlements. Add to that the tsunami of personal misery. Great news for Islamists, tearing at America's economy and sagging public image worldwide.

4) While we – the news media and our government—focused on the bad guys bearing arms in Afghanistan and Iraq, the truly bad guys bearing cash and influence have been infiltrating the infrastructure of America ever since, much of it with the aid and blessings of two presidents. In essence, the enemy is well on its way to conquer "from within" as they had promised. It is entirely possible that the 9/11 attack was a diversionary tactic that worked exceedingly well. It is reminiscent of the infamous tricks of professional robbers – set fires in one part of town, draw all the attention to one place, and then commit crimes at another part of town.

And now? We are still playing into the hands of the enemy.

The Rise of World War III (Holy War):

Prior to the Iranian Hostage crisis, there was no effective or ongoing Holy War being waged against the West. The United States had not been the target of systematic Islamic terror attacks before 1979. That all has changed. As the years passed, the United States would be tested again and again.

- April, 1983 – Beirut, Lebanon. US embassy destroyed by a suicide car bomb. Sixty-six deaths, including seventeen Americans.
- October, 1983 – Beirut, Lebanon, US military barracks bombed by suicide fanatics, killing 241 Marines.
- September 12, 1983 - Kuwait City, Kuwait. Truck bombers attacked the US Embassy killing five.
- September, 1984, East Beirut, Lebanon. Truck bomb at the US embassy, killed twenty-four.
- December, 1984, Kuwait Airways Flight 221, to Pakistan, hijacked and diverted to Tehran. Two Americans killed.
- April, 1985, Madrid, Spain. Restaurant bombing where Americans frequented. Eighteen dead.

- June, 1985, Beirut, Lebanon. TWA Flight 847 from Athens hijacked to Beirut by Hezbollah terrorists and held for seventeen days. One American diver killed.
- October, 1985. Mediterranean Sea. Islamist gunman attack cruise ship, Achille Lauro, killing one elderly American Jew by throwing him overboard in his wheelchair.
- December, 1985. Airports in Rome and Vienna bombed, killing twenty, including five Americans.
- April, 1986, Athens, Greece. A bomb explodes aboard TWA flight 840, killing four Americans.
- April, 1986, West Berlin. A bomb explodes in a nightclub frequented by Americans. Two servicemen killed, hundreds injured.
- December, 1988, Lockerbie, Scotland. Bombed Pan-Am Boeing 747 explodes in mid-air, killing 270 people, mostly American.
- February, 1993, New York City, World Trade Center bombing by Islamic terrorists. Six killed, over one thousand injured. Their objective was far greater.
- June, 1996, Dhahran, Saudi Arabia. Truck bomb exploded outside military complex killing nineteen American servicemen.
- August, 1998, Kenya and Tanzania. Simultaneous truck explosions at two US Embassies, killing 224 people.
- October, 2000, Aden, Yemen, suicide bombers strike the USS Cole killing seventeen American sailors.
- September 11, 2001, four American planes were hijacked by Islamic Jihadists; two impaled into the World Trade Center, another into the Pentagon and another crashed in Pennsylvania. Total victims killed: 2,977, (not including perpetrators).
  Since the 9/11/01 attacks, and as of July 20, 2016, there have been another 42 random attacks by radical Islamists on US soil resulting in the deaths of 139 innocent people, including the Orlando night club in 2016, killing 49. Weapons used have been bombs, guns, knives and vehicles. Some of the most notable include:
- July 4, 2002. Los Angeles airport. Two people were shot to death by a Muslim while standing at the counter for an Israeli airline.

- October 3, 2002. Montgomery County, Maryland. Two Muslim snipers randomly killed five people in a 15-hour spree.
- June, 2009. An Islamic Jihadist shot two Army recruiters in Arkansas, killing one.
- November 5, 2009. Fort Hood, Texas. Forty-one military servicemen were ambushed and shot, thirteen killed, by an Islamist military officer. The killer had been viewed by many military associates as an Islamic extremist and was known to engage in dialogue with a known terrorist leader. According to a report in the *New York Times*, intelligence agencies had intercepted multiple communications between the killer, Major Hasan Nidal and Anwar al-Awlaki, a known supporter of terrorism. The military was aware of this, but it was politically incorrect to take any action against – what else? A Muslim. The president refused to call it an act of Islamic terror, instead, "workplace violence."
- December, 2009, the so-called "underwear bomber," (an Islamist Jihadist) attempted to blow up a Northwest Airlines flight, but was foiled.
- December 4, 2009. Binghamton, NY. A college professor was stabbed to death by an Islamist as revenge for persecuted Muslims
- April 14, 2010. Marquette Park, Il. A Muslim convert shot and killed five family members to "take them back to Allah and out of the world of sinners."
- September 11, 2011. Waltham, Ma. Muslim terrorists killed three Jewish men by slashing their throats.
- February 7, 2013. Buena Vista, NJ. A Muslim killed and beheaded two Christian Coptic immigrants.
- March 24, 2013. Ashtabula, Oh. While praising Allah and carrying a Quran, a Muslim convert walked into a Christian church and gunned down his father.
- April 15, 2013. Boston, Ma. Boston Marathon finish line, three innocents were killed and another 264 injured by a homemade bomb perpetrated by two foreign-born Muslims. A police officer was gunned down by one of the Jihadists.
- October, 2014. An Islamic radical attacked four New York City police officers with a hatchet before being shot dead.

- July 16, 2015. Chattanooga, Tn. A devout Muslim went on a shooting spree, killing five military personnel at recruit stations.
- December 2, 2015. San Bernardino, Ca. A Muslim couple with loyalty to ISIS embarked on a terror attack at Christmas party, killing 14 and injuring 17.
- June 13, 2016. Orlando, Fl. An Islamist killed 49 innocent people at a gay nightclub.

There will likely be more before this book is published.

In every terror attack, perpetrators screamed "Allahu Akbar" as they fired weapons, stabbed people or detonated themselves and their victims into oblivion. Yes, we have a president and a Department of Homeland Security who refuses to categorize these murders as "Islamic" terrorism. Rather, they are sanitized now as "man-made disasters" in order to avoid offending Muslims. It is unbelievable that we cannot offend the very people who support killing us. Where does the priority lie? Protecting radical Muslims or protecting innocent Americans?

This would be like refusing to label Nazis as murderers in World War II, and instead, calling them man-made calamities.

This list does not include the on-going array of terror attacks resulting in thousands of murders perpetrated by Islamic Jihadists against innocent human beings—including thousands of Muslims—in other parts of the world since the 1979 Iranian revolution. The citizens of the world are suffering from an epidemic of "man-made disasters." According to reliable sources, including thereligionofpeace.com, there have been over 29,000 deadly terror attacks by Islamists around the world in the name of the religion of peace since the 9/11 attack in the US.

It was not until the attacks of September 11, 2001, that the United States finally engaged in significant retaliatory action against Jihadists, other than prosecuting perpetrators in civilian court as though they were local criminals. Taking firm, military action was seen by most staunch, pro-Americans as a positive step.

But it also had its downside. By engaging in wars in Afghanistan and Iraq, we openly defined our enemy as being inhabitants of remote areas elsewhere, not here, but twelve thousands miles on the other side of the planet. Rarely did our leaders recognize or admit that the supporters of Jihad – the haters of America – were operating inside our own country. To the contrary, our nation's leaders gratuitously stood with Imams and other Islamic leaders declaring Islam to be a religion of peace, only to learn later that those same Imams and leaders had been espousing hatred of western values to their followers, with incendiary speeches against America behind closed doors. They were also proven to be raising and funneling money to support Hamas and other terror organizations around the world.

So, while our sons and daughters were gallantly fighting the Jihad enemies overseas, their less violent compatriots—with the same goals—were infiltrating our country with impunity, under the guise of "moderation."

Some were eventually caught and imprisoned, like Islamic Supremacist Abdurahman Alamoudi, who had previously been courted and embraced as a friend by presidents William Clinton and George W. Bush. Turns out, Alamoudi is a stepchild of the Muslim Brotherhood who supported Hamas and Hezbollah. In 2003, Alamoudi was sentenced in federal court to twenty-three years in prison for working with al Qaeda to plan an assassination and funneling money to terror organizations. According to the Investigative Project on Terrorism, the Obama Administration's Department of Justice successfully sought to have his sentence reduced by six years in 2011. Little or nothing was reported on this in the media.

These are only a smidgen of the vast army of stealth Jihadists working every day to bring Sharia to our nation to replace the Constitution.

Clearly, the Islamic Jihadists enjoyed a free ride at beating up the sleeping giant until the 9/11 attacks. Then we took action. The wars initiated under the Bush Administration have been credited by their supporters as having kept America safe for the remainder of that decade. That may be true to an extent, but the Afghan and Iraqi engagements have not put a dent into their long-range objectives. If anything, the wars may have served as a welcomed distraction while their clandestine strategies have been positioned and activated inside our borders. Despite all the dead on both sides of the battle lines, the enemy remains right here among us, growing by the day, and laughing all the way to the Sharia bank.

THREE
GOALS OF THE MUSLIM BROTHERHOOD IN NORTH AMERICA

"War is Deceit" the Prophet, Muhammad

■ Hadith: Vol. 4, Book 52, Numbers 268 and 269

In 2004, when Muhammad Mahdi took over leadership of the Muslim Brotherhood, he made this statement:

"I have complete faith that Islam will invade Europe and America, because Islam has logic and a mission." Then he said, "The Europeans and the Americans will come unto the bosom of Islam out of conviction."

If such a statement came from a Central Park speaker on a soap box, we would totally ignore it. But it was made by the leadership of the most powerful and well organized enemy in the world of Islam, an organization that represents global Jihad—stealth and violent—with sights set on conquest of the Western Hemisphere. Yet, we still continue to ignore it.

Oddly, American authorities also ignore important and prophetic documents recovered by law enforcement agencies. Authored by the Muslim Brotherhood hierarchy, these documents explain and outline the nefarious goals, tactics and methods that must be practiced by the Muslim Brotherhood in pursuit of Jihad.

The basic tenets of the Muslim Brotherhood have not been changed since its inception in 1928. Yet, our government representatives continue to apologize, legitimize and defend this dangerous organization and its minions, including presidential candidate, Hillary Clinton, President Barack Obama and, as mentioned earlier, James Clapper, head of America's National Intelligence.

Thousands of experienced intelligence agents, military and other authorities who have studied the Muslim Brotherhood inside and out, know they are far from secular. They are a strict fundamentalist, Sharia-compliant organization. The intelligence, the reports, the books and the intrinsic knowledge of experts, are endless. So why does the best of our journalists not press for honesty and truth in government?

Strategic Goals of the Muslim Brotherhood:

The information revealed in the forgoing paragraphs are essential for understanding the motives, intentions and power of the Muslim Brotherhood and its self-declared role in effectuating Islamic conquest over all nations in North America.

Mohamed Akram was a top operative and member of the Board of Directors for the Muslim Brotherhood in North America as well as a senior Hamas leader. Akram authored the Explanatory Memorandum in 1987, not published until May 22, 1991, which spells out the "General Strategic Goals for the Group in North America," for the Brotherhood. Written in Arabic, this 18-page document was discovered in 2004 by federal authorities hidden in the sub-basement of a Virginia home owned by Ismael Elbarasse in one of 80 boxes of archives of the Brotherhood. Elbarasse was a founder of the Dar Al-Hijrah mosque in Falls Church, and a member of the Palestinian Committee that the Muslim Brotherhood created to support Hamas in the US. This enforcement action was pertinent to an investigation of the Holy Land Foundation's funneling of money to Hamas. The documents were vetted and introduced into evidence during the federal trial in 2007.

To repeat (for emphasis), part of that document states:

"The Ikhwan (Brothers) must understand that their work in America is a kind of grand Jihad in eliminating and destroying the western civilization from within, and sabotaging its miserable house by their hands and by the hands of the believers (Muslims) so that it is eliminated and Allah's religion is made victorious over all other religions."

From within!

Translated: The Brotherhood is *duty-bound* to eliminate our Constitution and replace it with the Quran and Sharia Law, and to convert North America into an Islamic caliphate. They intend to accomplish this takeover through subterfuge, deceit, government infiltration and the gradual incursion of Islamic culture and laws, further enabled by rampant immigration and a robust birth rate far exceeding non-Muslims. It should be noted that the use of terror is a low priority among their primary strategies.

The Holy Land Foundation Case:

The Texas-based Holy Land Foundation was the largest Islamic charity organization in the United States. In 2007, the foundation and five of its top operatives were convicted in 108 counts of laundering money and providing material support to a foreign terrorist organization (Hamas). They all went to prison. Another three hundred persons were named in the investigation as unindicted co-conspirators.

It is important to remember that we are referring to deceit as a mechanism and a weapon by which the Jihadists fight this Holy War. The Holy Land Foundation was portrayed as a "feel-good" organization helping needy people. Then the truth came out. It was a front to fund Islamic Jihad. While non-profit organizations are often formed to establish funding methods for worthy charities, they can also be a convenient subterfuge for radical Islam in disguising many of those contributions from its intended purpose—Jihad.

Today there are hundreds of Islamic organizations administrating Zakat (Muslim charity) and personal contributions from wealthy radicals. Zakat is one of the five pillars of Islam in which all Muslims are expected to donate two and a half percent of their income to Islamic charity, usually via the local mosque. While the Holy Land Foundation was nailed for criminal activity by the Justice Department during Bush's administration, there are undoubtedly others that are still funneling money to Jihad operations all over the world.

More than convicting supporters of terrorism, the *most important* outcome of this investigation were the revelations that surfaced via secret documents authored by the hierarchy of the Muslim Brotherhood. Their sinister objectives could not have been more plainly stated. It was – by any standards – a declaration of war. One wonders how many other documents and plans exist in other parts of the world, not yet discovered, that enumerate diabolical and specific plans for destroying the United States from within.

From within!

It's like having discovered Hitler's *Mein Kampf*, only more explicit, and then ignoring it until it was too late. It's like having discovered Imperial Japan's schedule of Pacific attacks and then ignoring them until it was too late.

We are ignoring the war plan of our enemy though it is right under our noses! The entire government including The Departments of State and Defense and the White House of two presidents are equally guilty. I can count on one hand the number of congressmen that have made reference to the manifestos of the Muslim Brotherhood. Those that do are ultimately humiliated and marginalized by the leftist side of the mainstream media. Start with Representatives Peter King (R-NY), Sue Myrick (R-NC), and Michele Bachman (R-MN). There are very few others who have had the courage to be politically incorrect.

During the Holy Land Foundation investigation, the big break came in August 2004, during a search of one of the Brotherhood leaders' homes in Annandale, Virginia. He had been arrested for casing the Chesapeake Bay Bridge and other bridges for possible terrorist attack. In a sub-section of Ismail Elbarasse's basement, FBI agents uncovered a stash of secret manifestos and other documents unveiling the depth of the conspiracy against the United States. When the Arabic-written papers were translated into English, federal investigators knew they had stumbled upon the archives of America's power branch within the International Muslim Brotherhood.

We rarely hear about this discovery and its contents from government sources. Senators, congresspersons, even the president and his cabinet are seemingly oblivious to the dangers that lurk from the stealth Jihadists within our nation. The same disappointment exists within the news media, which seems to deliberately avoid showing the Muslim Brotherhood in a negative light. Rather, our news information highway narrows their focus on ISIS, al Qaeda, Hamas, and the "war on terror" as our enemies, with rare mention of any stealth enemies represented within the Brotherhood and its sub-groups. They also ignore the evidence of how these terror organizations are spin-offs of the Muslim Brotherhood.

One can only wonder if that is an act of omission or commission. Is the media under control of moguls who are financed by oil cartel nations, thereby muzzled from uncovering certain facts about the entities involved in the stealth Jihad inside America? Must Americans be forced to reach out to the Internet and other compromised news sources for the truth about radical Islam in America? We shall see.

The FBI had the courage to name the Muslim Brotherhood as an organization with ties to terror groups, including Osama bin Laden. In February of 2011, FBI Director Robert Mueller and other law enforcement officials testified before a House Committee on Intelligence that the Muslim Brotherhood is closely tied to Hamas and other terror groups around the world, and that they are operating within the United States as the umbrella organization controlling at least sixty-one entities in North America, including CAIR.

According to testimony before Congress of FBI Agent and terrorism expert, John Guandolo, "The most prominent Islamic organizations in the United States are all controlled by the Muslim Brotherhood."

It was in those same hearings that the astounding false testimony came from the president's National Intelligence Director, James Clapper who conveniently ignored the history of the Brotherhood and all the data collected during the Holy Land Foundation investigation. He disregarded the Muslim Brotherhood's parenting of Hamas. Neither did he seem aware that the Brotherhood was responsible for the assassination of Egypt's Anwar Sadat, in 1981. He, and perhaps our president, needs to be reminded of the Muslim Brotherhood's motto, that includes, "Jihad is our way."

Congresswoman Sue Myrick of North Carolina sat on that committee. As one of the few politicians who aggressively pursued the bane of Islamic Jihad in the United States, she was astonished by Clapper's testimony. "Either the administration doesn't know who the Muslim Brotherhood is, which shows incompetence, or they are apologizing for them which is inappropriate for those in charge of protecting the American people. Let's be clear. The Muslim Brotherhood is not secular."

The Muslim Brotherhood Front Organizations:

According to the FBI and investigative reporter, Paul Sperry, author of the revealing book, *Infiltration,* writing for *Front Page Magazine,* and P. David Gaubatz, author of *Muslim Mafia,* the key front organizations of the Muslim Brotherhood currently operating in the United States are listed below. Several of these groups have often been represented in the Obama White House.

- African Muslim Agency
- Al-Aqsa Education Fund
- All Dulles Area Muslim society (ADAMS)
- American Muslim Armed Forces & Veterans Affairs Council (AMAFVAC)
- American Muslim Council
- American Muslims For Constructive engagement (AMCE)
- American Muslim Foundation (AMC Foundation)
- American Muslim Task Force On Civil Rights And Elections (AMT)
- Association of Muslim Scientists And Engineers (AMSE)
- Association of Muslim Social Scientists of North America (AMSSNA)
- Baitul Mal Inc. (BMI)
- Council of Islamic Schools of North America (CISNA)

- Council on American Islamic Relations (CAIR)
- Dar al-Hijrah Islamic Center
- Dar El-Eiman USA Inc.
- Figh Council of North America (FCNA)
- Global Relief Foundation
- Graduate School of Islamic & Social Sciences (GSISS aka Cordoba University)
- Happy Hearts Trust
- Holy Land Foundation For Relief And Development (HLF)
- International Institute For Islamic Thought (IIIT)
- International Islamic Federation of Student Organizations (IIFSO)
- International Islamic Forum for Science, Technology & Human Resources Development, Inc. (IIFTIKHAR)
- International Relief Organization (IRO)
- Islamic Academy of Florida
- Islamic Assembly of North America (IANA)
- Islamic Association for Palestine in North America (IAP)
- Islamic Circle of North America (ICNA)
- Islamic Free Market Institute
- Islamic Media Foundation
- Islamic Medical Association of North America (IMANA)
- Islamic Society of North America (ISNA)
- Makkah Mukarramah Charity Trust
- Muslim American Society (MAS)
- Muslim Arab Youth Association (MAYA)
- Muslim Public Affairs Council (MPAC)
- Muslim Students Association (MSA)
- Muslim Youth of North America (MYNA)
- Muslim World League (MWL)
- North American Imams Federation (NAIF)
- North American Islamic Trust (NAIT)
- SAAR Foundation
- Safa Trust

- Success Foundation
- Taibah International Aid Association
- United Association For Studies And Research (UASR)
- World Assembly of Muslim Youth (WAMY)

The full text of the Muslim Brotherhood document explaining the General Strategic Goal for the Brotherhood in North America, as authored by Mohamed Akram for the Shura Council of the Muslim Brotherhood, is provided in its entirety in Addendum One at the back of this book. Here is one more notable paragraph from that document:

In order for Islam and its Movement to become 'a part of the homeland' in which it lives, 'stable' in its land, 'rooted' in the spirits and minds of its people, 'enabled in the life of its society and has firmly-established 'organizations' on which the Islamic structure is built and with which the testimony of civilization is achieved, the Movement must plan and struggle to obtain 'the keys' and the tools of this process in carry out this grand mission as a 'Civilization Jihadist' responsibility which lies on the shoulders of Muslims and—on top of them—the Muslim Brotherhood in this country.

The foregoing documents are not the only source by which we have learned the intention and strategies of the Muslim Brotherhood. Another chilling discovery was made shortly after the 9/11 attack in 2001.

FOUR
THE PROJECT

"Use deception to mask the intended goals of Islamic actions."
■ The Muslim Brotherhood, from *The Project*

This discovery was a gold mine. It was like stumbling into the war strategy room of the Nazi Party in WW II.

Again, we've turned a blind eye.

In November of 2001, two months after the 9/11 attacks in the United States, Swiss law enforcement officials conducted a raid at a luxurious villa where the target suspect was an Egyptian man named Youssef Nada, a banker and chief financial strategist for the Muslim Brotherhood. The Swiss police were in search of evidence to prove money laundering and funding of terror organizations, including al Qaeda, the Algerian GIA (armed Islamist group), the Tunisian Ennahdah (Islamist political party) and Hamas. But what they inadvertently found, hidden away, was something far more valuable to intelligence sources and far more important to protectors of freedom around the world. Nada, whose assets were subsequently frozen by Swiss authorities and by the Egyptian government, was known as the Muslim Brotherhood's International Political Foreign Emissary.

Among Nada's hidden belongings that officials recovered was an unsigned, fourteen-page document, written in Arabic, and dated December 1, 1982. Known as *The Project,* the document outlines the specific strategies and tactics that would be employed toward achieving long-range goals of expanding Islamic settlements in the West, and eventually a global caliphate. It is a multi-phased, long-term approach to the cultural invasion of the West. In other words, it is a step-by-step, "How-To" manual for conquering Europe and North America. It also adjoins and confirms the "Strategic Goals for North America," also authored by the Muslim Brotherhood, outlined previously.

What sets this document apart from all other declarations from radical Islamic groups is that it represents a multi-phased, long-term plan for a cultural invasion of Europe and North America. It would appear, based on the enormous strides that radical Islam has made over the last three decades, that these strategies have served as the master plan for the Muslim Brotherhood for their cultural invasion; the manifesto, so to speak.

It is comprehensive, well planned, carefully worded and obviously the product of much consideration and discussion among its authors. It is, unequivocally, a war plan. It is authored by the top echelon.

One would think that this would be a valuable resource for agents of European and North American governments. After all, it reveals an array of stratagem from which authorities could establish counter-intelligence, new laws and retaliatory actions to protect our citizens and our cultures in the forthcoming decades. Alas, that has not been the case, as we will see.

Listed below are the unambiguous goals, tactics, strategies and techniques outlined in *The Project* that provide the scheming outline for global conquest. It is important to remember that the purveyors of Jihad are not forthcoming and honest, for if they were, their plans would surely fail. Nor are they impatient. It doesn't matter if they see the end result in their lifetime, because they are convinced they will see it from Heaven as martyrs down the road.

The Project tells us what we should watch for. But we have failed.

The Project is the opponent's game plan, but we have stupidly ignored it.

The Project is like a general's strategy plan in which operatives receive their instructions.

The Project is, in fact, genius. It is on track. It is succeeding. And as readers absorb the forthcoming chapters, they will see how each and every tactic and strategy is being successfully employed while our representatives slumber.

Why is it succeeding? It's not because the enemy is so competent. It's because we are so inept. We are stupidly in denial, stupid because we only acknowledge war strategy when it comes in form of a bomb or a gun. We are stupid because we choose to believe people who lie to us, and then elect them into powerful government positions. Our infrastructure, including government and media, is collapsing before our very eyes and we're too stupid to see it.

This is all about conquest: *From Within.*

The Strategies:

These are the documented strategies as enumerated in *The Project:*

- Develop a comprehensive one hundred-year plan to advance Islamic ideology throughout the world.
- Collect sufficient funds to indefinitely perpetuate and support Jihad around the world.
- Establish financial networks to fund the work of conversion of the west, including the support of full-time administrators and workers.
- Inflame violence and keep Muslims living in the west in a Jihad frame of mind.
- Support Jihad movements across the Muslim world through preaching, propaganda, personnel, funding and technical and operational support.
- Make the Palestinian cause a global wedge issue for Muslims
- Adopt the total liberation of Palestine from Israel and the creation of an Islamic state as a keystone in the plan for global Islamic domination.
- Instigate a constant campaign to incite hatred by Muslims against Jews and reject any discussions of conciliation or coexistence with them.
- Actively create terror cells within Palestine.
- Link the terrorist activities in Palestine with the global terror movement.
- Infiltrate and take over existing Muslim organizations to realign them toward the Muslim Brotherhood's collective goals.
- Avoid open alliances with known terrorist organizations and individuals to maintain the appearance of 'moderation.'
- Build extensive social networks of schools, hospitals and charitable organizations dedicated to Islamist ideals so that contact with the movement for Muslims in the West is constant.
- Avoid social conflicts with westerners locally, nationally or globally that might damage the long-term ability to expand

the Islamist power base in the West, or provoke a lash back against Muslims.

- Balance international objectives with local flexibility.
- Put into place a watchdog system for monitoring western media to warn Muslims of international plots fomented against them.
- Instrumentally use existing western institutions until they can be converted and put into the service of Islam.
- Involve ideologically committed Muslims in democratically elected institutions on all levels in the West, including government, NGOs (non-government organizations), private organizations and labor unions.
- Institute alliances with western 'progressive' organizations that share similar goals.
- Conduct surveillance, obtain data, and establish collection and data storage capabilities.

Make particular note of the final bullet:

- Use deception to mask the intended goals of Islamic actions as long as it does not conflict with Sharia Law.

In other words, lie, pretend, fake, deceive, mask, distract or do anything dishonest.

If it furthers the cause of expanding Islam, God will be forgiving and Heaven awaits.

Unmentioned in this global plan is the simplest method of all for expanding Muslim dominance in the world – population growth. This is probably the most successful of all, because the results have been astounding, particularly in Europe, which is an ominous omen on the other side of the Atlantic Ocean.

We will define, more in detail, all of these strategies and tactics, including the progress that radical Islam has made in the last thirty years toward western dominance. First and foremost, none of the strategies could ever have been accomplished without the employment of final strategy listed: "Deception."

FIVE
DEFINING DECEIT

Taqiyya:

From the Quran:

3.28: Let not the believers take the unbelievers for friends rather than believers; and whoever does this, he shall have nothing of (the guardianship of) Allah, but you should guard yourselves against them, guarding carefully; and Allah makes you cautious of (retribution from) Himself; and to Allah is the eventual coming.

Defined, this means a radical, fundamentalist Muslim may lie to non-Muslims if it is done to advance the expansion of Islam, and if a Muslim still holds Islam dear to his heart, he may be deceitful.

If needed to achieve a special mission, a Muslim may say he is a Christian, when he is not, as long as it is for the purpose of advancing the cause of Islam. That is called, "Taqiyya." He may claim to be your friend, when he is not. That is still called "Taqiyya." He may run for office as a Democrat or Republican, or claim beliefs that are not true, just to fit into the long-term scheme.

Religious fanaticism is much like addiction. Any of us whose family members and loved ones have been touched by the tragedy of substance addiction from drugs or alcohol, will know what lying and deceit is all about. Addiction (or obsession) will invariably cloud rational judgment. Deceit is the bedrock of coping with addiction.

All addicts lie. The longer someone is an addict, the more that person becomes fixated. An addict or serious alcoholic will go to great lengths to deceive a spouse, a parent, a child, a cop, or anyone else, in order to advance their needs to sustain the addiction. Cocaine, heroin, Oxycodone or a bottle of whiskey are far more important to an addict that telling the truth to a mother, wife or daughter. Some are so fanatical they will even rob and kill loved ones, or strangers. Those who have never had close exposure to people with major substance dependency haven't a clue about the power of addiction.

Some religions, particularly Islam, can be likened to addiction. Extremely devout Muslims are not only obsessed, but intoxicated with their religion, thinking that their faith supersedes all other religions. They live, eat and breathe religion daily. For the great majority, it is not a choice, but a life they were born into. Through intense dogmatic teachings experienced as a child, they pass that obsession on to their children and spouses. In essence, fundamentalist Islamists are virtually marinated in hate dogma from birth.

We should note that other religious sects may be as devout and dogmatic as Islamists. Orthodox Jews in the US and in Israel are very strict with their customs and the manner in which they raise children. Many of their customs are similar to Islamic teachings, particularly about dietary rules and the role of women in the family. *But they do not teach hate.* Devout Jews do not declare themselves as the only true religion, or do they evangelize or demand that non-Jews must convert for fear of punishment. And they do not commit mass, indiscriminate murders throughout the world in the name of their God. Note also, the number of Jews in the world is only one percent of the number of Muslims.

I know of no other faith besides radical Islam that is so powerfully addictive that it will send out sons, brothers and sisters to kill themselves in the name of their God so they can succeed in murdering innocent people and call that "defending" their faith.

Mass murder through terror has become the rule, not the exception. According to thereligionofpeace.com, a web site dedicated to tracking acts of terror around the world, approximately 1,900 deadly terror attacks have taken place in the world annually since the 9/11 attacks in the United States. An average of at least ten people have been killed in each attack, with thousands of injured left without limbs and eyesight. Most take place in Islamic countries like Pakistan, Afghanistan, Iraq, Sudan, Mali, and so forth, where the majority of victims are also Muslims. With rare exception, all random terror attacks against innocent people are committed by Islamists.

Virtually thousands of Islamist fanatics have fired guns randomly at people or blown themselves to bits over the years in order to commit mass murder, all in the name of God. Clerics and other fundamentalist leaders have convinced these bombers and shooters they would be rewarded in Paradise for being a martyr. The ideology of hate and war is so entrenched within the extremist community that they are virtually "addicted" to Jihad. With that comes the most dangerous element of deceit: Non-violence.

Why dangerous? Because it lulls well-meaning people into a false sense of trust.

It's more dangerous because you can't see it, smell it, feel it, hear it or taste it. It is more pervasive and eventually more destructive to our way of life. It's more dangerous because average, unsuspecting Americans are easily fooled... and that includes our politicians.

Mohammed's decree that "War is deceit," is not a profound quotation; it has been echoed by many others in wartime through the annals of history. Playing cat and mouse on the battlefield is as old as the Trojan Horse ploy, and older. What makes the Holy War different is the element of stealth and infiltration, the absence of battlefields and the cloak of "moderation" that is designed to dupe us all. Rather than the predominance of weaponry, this war is being fought from the deployment of wits, intelligence and pretense. Unfortunately, too many well-intentioned folks in the Western world easily fall for the ruse, much the same as the Jews fell for the many ruses of the rising threat of extremism in Germany during the early 1930's.

Though warning signs were seething everywhere in the early 20th century, European Jews basically ignored them. Jewish people were so accustomed to anti-Semitism they disregarded the ominous signs, believing they could still operate businesses in Germany. Then the Nazis smashed their windows and closed their shops. They thought they could still live in their homes until the Nazis surprised them with the ghetto round-ups. They thought they were being sent by train to labor camps. Another ruse. They thought they were going to take showers at Auschwitz. Again, another ruse. At what point does a ruse become too late?

Secular Muslim scholar, Tarek Fatah, wrote a chilling revelation in his book, *Chasing a Mirage*. Pay close attention to his words:

Since 9/11, the modus operandi for those Islamist individuals and organizations who want to manipulate Western pluralism has been to pass themselves off as moderates. They use the language of left-wing activists, they sprinkle their language with references to the World Bank, social justice, debt relief, poverty, and that key word "equity' to get well-meaning leftist liberals on their side. And it has worked.

The 9/11 terrorists were known to have spent months in advance of their mission, mingling and commiserating with American non-Muslims in order to blend in and not attract suspicion. They ate pork, drank alcohol, caroused with women and violated other tenets of the Islamic faith that is forgivable because their ultimate mission was to murder thousands of infidels in the name of Allah. And they succeeded.

But they were the *violent* Jihadists. Worse yet are the *non-violent* Jihadists who have infiltrated our nation. Sometimes the highest level of scholars within Islam will even deny knowledge of the word "Taqiyya" though it is easily accessed on the Internet and has been used in dialogue in Hollywood movie scripts about terrorism. It's no secret to anyone who has studied deceptions within Islam.

It was sometime in 2010 that Mr. Ibrahim Ramey, a prominent director with the Muslim American Society (MAS), was a guest on the Joe Citizen radio talk show in Broward County, Florida, when he was asked about "Taqiyya." Mr. Ramey played dumb and claimed he didn't know what Joe Citizen was talking about, that he had never heard the word. He lied about lying.

In truth, Mr. Ramey was accessing the forgiveness due him by Allah, for employing Taqiyya himself. The MAS is one of the organizations in the United States that was born of, and strongly tied to, the Muslim Brotherhood.

All prominent Muslims know Taqiyya. It's like a Mafioso hit man claiming he didn't understand the meaning of "whack."

When Mohammed declared "war is deceit," he was not only talking about wars of bloodshed, but all wars involving Islam and its perceived enemies, which generally mean non-believers or "infidels." Therefore, anyone entrenched into the Jihad movement, or Holy War, is actively employing Taqiyya on a daily basis, whether in the Middle-East, or right here in the United States.

Unfortunately, as Mr. Fatah writings state, Americans tend to be hugely gullible, which is what the enemy is counting on.

Major Nidal Hasan, the Fort Hood Jihadist murderer who shot forty-one and killed fourteen people in November 2009, pretended for months and years to be a loyal American soldier, attending medical and psychiatric schools on the backs of taxpayers, and fooling everyone in his military environment, including top level officers, that he was a harmless fellow who only wished to practice the religion of peace in his private life, like others practice Christianity and Judaism.

How many other radical Islamist officers and soldiers have infiltrated our military for sinister purposes, other than violence? How many others are still being ignored by political correctness though the signals exist that these people may not be true Americans at all?

Some see what they wish to see, not what it is front of their noses. That goes for US presidents as well as the common man.

President George W. Bush and his staff, made some notorious errors in judgment in dealing with Islamists who successfully passed themselves off as "moderate" in order to gain access to high level influence. The current president is guilty of the same, which will be addressed later.

Here are some examples:

Within days after 9/11, President Bush stood side by side with two noted Imams declaring Islam to be a "religion of peace." With three thousand murdered Americans still buried in the rubble created by four crashed airplanes at the will of Islamists, one can only imagine who he was trying to appease, Muslims or the United States people in general?

Imam Muzammil H. Siddiqi was one of those clerics standing with the president. He was an honored guest in the Bush White House. It didn't matter to Mr. Bush that Mr. Siddiqi was known to have given speeches that were anti-American, praising Palestinians and issuing warnings to America that we should side with them against the Jews. Two years later, Siddiqi, who pretended to be "moderate," issued a Fatwa to the Fiqh Council of North America: *"As Muslims we should participate in the system (American) to safeguard our interests and try to bring gradual change. We must not forget that Allah's rules have to be established in all lands..."*

Omar M. Ahmad is another "moderate" Islamic leader who helped establish the CAIR and had been an honored guest in Bush's White House. In 1998, while speaking at an Islamic conference in Fremont, California, he said, *"Islam isn't in America to be equal to any other faith, but to become dominant. The Quran should be the highest authority in America and Islam the only accepted religion on Earth."*

In my 2006 book, *Militant Islam in America*, I cited numerous examples of the Bush Administration's capitulations to radical Islamists, including the secret shuttling of 142 Saudi nationals from the United States back to Saudi Arabia two days after the 9/11 attack, when all airports were still closed to routine travel, despite the fact that fifteen of the terrorists were Saudi Arabian.

As mentioned, notable Islamists from universities and private business had been honored guests at the White House, only to find themselves behind bars later for aiding and abetting the money trail to terrorists. Previously mentioned, Mohammed Hussein Al Amoudi, a hater of America and vocal supporter of Hamas and Hezbollah, was one of those who eventually went to prison. In 2011, Abdul Rahman al Amoudi was being recommended by the Obama Department of Justice for release after serving only nine years of his 23 year sentence. They managed to convince a judge to lop six years off his sentence.

Sami al Arian, a university professor, was also honored at the White House along with 160 Muslim-American activists in 2001, though he had been under investigation by federal authorities for years for his connection to money laundering and for funneling funds to terror organizations. Sami al Arian ended up in prison after several plea arrangements and has since been released.

These are the types of people who live lies every day, determined to make Americans believe they are harmless Muslims who pray five times a day and practice dietary laws and wish no ill will on the American people. Yet, they practice stealth Jihad and apply Taqiyya daily in order to blend in and appear harmless while they carry out their sordid duty to Allah behind closed doors.

For certain, all Muslims who work and live in the United States are not Jihadists or do they practice Taqiyya. But how does one recognize a “radical” from a “moderate?”

You don’t.

Not long ago, I attended a lecture by a respected Muslim college professor who addressed a liberal, curious and friendly audience. He used a Power Point showing that Islam also recognizes Jesus and many other prophets of the Old Testament and it is completely misunderstood by mainstream America. While much of what he conveyed was true, he cleverly omitted verses the Quran that are not peaceful (109 of them) and failed to explain to the audience that the Quran was formed in two segments of Mohammed’s evangelical life, the peaceful segment in Mecca, and the violent segment in Medina. When I raised my hand to ask a question, I asked about two verses from the Quran (9.5 and 5.51) that command death against infidels and prohibits Muslims from taking non-Muslims as friends. My question was summarily dismissed as “misinterpreting the Quran” and the session ended suddenly. Clearly, the professor had presented a sanitized version of Islam in order to impress and pacify.

In 2008, when I addressed a library audience to promote my book, *Militant Islam in America,* one nice-looking gentleman, about thirty, sat through the talk. He then raised a question announcing he was a Muslim convert. His questions challenged my sources. The man said he was a furniture salesman, seemingly a gentle fellow, though visibly perturbed. I posed a question to him in return.

"Sir, do you ever pledge allegiance to the United States"

Unabashed, his answer was, "Never. My only allegiance is to my God."

Even more disturbing is the appointment of Anita Najiy to become Assistant Chief of Police for the Miami Police Department in April of 2015. Ms. Najiy, a Muslim, refused to pledge allegiance to the United States flag during the appointment ceremony, leaving many to feel that a defender of American laws should, at the least, show enough patriotism to her country by reciting the pledge.

An Assembly of Muslim Jurists of America (AMJA) paper in 2009 stated that "The basic conflict between the declaration of faith and testimony that there is no God except Allah... and the declaration and pledge of Allegiance of the USA is irreconcilable."

Noted moderate Muslim, Dr. Zuhdi Jasser, a physician in Phoenix, often appears on cable news warning Americans of the dangers of creeping Sharia and Islamic extremism. He penned an article published in the *Wall Street Journal* on August 18, 2011, cautioning our government about indiscriminate recruitment of Muslims in the military.

He wrote:

How many Islamists-gone-militant do we need to attack us before our military addresses radicalization among its Muslim members? Political correctness and denial are not working. The vast majority of Muslims serve with honor and distinction. They are not the problem. The problem is the subset of Muslims who are Islamists.

Dr. Jasser is correct. But how can one know who is a loyal American versus who is an Islamist? Islamists, like Nidal Hasan, practices Taqiyya until the time is ripe to commit murder.

In 2011, the owner of a Buffalo television station who was in business to portray Muslims as good and decent people was convicted of murdering and violently beheading his wife for daring to want a divorce. Pakistani born Muzzammil Hassan was a respected citizen and popular show host, but nevertheless a fundamentalist Muslim. He may not have been a Jihadist (unless he was sending money to terror organizations), but he was an abuser and killer in the name of Allah. According to his belief, her beheading ensured she would not go to heaven. Mister Hassan was a "moderate" Muslim, of course.

This chapter could cite numerous examples of honor killings that have infected our country, where fathers, husbands and brothers embarked on vicious murders of young women because they violated some tenet of Islam, or wished to convert to another religion. All of these killers were "moderate" Muslims before they slashed their sister's throats or blew their heads off.

It is without doubt that Taqiyya is being practiced today inside the halls of the US government by officials and employees for the very purpose of long-range Jihad. And we stand by, in denial, uncaring, blind and indifferent, blaming ho-hum partisan politics when enlightened people bring out the truth.

What's ironic is that some folks accuse this author of being a hater. They say I stir up hard feelings toward Muslims. In fact, the only people I hate are haters who impose their hatred upon others.

Muruna:

This is another term, similar to Taqiyya that permits violating Islamic law if it is to further the goals of Jihad. *Muruna* justifies deceit against western institutions. It was designed to advance Sharia by using or infiltrating western means. *Muruna* is accomplished by permitting behavior normally so eschewed by Sharia that westerners logically assume a more moderate version of Islam is in place when such prohibitions are permitted. Westerners' eyes are, in fact, deceiving them. *Muruna* is about going to great lengths to gain interests through a much deeper level of deception while simultaneously lowering the guard and gaining the support of the infidels.

Note the following quote taken from the series Preparing the Atmosphere under the title, *The Workings of Al-Si'a and Muruna*: (numerous sources, including *PJ Media* and Robert Spencer in *Jihad Watch*).

Sharia's ability to be flexible and inclusive is that it cares for their needs while excusing the burdens Muslims have to endure. For the sake of their destiny, it was made lawful for them to have exceptions from the law that are appropriate for them since these exceptions match their general goals to make it easy for humanity by removing the chains of [Sharia] rules they were made to adhere to in previous Sharia rulings.

Muruna provides for flexibility, allowing the Islamists to put on a smiling face while holding animosity and hatred toward the enemy. It is a strategy for fooling the naïve into believing something that is not. The so-called Arab Spring is a good example of a movement that garnered support from the West, including the media and the President of the United States, in calling for the removal of Mubarak, Gadhafi, and others. Why? Because we were fooled into believing the rebels and protesters were "moderates" seeking a democratic government, when in fact they were the Muslim Brotherhood assuming power by deceit and turning Egypt into a strict, fundamentalist Islamist state. When their power rooted in, the Egyptian people realized they'd been had been fooled by a fascist movement, which triggered the secular revolt currently under way.

When the Muslim Brotherhood claimed victory in the streets, their supreme leader, Sheikh Yusaf Abdallah al-Qaradawi, proclaimed the Brotherhood's Doctrine of Balance, as follows:

"...if the good and evil conflict with each other, we make priority as to when we put ahead evil for the sake of an interest, and determine when an evil deed is forgiven for the sake of an interest."

In other words, it is against Islamic law to behave in an evil manner, unless it is to advance the cause of spreading Islam against the infidels. That makes evil acceptable. It is forgivable to lie, deceive, kill, maim, rape, plunder, conquer and destroy innocent people, because all non-Muslims are, in fact, not innocent.

SIX

THE TIMELINE

We may refer to this chapter several times as we journey through the details of the book. It is important for the reader to oversee the war operation of the Muslim Brotherhood from a global perspective and not by nit-picking each individual act or terror or example of government infiltration. It's the entire picture that forms the mosaic, not each individual tile. Therefore, it is counter-productive to mire into one or two single incidents or profiles. We must see the entire picture to understand how and why we arrived at where we are today.

The issue of radical Islam here and abroad was not on the edge of our lips prior to the 1979 Iranian Revolution. Few Americans paid any attention to Islam or Muslims in general. While we knew Muslims existed in the United States, the population was very small—less than one million—and the number of mosques stood at around four-hundred across the land. Now, there are over 3,000 mosques in the United States—nearly doubled in the last ten years—plus hundreds more "Learning Centers." Muslim population figures vary depending on who is doing the research. However, most Islamic sources claim eight million Muslims live in North America, with one million in Canada. The Pew Research Center puts the number at less than three million. It is impossible to count accurately because the census systems do not tabulate numbers by religious base. Comparatively, immigrants—legal and illegal—cannot be tabulated.

Suffice to say that terrorism and Islamic radicalism was not a primary concern prior to 1979, nor was Islamic politics. Enormous changes have taken place since 1979.

The Islamic war against America and the free world in general might have been technically born in 1928 when the Muslim Brotherhood was formed. But it never reached full steam until five milestones, mentioned in Chapter Two were achieved; Oil wealth, Israel's formation, Iran's Revolution, 9/11 and the Holy War in general.

Fundamentalist Islam has been on a hate campaign against Jews since the 7th century. The leadership has now been passed on to the Muslim Brotherhood, which has helped carry out that campaign since 1928, to and including their assistance to Adolf Hitler in working toward the "Final Solution" in World War II. So, it was not the formation of Israel that is an issue, but the pervasive establishment of hatred toward Jews in general throughout history. In 1948, Israel merely provided a global wedge for Muslim fundamentalists to unite behind once the state was formed.

The Muslim Brotherhood has been successful at realizing its strategies spelled out in *The Project,* where it states: *"Instigate a constant campaign to incite hatred by Muslims against Jews and reject any discussions of conciliation or coexistence with them."* It also states: *"Make the Palestinian cause a global wedge issue for Muslims"*

By reading these edicts, it becomes clear that no amount of negotiations, no amount of appeasement and no treaties will ever satisfy the Israeli/Palestinian conflict until Israel is destroyed. The Muslim Brotherhood has been very successful in fanning the flames of hatred, especially behind the scenes.

Here are the essential components of the timeline:

- 1928 - Muslim Brotherhood formed in Egypt as a fundamentalist Islamist organization to work toward reestablishing a caliphate that crumbled after WW I.
- 1936 - Muslim Brotherhood grows to 800 members.
- 1946 - Egypt's Prime Minister, Mahmoud Pasha is assassinated by agents of the Muslim Brotherhood.
- 1948 - Muslim Brotherhood grows to 500,000 members.
- 1952 - Muslim Brotherhood ignites the Cairo Fires of 1952, leaving 750 buildings destroyed.
- 1978 - Muslim Brotherhood operatives kill President Anwar Sadat of Egypt for signing a peace treaty with Israel.
- 1979-1980 – Iranian revolution brings fundamentalism back to Iran.
- 1981 - The politically powerful Islamic Society of North America (ISNA) is formed in the United States, an offshoot of the Muslim Brotherhood. The ISNA eventually becomes

its own umbrella organization for many other Islamic organizations in America.

- 1982 - The United Muslims of America (UMA) is formed to provide a voice for Muslims in the political arena. It is the first of many operations seeded in the United States by the Muslim Brotherhood.
- 1982 - "The Project" is first drafted by the hierarchy of the Muslim Brotherhood
- 1987 - The Muslim Brotherhood authors the "Explanatory Memorandum" citing the goals to destroy western civilization *from within*. It is published in 1991.
- 1988 - Osama Bin Laden, formerly of the Muslim Brotherhood, establishes al Qaeda terrorist network. Bin Laden's assistant and current leader of al Qaeda, Ayman al-Zawahiri, was also a member of the Muslim Brotherhood before joining al Qaeda.
- 1988 - The Muslim Public Affairs Council (MPAC) is established to work for civil rights for American Muslims and for the integration of Islam into American pluralism.
- 1990 - The American Muslim Council – another offshoot of the Muslim Brotherhood – is established to increase effective participation of American Muslims in the political arena. These organizations were spawned by the Muslim Brotherhood in the United States for the purpose of exerting influence over American politics and society in general.

Note the rapid increase in Islamic organizations and political power following 1980 and the Iranian revolution.

- 1993 - The first bombing of the Twin Towers in New York by Islamic radicals, killing six and injuring more than one thousand. This signaled radical Islam's dogged interest in bringing down the United States and establishing fear and power over the nation.
- 1994 - CAIR is established, calling itself the counterpart to the ACLU for Islam. This is another powerful oil-rich army of legal teams spawned by the Muslim Brotherhood to fight for Islamic rights and, ultimately, the establishment of Sharia in the West.

- 2001 - The 9/11 attack by nineteen radical Islamists, fifteen from Saudi Arabia, kill nearly 3,000 people at the World Trade Center towers, The Pentagon and a field in Pennsylvania.
- 2001 - Within two months after 9/11, the secret document "The Project" is discovered by Swiss police in the home of a high-ranking member of the Muslim Brotherhood, spelling out in detail the plan for methods and strategies in conquering the West.
- 2004 - The Holy Land Foundation, a charity-based organization run by Islamists, is designated as a terrorist organization because of funds funneled to organizations such as Hamas. During this investigation, the "Explanatory Memorandum" (see Chapter Three) is found hidden in an Islamist's home in Virginia. Written in 1991, this document specifically cites the intent of the Muslim Brotherhood to "destroy the United States from within."

The Holy Land Foundation trial was held in 2007 resulting in the convictions of five Islamists who were sent to prison. CAIR was identified by the Justice Department as an un-indicted co-conspirator in terror financing).

- 2007 -- Keith Ellison of Minnesota is sworn in as the first Muslim in the US Congress.
- 2008 -- Andre Carson, Democrat from Indiana, is the second Muslim elected to the US Congress.

2008 -- Barack Hussein Obama, whose roots are anchored in Islam though he claims to be a Christian, is elected President of the United States. Islamists around the world and in America could not have asked for a better ally within the government of the United States. More on this appears in Chapter Thirteen.

SEVEN
EUROPEAN EXPANSIONISM

History has often told us that the political tides of Europe are a forecast for the future of the United States.

As this book title implies, war tactics of the 21st century do not, and cannot, rely on military victory. The most efficient and certain methods for winning a struggle for conquest is to infiltrate, commandeer and effect change from within. That can be accomplished in three ways: Politically, culturally and legally.

Now that we established the framework and motivations of the Muslim Brotherhood, let us address the various methods, tactics and strategies laid out in "The Project" and evaluate their progress as of 2016. These ensuing chapters will highlight the present status of various strategies and objectives enumerated in "The Project." How far have they come toward reaching their long range goals?

Let us start with the frightening, broad range prognosis that is described in the document. It is important to remember that this was published in 1982, so we are already over thirty-four years into the scheme.

Develop Hundred-year Plan to Advance Islamic Ideology Throughout the World:

Now that thirty-four years have passed since "The Project" was adopted, the Ikhwan (Brothers) must be absolutely delighted. Not only have Muslim Brotherhood operatives infiltrated the United States and Canada, they have saturated Europe with immigrants, their families and converts, to the point that "Mohammed" has become the most popular name for babies in many countries, including the Netherlands, Belgium, England and more. It's only a matter of mathematics for predicting where this will be going in the next generation.

Prior to 1979, there were no significant issues in Europe or America concerning the infiltration of Islamic ideology. Today, Islam is the focal point of numerous political, social, religious and cultural strife. It has become a serious problem in the European arena. If thirty-plus years made such significant changes, one can only imagine what the next thirty years will bring, particularly considering the enormous refugee migration that has been on-going from Syria and other countries since 2013.

All one has to do is access any search engine on line and query a European country along with the word "Islam" to see the remarkable impact of dominance in the last thirty years. Europe's greed in search of cheap labor and domestic services brought millions of immigrants from Africa and the Middle-East since the 1970's. The European people were not thinking ahead. To their chagrin, they learned that Muslim immigrants, for the most part, do not assimilate into the culture as they had hoped. Instead, Islamic communities and enclaves have imposed their own brand of apartheid, establishing parallel governments of their own in defiance of national customs and laws. All the children born to Islamic parents grow up as legal citizens of countries like Germany, France, Norway and England. Thus, the children of following generations multiplied likewise in larger numbers, all become voters, all are eligible to run for office and expand their power.

According to the Pew Research Center, virtually every European country shows a significantly higher birth rate for Muslim families than non-Muslims. Most notable is the United Kingdom, Serbia, Norway and Finland that records Muslim birth rates over 3.0 per mother versus non-Muslim birth rates at 1.3 to 1.8. This does not take immigration into account and the fact that polygamy is rampant in strict Islamic communities. Women may be mothering four and five children, while men are fathering twenty or more.

Countries like Sweden, Austria, France, Norway and the United Kingdom are expected to see Muslim populations double by the year

2030. Likely double that again in another twenty years. If Sweden, for example, grows from five million to ten million Muslims in 2030, the same rate will bring them to twenty million Muslims in 2050 while the native Swedes remain relatives static. As legal citizens, the children of immigrants are entitled to run for public office, thus imposing significant influence on existing laws and government policies in the future. As the population grows rapidly, so will their power. By the end of this century, based on population growth alone, Sweden as we know it will no longer be Swedish. And they are not alone.

Islam doesn't need weapons or terror, it only needs a welcome mat and the freedom to out-procreate the native population. Since the early 1970's, the Islamic populations in Europe have mushroomed into positions of influence.

But it's only a religion, some say. What's the worry? As shown throughout this book, Islam *is not* just a religion; it is also strict form of government with an unwavering culture, with harsh, restrictive laws known as "Sharia." Daniel Pipes, author, scholar and historian on Islamic studies, stated in a 2010 interview on line with *The Citizen Times*, "Islam is a religion like Christianity and Judaism. It is also a radical utopian ideology like fascism and communism."

With the exception of less important topics like dress and dietary rules, Sharia laws are not compatible with any laws espousing or protecting freedom in the western world. Freedoms as we know them do not exist in Muslim-dominated nations. In predominant Islamic countries today, the freedoms guaranteed Americans in the First Amendment—speech, religion, assembly, and press—do not exist. Saying anything aloud that criticizes Islam can bring, and has brought, severe punishments.

In the most populated Islamic countries, it is a crime punishable by death to convert to any religion other than Islam. Carrying a Bible in public in strict Islamic countries like Saudi Arabia can result in the arrest of an "offender." A woman's hair exposed from her Abaya can result in a beating or reprimand by the "Morality Police" that patrols the nation's population to ensure Islamic law is being strictly adhered to.

So, the immigration experiment has evolved from economic benefits and gestures of good will into a virtual crisis that threatens the very fabric of the unique cultures that make up the European mosaic.

Here are a few examples of the looming European conversion:

France:

Islam is now the second largest religion in France, behind Catholicism. It supersedes Protestants and Judaism. Muslims make up approximately 5 million of the 59 million population, which surely will expand after millions resettle in Europe during the refugee crisis. It doesn't sound like much, but they are separatist, vocal and the numbers are growing. Two-thirds of French Muslims come from scores of countries, with Algeria most predominant. There are several conflicting sources that project the future of Islam in France, but the general consensus is that France will definitely be a Muslim majority nation before half of the 21st century is over, if not sooner. With that, comes Sharia and Muslim rule.

Today, there is very little assimilation into the French culture, signified by an establishment of over 700 "No-Go Zones," or Sharia zones, throughout the country, which are not unique to France. These are Muslim neighborhoods and enclaves that basically act as their own country within a country, ignoring national civil and criminal legal systems. It's like saying, *"We settle in France and accept the benefits, but we don't believe in France."* French authorities have lost control in these enclaves and, in most cases, are unable to provide even basic public aid such as police, fire, and ambulance services. It is widely believed that the French Muslims ignore state law and are guided by Sharia where acts such as forced marriages to minor females, honor killings and female circumcision are practiced with impunity. If French authorities dare to intervene, the resistance would likely explode into riots. The government's ban on burkas in 2011 had sparked motives for civil unrest.

Riots perpetrated by Muslim youths are commonplace throughout France, with several outbreaks starting in 2005 and continuing to the present time. Thousands of automobiles and buildings have burned as the rioters blame unemployment and civil rights violations as their basic cause. In truth, riots produce fear and intimidation and with that, comes acquiescence by the host nation in order to broker peace. But with that brokering, the foundations and cultures of each country are chipped away, riot by riot.

The wake-up call of mass terrorism occurred in November 2015, when three teams of Islamic terrorists in Paris randomly killed 130 innocent people leaving hundreds more injured. The nine dead suspects were living as residents or citizens, or both, of France. Credit was given to ISIS. The French Prime Minister called it an act of war.

Netherlands:

Approximately 1.2 million Muslims comprise about six percent of the Muslim population of The Netherlands. Those numbers are increasing and "Mohammed" is now the most popular name for newborn babies in the four largest of Dutch cities.

In one of the most liberal countries of the world known for its tolerance and welcoming attitudes, things are changing in regard to, or because of, Islam. The Dutch government has recently abandoned efforts toward multiculturalism in an effort to retain and reignite its rich culture. New laws have been passed that will require immigrants to learn the Dutch language while newer, tougher approaches are being centered on those who disobey Dutch law. Special subsidies for immigrants have been discontinued. The government is fighting the emergence of Sharia by banning forced marriages and outlawing full face coverings in the style of burkas and abayas. A documentary aired in 2009 by the television program *Netwerk* reported how Dutch law was being systematically undermined by the growth of Sharia.

Dutch polls in 2011 show that 74 percent of voters say that immigrants must conform to Dutch values and laws and 83 percent support a ban on burkas in public places.

It is dangerous, indeed, to speak out against Islam in The Netherlands and other places. In 2002, Dutch politician Pim Fortuyn was assassinated by an unrepentant Islamist for espousing critical views about Muslim immigration. In 2004, Dutch filmmaker Theo Van Gogh was stabbed to death in the streets of Amsterdam for daring to produce a ten-minute documentary movie (*Fitna*) about the rise of radical Islam.

Geert Wilders, a Dutch politician and member of the House of Representatives, was put on trial in 2011 in Amsterdam for "inciting hatred" against Muslims. He was acquitted. This was another example of Islamic appeasement. Wilders has emerged as an outspoken critic of creeping Sharia, warning of future threats to the Western world by the rise of fundamentalist Islam. His talks are so worrisome and candid that the British banned him from entering the United Kingdom in 2009 saying that his presence would create a threat to national security. Islamic intimidation was victorious over free speech. Wilders, who compares the Quran to *Mein Kampf,* focuses his campaign on the Islamization of his native land.

Germany:

This is another liberal-minded nation that has welcomed immigrants with open arms over the last forty years, mostly Muslims from Turkey and some from other Islamic nations. Times have changed. In 2010, the Chancellor of Germany, Angela Merkel, spoke out and claimed that their attempts to create a multicultural society have "utterly failed." The four million Muslims that now live in Germany are basically a nation within a nation, assimilating only when necessary and maintaining separatism.

Similar to our own Holy Land Foundation investigation, Germany outlawed a huge "charity" organization in 2010 because it was learned it had been funneling monies to Hamas. (Internationale Humanitaire Hilfsorganisation) According to Wikipedia, over eight million dollars had been collected in German mosques for distribution to that terror organization.

A ten-year survey by the University of Bielefeld indicates that the enormous welcome once extended to foreign Muslims has worn out. Only 19 percent of once-liberal Germans believe that Islam is compatible with their culture.

Author Nasim Ben Iman is an Arab-born former Muslim (apostate), raised and living in Germany, who has risked his life not only to convert his religion but to speak out warning the West of the grand plans for Islam to rule the West through Islamization. His video talks are accessible on line in which he speaks openly about the indoctrination process of Muslims from the time they are born, why death in the name of Allah is considered an honor, how all Muslims are potential terrorists and that according to fundamentalists, no other religion should exist on the planet. In particular, he laments the naivety of Western liberalism, the greatest asset for Islamic expansionism. Extrapolating from his talk:

I can confirm that what is said publicly (by the Muslim community) and that what is said behind closed doors in Muslim society and in the mosque is as different as day and night. Sometimes I am stunned by the naivety of the West—and the naivety of Christians—because they are so blind and let themselves be so seduced.... To give sleeping pills to the West so that they sleep through their own Islamization: That's the aim.

Mr. Iman claims his life is in perennial danger for being an apostate, and that a sword hangs over his head.

Meanwhile, when the flood of refugees began the mass odyssey into Europe in 2015, Angela Merkel did a flip-flop and welcomed 1.2 million desperate Muslims into her country. The Gatestone Institute Study reports, as a consequence, that sexual assaults skyrocketed, considering that the majority of immigrants are young Middle-East males.

Like France, the general consensus of studies agree that Germany will be a Muslim majority nation by the middle of this century.

Belgium:

Abu Imran is an Islamist leader in Brussels who makes no apologies for forecasting the end of Belgium as we know it by the year 2030, and that Sharia, which he states is synonymous to Islam, will rule. Imran heads a vocal Islamic organization called "Sharia 4 Belgium," which hosts a web site of the same name.

In September 2011, Belgium capitulated and established its first Islamic Sharia Law court in Antwerp. This is intended to create a parallel legal system in order to challenge the Belgium authorities. Basically, it means Muslims may answer only to Islamic law, not to the nation they live in.

It has only just begun.

As in the Netherlands, "Mohammed" is the most common name for newborns in Brussels and Antwerp though the Muslim population is only at six percent. In 2012, two Muslim politicians won municipal elections in Brussels vowing, one day, to implement Sharia Law in Belgium. Muslims now make up one-quarter of the population in Brussels, thus emerging as a powerful political group for the future. A 2006 opinion poll in Belgium revealed that 61 percent of the population believe tensions will increase with Muslims in the future.

Novopress, a press agency founded in France, reports 232 gang rapes in Belgium, an average of five gang rapes a week. Perpetrators, though not listed by religion, are overwhelmingly immigrants or sons of immigrants. Rape was a rarity in many of these peaceful European nations until the advent of Islamic immigration. The figures are believed higher but many victims are fearful of filing reports. Between 2009 and 2011, forty-four percent of the reported gang rapes resulted in no prosecution. It is believed that threats and fears of family retribution were the basis of many non-prosecutions.

Islamists have been known to grant moral sanction to that crime, blaming the victim for allegedly appearing in a seductive manner. Basically, it's like saying, "It's okay to rape a deserving woman. Men need to be protected from prosecution." Rapes by Islamists are not uncommon in other European nations, as we shall see.

Various media and newspaper sources, including the *New York Post,* have reported on intensifying terror activity in Brussels, especially in the wake of the Paris attacks, since one of the masterminds was apprehended in a Brussels slum area that had long been a hotbed for radical Islamic lawlessness. In March of 2016, 35 people were killed and another 200-plus injured by suicide bombers in a Brussels subway station and the airport, for which ISIS was assigned credit.

Sweden:

Most recent estimates stand at about 500,000 Muslims in Sweden, which would comprise five percent of the population. This nation is no longer the picture of Scandinavia it once was forty years ago.

Dominant Muslim populations primarily live in three Swedish cities including Stockholm, Goteborg and Malmo. Riots, perpetrated by immigrants and sons of immigrants, have ravaged the city streets of Sweden, particularly in Malmo, the most Islamized community in that nation. Rioters who set fires to buildings and cars, allegedly blame their behavior on unemployment and the demand for more welfare. As in France, the non-assimilating Muslims have been establishing enclaves, considered "No-Go" zones for local non-Muslims. Fire and emergency workers refuse to enter these neighborhoods without a police escort. In one instance, when firefighters were attempting to put out a blaze at one of the mosques, they were pelted by young Muslim men with rocks.

Muslims comprise eighty percent of the town of Husby, a suburb of Stockholm, where many of these riots begin and spread into the big city.

Once a peaceful nation, crime has exploded in Sweden since the mid-1990's, with most of the violent crimes being perpetrated by Muslim immigrants and offspring. These figures are confirmed by nearly every study and web site pertaining to the subject. United Nation statistics reveal how the risks for a woman being raped in the streets of any Swedish city are the second highest in the world, with

53.2 reported rapes per 100,000 population. Of course, those statistics apply to cities where rapes are actually reported. Many, it is believed, go unreported for obvious reasons. The National Crime Prevention Council reports that one in four women in Sweden today will be raped. Although political correctness prohibits tallying statistics by religion, the general, educated consensus is that 85 percent of all rapes are perpetrated by Muslim men.

In 1970, rapes were nearly unheard of in Sweden.

In 2009, when Malmo hosted the Davis Cup tennis matches, which included Israeli players, Muslims erupted into a wave of anti-Semitic violence, causing a near-empty stadium for the games. Malmo is home to only 700 Jews, yet the Swedes report between 50 and 100 anti-Semitic incidents a year, most by first and second-generation Muslim immigrants.

Israeli tennis player Andy Ram was quoted by author, Pam Geller: "… a sad moment for tennis. Never in my career as an athlete have I encountered such hatred."

On March 27, 2016, *World Net Daily* published a report titled, "Sweden Buckling Under Muslim Immigration." Besides crime and fear, the report cites a study that identifies the 2015 crisis as costing much more to the country than what it spends on defense. G.M. Davis, author of *House of War: Islam's Jihad Against the World,* notes how Sweden's famous welcoming approach to immigrants has led to contempt among the Muslim population for their adopted country. The WND report adds: "Mass immigration, mostly from Muslim nations, has utterly transformed many Swedish cities, leading to the development of No-Go zones where law enforcement fears to tread."

Norway:

This is another evolving Scandinavian country gradually succumbing to the yoke of radical Islam.

In 2009, Anders Behring Breivik, a 32 year-old non-Muslim Norwegian, went on a murder spree slaughtering some 77 men, women and children as young as fourteen. His primary targets were the bombing of government buildings in Oslo resulting in eight deaths and then firing several guns at a nearby youth camp event being held by the National Labor Party. He was apprehended and sentenced to life in prison. While there can be no excusing such a horrific crime, it is worthwhile noting the killer's mentality because it symbolizes a growing fear and frustration with the Islamization of Norway, and the gradual destruction of its rich and beloved culture.

Breivik, who planned the terror event for nine years, made no secret of his motive which he recorded in writing. It highlights the frustrations undoubtedly shared by many nationalists throughout that country. According to *The Week* on-line magazine, Breivik was incensed by the rise of multiculturalism in Norway. In the 1,500-page manifesto, posted on line, the killer hoped to use the attack as a "declaration of war against the Islamization of Western Europe." According to his subsequent confession, he wanted to save Norway from a Muslim takeover, and the Labour Party had to pay the price for "letting down the Norwegian people."

This was truly an act of terror, not by Islam, but inspired by fear and hatred of Islam by an extreme nationalist whose love of country propelled him into a despicable violent act.

While Norway has not seen the burgeoning size of Muslim populations when compared to Sweden, the two countries share the same peninsula, so it's only a matter of time. Pew reports that Norway's indigenous birth rate is at 1.8 while the Muslims rate is 3.1. The current population is under five million, 144,000 of which are Muslims. That number is projected to increase by 148 percent – to 359,000 – by the year 2030. (In 1980, the Muslim population stood at only one thousand.)

Alan Dershowitz, famed American lawyer, Harvard professor and author, encountered a strong dose of Muslim-inspired anti-Semitism in 2011 when he was invited by a Christian group to speak about the Israel-Palestinian conflict. Meanwhile, he was also scheduled to speak at three different universities on the Israeli situation, of which he has written six books, but was stonewalled by college authorities telling him the subject was off-limits. They told him to talk about the O.J. Simpson case instead. According to Mr. Dershowitz, "Hamas and its supporters are invited in the dialogue, but supporters of Israel are excluded by an implicit, yet very real boycott against pro-Israel views."

United Kingdom (UK):

In June of 2016, the citizens of Great Britain went to the polls and shocked the world when 52 percent of the populace voted for England to break away from the European Union (EU). A record 71 percent of voters turned out, a show of intensity and purpose for the English people. Some folks attribute the shocking withdrawal to a sagging economy and other issues, but the bottom line, according to well-informed pundits, is the runaway immigration problems that are not only pecking away at an overloaded economy, but eroding the culture of the English landscape as the Islamization process forges ahead like a steamroller.

In 2010, Pew Research reported that the Muslim population of the UK is slightly more than 2.8 million, and that number is expected to rise to 5.5 million in 2030 while the indigenous British population remains static. This author has spoken with folks who are British, or who recently visited London, saying there are parts of the city that feel like another country.

With the possible exception of France, nowhere has Europe been more inundated with Sharia demands and Islamic unrest. Nowhere does the indigenous government capitulate more than the British.

Islamic demands have succeeded in eliminating Israel from the map in school books, replaced by "Occupied Palestine." (Source: Gatestone Institute). That same source reports in 2011 that the numbers of Christians declined in Wales and England by eleven percent. In that same decade, Islam increased by 80 percent.

Conversions have been plentiful in the UK, with many young people from prisons being lured into the Islamic faith for a variety of reasons such as security, acceptance, food, etc. (Prisons, likewise, have been a fertile source for Muslim conversions in the United States.)

Gatestone reports approximately 1,700 mosques in the UK, many of which have been converted from abandoned Christian churches. In Britain, Islam has taken over Anglicanism as the dominant religion. More people attend mosques than those who attend the Church of England.

The nascent Muslim population has also had an impact on British politics as the House of Commons now seats six Muslims as Members of Parliament. In May of 2016, 1.3 Londoners cast their votes for Sadiq Khan, son of Pakistani immigrants, to become the first Muslim mayor of London. That number, ironically (according to Gatestone), is roughly the number of Muslim residents in London.

It is not uncommon for hundreds of Muslims to commandeer a city street in London or Birmingham for mass prayer. It is illegal, but no one dares to enforce the law. Riots and mob burnings by Islamists are equally common in urban areas, as British Muslims gain more numbers and power, making more demands.

As though living in Saudi Arabia, not England, Islamic centers are dispatching the "Sharia Police" harassing and chasing people away who do not conform to Islamic laws, i.e., wearing short skirts, tight pants, being gay, carrying a beer, etc. Muslim No-Go zones are strictly enforced for Sharia compliance. Many of these enclaves have signs posted stating: "You are entering a Sharia Controlled Zone, No gambling, No Music, No Alcohol," and *et al.* There is no statistical count of "No-Go" zones in Great Britain.

The Brits have capitulated to Islam by allowing Sharia law to usurp British law in many urban centers, specifically in reference to domestic matters. Women, in particular, are at risk because Islamic law generally rules in deference to men when it comes to marital or other domestic disputes, such as child custody, sexual activity, etc. Women have huge barriers to cross in achieving parity from a Muslim cleric since Sharia cites men as being twice the worth of women, and any woman who wishes a divorce generally fails. A woman who refuses to give sex to the husband is entitled to be beaten. According to Quran Sura 4:34:

Men are the maintainers of women because Allah has made some of them to excel others and because they spend out of their property; the good women are therefore obedient, guarding the unseen as Allah has guarded; and those on whose part you fear desertion, admonish them, and leave them alone in the sleeping-places and beat them; then if they obey you, do not seek a way against them; Allah is Great.

Honor killings are not uncommon in the world of Islam. They are technically illegal, but often result in Islamic blindness since authorities routinely ignore them, particularly those that receive no media attention. Any woman; wife, daughter, mother, who shames the family, especially through apostasy, may likely find herself in an early grave, while the Islamic community turns a blind eye.

Muslims believe Sharia Law is revealed by God. In cases where a divorce was granted by a civil court, the parties will still go before a Sharia Council. There are now 85 of these councils in the UK that rule on every domestic or civil matter imaginable, contrary to any British law. According to UK barrister, Charlotte Proudman, "They are totally unregulated, unauthorized, there is no accountability and do not operate within UK laws."

Of major concern to the UK economy is the state of welfare that often must support the products of polygamous marriages. It's not uncommon for a male immigrant to have four wives, each bearing three or four children requiring health and social benefits from the government. However, because English law does not recognize bigamy/polygamy, most of these women are considered "single mothers" and therefore entitled to a plethora of welfare benefits from the taxpayer. While the government estimated in 2007 that there were about 1,000 polygamous marriages in the UK, reporter Sue Reid of *Mail On-Line*, a British journal, claims her sources put the estimate closer to 20,000.

If this much Islamization has succeeded in the UK since 1980, one can only wonder if there will be an England remaining by mid-century. This is the primary reason the people voted to become independent of the EU, because the central power in Brussels was exerting more control over Great Britain's immigrant crisis, and thus,

British culture and the British economy. Basically, the English took their country back.

The seven countries described above serve as a sampling of the pervasive spread of Islamic culture, religion, and Sharia, that have, to one degree or another, affected virtually all of the fifty-one countries that make up the European continent. Four of these—Bosnia, Turkey, Albania and Kosovo—already have majority Muslim populations.

Consider the landscape in another twenty years.

Europe in the Crosshairs:

According to Pew Research studies, the overall population of Europe will decline 28 million by 2030 while the Muslim population will increase 29 million. At present, there are 44.1 million Muslims living in Europe. With those population increases and burgeoning citizenship comes political power and influence to slowly convert the nations into bastions of Sharia law, while the cultures of Europe, as we know it, are slowly eradicated. Later in this century, the native French, German and British will become the prevailing minorities.

Europe has been a consistent target of Islamic expansionism since early in the eighth century. The following is a brief synopsis of significant historical events and milestones:

In the year 711 A.D., Islam conquered what is modern day Spain and ruled the Iberian peninsula for 780 years. Apologists for Islam will say that Islam lived in peace jointly with Christians and Jews. What they often fail to share is that Christians and Jews had to pay Dhimmitude, a special tax for refusing to convert. No pay, no live.

In 732 A.D., Muslim armies invaded France in another attempt at conquest, but were defeated at the Battle of Tours. Historians cite this event as the turning point lest Islam would have been ruling the entire European continent. Had that been successful, it would have changed the future course of America.

In 827 A.D., Muslims invaded Sicily, initiating a war of seventy-five years until the Sicilians finally capitulated in 902 A.D. Muslim rule would last 264 years.

The Ottoman Empire began its thrust toward European conquest in the end of the 14th century. Between 1385 A.D. and 1683 A.D., the Muslims engaged in a number of smaller conquests—Serbia, Albania, Bosnia, Croatia, Bulgaria, Hungary, *et al.* Constantinople fell in 1453 A.D. and Greece fell in 1460 A.D.

1683 A.D., Muslim armies of the Ottoman Empire initiated the Battle of Vienna, and lost.

These few examples, alone, should tell the story of unrelenting campaigns toward conquest either by violence or infiltration.

There have been smaller wars, far too numerous to name here, all the result of Muslim invaders. It is suffice to say that the continent of Europe has been in the crosshairs of Islamic conquest since the first invasion of Spain in 711 A.D., and it has never relented. Today, the Islamists have learned newer and better methods for conquest. In 2016, warriors don't need instruments of death to conquer other civilizations. All they need is Taqiyya, effective propaganda, money and a gullible populace ready to be eaten.

In killing, it doesn't matter how many people die as long as Allah triumphs in the end. Sadly, the Europeans of the 21st century have yet to catch on how or why they are being conquered and that their granddaughters are destined to live under the watchful eye of Sharia, owned by their husbands as though owning a useful camel.

Those who are aware of their granddaughter's destiny of slavery into fundamentalist Islam, must not care very much, because the European governments have basically capitulated to demands as Islamic influence grows stronger with each passing year.

EIGHT
NORTH AMERICAN EXPANSIONISM

Throughout parts of the Middle-East, particularly in the Palestinian arena, there is a saying: "First Saturday, then Sunday." Translated, it means the destruction of Israel will by followed by the conquest of the United States.

The Muslim Brotherhood acts as an immense control center for puppeteers engaged in manipulating, strategizing, propagandizing and infiltrating. After knowing and digesting the Muslim Brotherhood's "Explanatory Memorandum" and the notorious document, "The Project," the intentions and objectives of this organization are unambiguous. There are absolutely no doubts about their intentions. And if we examine all the actions and decrees from the Muslim Brotherhood in recent years, we can see the process is working.

The so-called "Arab-Spring" is a good example, which flooded into several countries as a sugar-coated subterfuge for conquest. Another is the 2014-2015 mass refugee crisis of biblical proportions as millions swarmed into Europe from Syria, Iraq, and other places. The enemy means what they say, even though they practice deceit in order to fool the general populous into believing they are secular and harmless. Some would say they even fooled our own president. That's highly questionable as we'll examine in future chapters.

While there is no single leader or person heading the expansionism, as there was with Hitler's Germany or Hirohito's Japan, there is definitely a central command with a leadership system. We can also call it a hierarchy that answers, in their minds, to Allah and together their cause is one; conquest. Die-hard Islamists have been so deeply indoctrinated in scores of countries around the world that they will commit suicide by the thousands and randomly kill other people they consider infidels in order to serve Allah. The innocent Muslim victims who often die in the process are rationalized as glorious sacrifices for Allah who will embrace them all in paradise.

Mothers have proudly sent their sons and daughters into the streets strapped with bombs for the glory of killing and being killed. Jihad has been a hallmark for Islam since the death of Mohammed. The struggle for conquest throughout the world has never ceased. Never.

Today, the advancement is going better than ever. The enemy is relying on the well-intended good nature and naivety of the Western world, coupled with unlimited resources and a complicit media. The protections of our constitutional freedoms that extend to anyone in America, including the freedom of religion that is used by the enemy as a Trojan Horse to invade our country with impunity.

For a moment, imagine several members of the Brotherhood hierarchy in a war room in post Iranian revolution, circa 1980-1981, planning for conquest. The top puppeteers place various colored pins on a map of Europe and North America determining who to target, where, what and why. The pins denote where they intend on forming Islamic settlements throughout the land, as they build mosques and learning centers. They will denote the most effective targets for political action, identifying which parties and politicians to flood under the radar. They will also need support from media in order to portray Muslims as harmless religious worshippers with no other agenda. They also need a plan for burgeoning the population in the manner of Europe.

Think of it as a control center arranging for expansion in all four corners of the world, particularly Europe and more so, America, the great Satan. How could they go about succeeding without terrorism?

Answer: by planting the seeds of population growth. With greater populations comes greater political power.

It's happening today, throughout Europe and North America, as we go about our daily lives.

There is no more efficient way of conquering a civilization than by a successfully proliferating people of one ilk. The proliferation of

Muslims translates to increased Islamic power throughout the land, in all facets of the infrastructure, including banks, schools, the justice system and the political arena itself. Once Islam grips the government leadership and the lawmaking bodies, the US Constitution, as we know it, will be worth nothing. When we hear about some examples of expansionism, they can make a cynic very curious.

For example, in the 1980s, just outside a small town of Cornwall, Ontario, there existed a large five-story hospital situated on eighteen acres along the highway parallel to the St. Lawrence River. In 2003, after several years of being vacated, the property was purchased and occupied by the Al-Rashid Islamic Institute for Learning. The curriculum is awash in religious studies for all Muslims, although younger students attend classes in grades one through twelve. The enigma of this immense project is that there were hardly any Muslims living in or near Cornwall in the early 2000's. So, why invest in such a huge Islamic learning center?

Another puzzle is Yellowknife, Canada, the provincial capital situated in the far regions of Northwest Territories, one of the most northern cities in the nation where winter residents live in twenty-four hour darkness. In the 1990's and early 2000's, approximately 125 Muslim immigrants from Pakistan, Somalia and other places, settled in Yellowknife to find jobs. Of course, who wouldn't want to live in Yellowknife where it's freezing eight months of the year?

Inch by inch, few here, a few there as the numbers grow. Make lots of babies. Indoctrinate them as small children and do not assimilate outside the culture. As the babies grow, they all have more babies, and very soon, those babies become political figures in towns, provinces and maybe more.

In all, nearly one million Muslims live in Canada, with the greatest concentration in the Greater Toronto Area, which is about five percent. It has the greatest concentration of Muslims of any city in North America. Other Islamic communities are thriving in Canada from the Atlantic to the Pacific.

Much like Europe, Islamic expansionism has been very successful in the North American continent, either through immigration, overstaying visas, anchor births of children from Muslim immigrants, and conversions. In 1980, approximately 400 mosques existed in the United States. According to *Salatomatic.com*, a guide to Islamic mosques and schools around the world, 3,186 mosques now exist in the US as of 2015, plus hundreds more Islamic learning centers. That's an increase of nearly 700 percent. What will the next twenty years bring? In fact, those numbers are deceptive, because they do not take into account the hundreds, or thousands, of storefront prayer and learning centers in most cities. That also doesn't include Muslim-only enclaves.

It's almost as though immigrants are being deployed from a central command to strategic locales in the US and Canada, like sowing the seeds of a population farm. We don't notice because most of us don't care. It's too big to comprehend. Sadly, today's populous is mostly concerned with the present and not the world our great-grandchildren will be living in.

Interestingly enough, the millions currently involved in the mass exodus from Syria and other Muslim nations were never invited or offered sanctuary by their fellow Arabs in countries such as like Saudi Arabia, Yemen, Qatar, Oman, Egypt, Libya and more. And, why not? It would seem far more logical and expeditious considering the masses could assimilate among people of their own culture, without language barriers, and with folks who mainly share the same religious beliefs. But no. The target is exclusively Europe and the United States. Saudi Arabia, or any other Arab nation, opened their doors to no one.

Statistics vary in determining the current population of Muslims. Islamic web sites claim about seven million, while other studies say it's two to three million. Pew Research puts the number just under three million, but that doesn't include inmates, illegals and American converts. Studies for growth are impossible to calculate. The influx of immigrants, legal and illegal, plus the enormous volume of Muslims coming to the United States on student visas is staggering and cannot be figured into the overall resident population. That's in addition to the 90,000 Muslims who routinely immigrate to the US.

annually, according to a 2010 study filed by the International Institute for Applied Systems Analysis. Then there are the converts, many of whom come from prisons.

According to a 2010 Religious Census, in a study released by the Association of Statisticians of American Religious bodies, Illinois ranks as the state with the highest per capita Muslim population (2.8 percent) with Montana the lowest (.034 percent). Islam is the largest non-Christian group in twenty American states, mostly in the south and mid-west. California has the most mosques with 525. Montana has three mosques, and a vibrant group of students at the University of Montana belonging to the Muslims Students of America (MSA), a spin-off organization of the Muslim Brotherhood. Vermont has only one mosque.

Visas:

The volatile issue of illegal immigration in this country focuses almost entirely on the Hispanic front, mostly from Mexico. Here we are again, with our attention being diverted from another problem the government does not want us to see. Virtually no attention is given to the problem of illegal immigration from people overstaying visas, which accounts for approximately 40 percent of an estimated eleven or twelve million illegals, according to the *Wall Street Journal*, (April 7, 2013) and *USA Today*, (January 20, 2015)

All the funding for additional enforcement personnel in the new immigration reform package offered by the US Senate in June of 2013 bolsters the Border Patrol by large numbers, but offers nothing to Immigration and Customs Enforcement (ICE) that are responsible for enforcing illegal overstays. In essence, the visa overstay situation is being ignored by the current administration. This includes all those who obtain visas for work, school or tourism. Violators easily blend into the American landscape without notice because they've already been here legally.

The *USA Today* report in January of 2016 concluded that nearly 500,000 foreign nationals overstayed their visas in 2015. Many are from counties that harbor Islamic Jihadists.

In 2007, A Jordanian, Hosam Smadi, came to the US on a tourist visa. Two years later he was caught plotting to blow up a Dallas high-rise.

In 2012, Moroccan Amine El Kahlifi overstayed his visa and was arrested for conspiring to detonate a bomb at the US Capitol.

Four of the 9/11 terrorists were in the US on overstayed visas.

According to *Judicial Watch*, there are about 1.2 million foreigners in the country on student visas, of which about 75,000 come from Muslim countries. Thousands of these students never show up for class and eventually blend into the landscape as illegal immigrants with legal papers.

One Pakistani man, who was indicted in Houston for aiding the Taliban in Jihad training against America, entered the US with a student visa. He remained long after the visa expired and joined with Muslim groups in Texas where he engaged in weapons training for terrorizing Americans.

We simply make it too easy for Muslims, and others, to enter this country, any one of whom could be associated with the Jihad movement. It may come under the heading of "profiling," which is non-politically correct in today's world, but it is only common sense to know that 98 percent of global terrorism and stealth Jihad is rooted in radical Islam. Even if only ten percent of Muslims could be categorized as "radical," we are taking a huge risk, knowing what we know about Islamic Jihad and the objectives of the Muslim Brotherhood.

It is a simple fact that extended visas are an ideal avenue for stealth illegal immigration into the US. There are no reliable numbers today that can tell us how many visas are overstayed from Islamic origins. Since 9/11, the numbers could be close to a million, or more. Yet, we continue with the idiotic open-door policy that will ultimately contribute to the downfall of this great nation.

Mr. Bob Beckel, a well-known Democrat and liberal commentator and columnist, said it best. He declared on Fox News in April of 2013 that the United States should stop accepting Muslim student visas until the ones already here are thoroughly vetted:

"The hatred for the United States runs deep. Given that fact, I think we have to consider cutting off Muslim students coming to this country for some period of time so that we can absorb what we've got, look at who is here, and decide whether some of the people here should be sent home or go to prison."

In another news interview, Senator Marco Rubio (R-FL), the son of immigrants, suggested that student visas are not a right. He stated he was open to the idea of halting student and other visas to people from Muslim countries.

While it's true that only a tiny number of terrorists came from the pools of student visas, we must never forget that "terrorists" *do not* comprise the majority of Jihadists. We should be focusing more on people who engage in anti-American subterfuge, who work with Jihad groups inside the United States to organize political takeovers, who strive toward implementing Sharia law, and who support Hamas and other hate organizations around the globe. There are more ways to undermine America besides terrorism. Though impossible to count, many more of the Muslim students who come over on visas are deeply programmed, as are most hard-core Muslim nations, to hate America and to aid and abet in the stealth Jihad process. Many of these people are not living in America because it's so wonderful; they are living in America with a sinister purpose.

This is just one method by which we're stupidly allowing the enemies of America access to our infrastructure.

Birth Rates and Immigration:

According the Pew Research Center, Muslim birth rates and immigration will see a doubling of the Muslim population in America in the next thirty years. I suspect that is a low estimate, based on *legal* immigrants. There was a time when nearly all Muslims in the US were immigrants. That's changing. Nearly half are now citizens or legal residents of the US.

Pew research finds that 64.5 percent of US Muslims were born abroad, but that number will fall to 55 percent as the numbers of native-born rises. That's good news for the Jihad movement because American-born Muslims are less noticed.

As stated earlier, it's nearly impossible to count the number of Muslims now living in the United States because there are no reliable statistics. Pew Research puts the number at 2.6 million, but doesn't take into account prison converts and illegals living in the US. Other estimates vary up to as much as nine million. President Obama and Secretary of State Hillary Clinton in 2009 told the world that seven million Muslim Americans live in the US

As this book is written, President Obama and his administration are brokering for a welcome mat for untold numbers of refugees that have been displaced from Syria and the Middle-East. Inviting refugees and migrants is another way of ballooning the Muslim population in the United States and Canada.

According to a 2010 article in the *Houston Chronicle* tracking estimated Muslim populations, the following are the most populated *per capita* major cities in the US

Detroit
Washington, D.C.
Cedar Rapids, Iowa
Philadelphia
New York
Atlanta
Peoria, Illinois
San Francisco
Houston
Chicago

Note: Cedar Rapids is the site of the first mosque built in the US in 1934.

This list omits the impact on Detroit by the suburb city of Dearborn. With a population of 98,000, forty percent of which (per Wikipedia) is Arab-American, Dearborn is also represented by other Islamic countries in smaller numbers, such as Lebanon, Iraq., etc. Dearborn hosts the Islamic Center of America, the largest mosque in North America. It is well-known as the Islamic hub of the United

States, and is often euphemistically referred to by cynics as "Dearbornistan."

Minnesota towns and cities are growing with Muslim populations, particularly with Somali Muslim immigrants who started arriving in the early 1990's. Their children are all now American citizens and so will be their children. According to Minnesota Public Radio, St. Cloud schools now boast an enrollment of ten percent Somali students. As of 2015, according to the American Community Survey, about 86,000 Somali settlers and refugees have come to the US, 40 percent of whom settled in Minnesota.

Numerous reports have been filed about Somali gangs causing unrest and raising crime rates. Several reports from reputable sources cite women and gays as the frequent target of harassment and assault. In 2012. Sheriff Rich Stanek, representing the National Sheriff's Association, testified before House Judiciary Committee on Crime, Terrorism and Homeland Security about the threat of Somali gangs in Minnesota. His state is now a designated "US Refugee Resettlement Area," with a Somali population between 80,000 and 125,000 people. Exact counts are impossible to calculate for a variety of reasons, thus the exact population of Somali Muslims is unknown. (According to the Department of Health and Human Services, resettlement sites exist in 49 states)

Typical crimes committed by Somali gangs range from burglaries, credit card fraud, and witness intimidation to connections with international terrorism. They're also known to specifically target gays and joggers whom they rob, assault and harass.

Muslim cab drivers made the news in the decade between 2000 and 2008, when they collectively refused to accept passengers, particularly from airports, who were carrying alcoholic beverages (in sealed containers) and guide dogs. They claimed it violated the laws of Islam. An ABC News report in 2007 stated that 5,400 passengers had been turned away over a five-year period. The cab drivers lost a law suit in 2008. Three-fourths of the 900 cabbies licensed at the Minneapolis-St. Paul airport are Muslim, mostly Somali.

Muslim gangs in San Francisco have reportedly been targeting gays for robbery, assault and harassment. In one case, there was a series of gay men being shot in the face as Muslim gang members videoed the events. One camera was found on the scene by authorities, in which eleven such attacks were recorded. Such crimes, like rapes, are not always reported because of fear of retribution by gang members.

Florida is a growing hub for Muslim expansion since 9/11. According to the Association of Statisticians of American Religious Bodies, as published in the *Orlando Sentinel,* the Muslim population of greater Orlando grew ten-fold in the decade between 2000 and 2010, from 2,691 to 27,939. In the suburb of Longwood, a 17,000-foot warehouse has been converted into an immense Muslim Community Center. Significant Muslim communities have been growing throughout Florida, in greater Jacksonville, Tampa, Miami, For Lauderdale and of course, the capital, Tallahassee.

In truth, the pattern of Islamic influence and supremacy is growing throughout America, particularly in other "gateway" cities such as Lewiston, Maine, Shelbyville, Tennessee, Clarkston, Georgia and Jamestown, North Dakota.

This brings to mind the previous chapter's reference to seeding.

Prison Conversions:

What better place to find vulnerable and needy young men who are disenchanted with America, mostly uneducated, lower-socioeconomic roots, and with low self-esteem, than in the nation's prison systems?

A typical scenario arises when young first-time offenders, particularly black males, enter prison in a state of fear. Horror stories abound, many of which are true, about what happens to young men in their initial days and nights in the prison world. The kids entering the jails certainly learn about it.

Enter Islam. The Brotherhood is a powerful lure. It is enticing, indeed, to be offered protection from harm by other inmates. Simply enter into Islam and follow the path of Mohammed. And for this, we must give credit to the Muslims in prisons, for they do, indeed, protect their own. Most bully convicts will not risk an assault against a Muslim in jail unless they are willing to face the wrath of Allah. In fact, they probably prevent hundreds/thousands of inmate assaults.

The Muslim Brotherhood is not stupid. Their leaders know where to recruit. Thus, prisons throughout America have become a fertile harvest ground for Islamic conversions, most of whom become dedicated Muslims after they leave incarceration, whether two years or twenty years later. With those conversions come strict indoctrination and in many cases, fanaticism with Islam, prime recruits for the mission of Jihad. Most of the Islamists in prisons are proponents of Wahhabi teachings, a strict form of Islam practiced in Saudi Arabia, from which the funding flows. Saudi Arabia and other Middle-East nations have been furnishing copies of the Quran by the thousands into the American state and federal prison systems, along with other reading materials germane to Islamist teachings.

This is not because they love America so much.

According to Wikipedia, which posted an entire page on this topic, approximately 17 to 20 percent of the prison population in America, about 350,000 inmates, are now comprised of Muslims. Eighty percent of the prisoners who "find faith" while in prison, convert to Islam.

The National Islamic Prison Foundation (NIPF) claims to be converting about 135,000 inmates a year to Islam, 95 percent of whom are African American with a small but growing Hispanic representation close behind. Non-Islamic sources put that conversion rate at about half that number. The NIPF was formed for the expressed purpose of converting inmates in the American penal system.

In February of 2003, the *Wall Street Journal* reported that Wahhabism is making serious inroads in the black inmate population. Inmates are told, when eventually set free, that they will be assisted at any mosque to find food, shelter and jobs. That's an attractive package for young men who come from dysfunctional families or no families at all.

The indoctrination of inmates is a strategy documented in al Qaeda training manuals which assert that non-Muslim prisoners should be targeted for conversion because they are likely to be disenchanted with their country. Moreover, say the manuals, those converts can be valuable to terrorist groups because they combine a desire for "payback" with an ability to blend easily into American culture.

Female Conversions:

According to an *NBC News* report in 2013, approximately 20,000 conversions to Islam take place among Americans each year (excluding prisons) 80 percent of which are female. These statistics are questionable and could be far more, but the fact remains that a huge number of free American women voluntarily take part in the conversion process to Islam.

Most will tell us, as many web sites post, that these women convert for a variety of reasons, most of which have to do with the positive aspects of Islamic life:

- Close family bonds
- Sense of loyal community
- Security; feeling of being protected
- Cleanliness
- Strong ethical and moral standards
- Purity of dietary requirements
- Disillusionment with their prior religion

There are two additional factors that have a subtle but powerful influence on female converts, not listed in studies of conversion.

Deceit and power.

First Additional Factor – Deceit:

American women are rarely told the entire truth. They are led to believe what the Islamists want them to believe as they are indoctrinated into blind faith: Do not question. Just believe.

Islam is a broad and complicated culture, religion and source of deep study. Imams and other Islamic leaders have been notorious in their ability to spin Islam as just another religion whose roots are found in the Old Testament, that acknowledge Abraham's role in religious history, and the role of Jesus as a prophet, though not a deity. This author has attended meetings and talks by Islamic leaders and professors, all of whom teach the goodness of Islam, how it is truly a religion of peace, selectively quoting from peaceful verses in the Quran. But that's the sanitized offering.

What the leaders fail to teach are the array of hateful and degrading Qur'anic verses and messages in the Hadith that subjugate women to the point of slavery to the male gender, and calling for Jihad, failing to point out that the Quran was not assembled in chronological order of Mohammed's life that led to abrogation of old verses by newer verses. Mohammed's early evangelical years in Mecca were peaceful, but his later years in Medina were rife with warring. Verses that appear in conflict with one another are resolved by the earlier verses (during the Mecca years) being abrogated by the later verses (during the Medina years), a period that rose Islam to world prominence through violence. Thus, we resolve why some verses speak of love and tolerance for other religions, and others speak of intolerance and even killing. The newer verses speak more about Jihad, conquest, violence, hatred of other religions and the subjugation of women.

From the Quran:

"Sura 2:256 - Let there be no compulsion in religion: Truth stands out Clear from Error: whoever rejects evil and believes in Allah hath grasped the most trustworthy hand-hold, that never breaks. And Allah heareth and knoweth all things."

Compare to:

"Sura 9.5 - And when the sacred months have passed, then kill the polytheists wherever you find them and capture them and besiege them and sit in wait for them at every place of ambush. But if they should repent, establish prayer, and give zakat, let them [go] on their way. Indeed, Allah is Forgiving and Merciful.

True, in parts of the world, Muslim men do not always hold these commands as literal. All do not treat women as they were animals possessed for servitude. But as a rule, the more fundamentalist a country becomes, the stricter women are held to the harsh laws of the Quran and the Hadith. That oppression exists in countries such as Saudi Arabia, Pakistan, Afghanistan, Somalia, Libya, and others. Much of the protests and uprisings that are taking place in Turkey as this book is being written are being conducted by secular women and men who are pleading for freedom from the yoke of fundamentalism.

Neither are women fully informed of the true nature of Mohammed's methods and tactics in his rise to power after moving to Medina in 622 A.D. His last ten years of evangelism is rife with raids of violence, robbery, murder, rape and conquest, particularly over those who refused to accept Islam as their new faith.

The life of Mohammed is well documented, more so than Jesus or any other prophet or figure in Biblical times. Those who have an open mind and seek answers from knowledgeable historians would be shocked to learn about Mohammed's years of Jihad, some of which entailed ordering local tribal women to be taken as concubines after beheading their men and seizing possessions in villages and towns.

In his lifetime, Mohammed took a dozen wives for himself, one of which was a child of six with whom he did not consummate until she was age nine.

Islamists in the United States seek out converts who will provide more support to the long-range stealth Jihad. Part of that plan is outpopulating the non-Muslims over time. That's an important role of women. Jihadists do not expect America to be an Islamic state overnight, and they don't care if they fail to see it materialize in their lifetime, for they believe deeply that all their efforts on behalf of Allah will provide them an ultimate passage into paradise and everlasting life.

Thus, deceit is an effective tool in luring females into Islam. A great example of that was exposed by journalist Laura Mansfield when she visited a mosque in a small southern town in 2005. The mosque had issued invitations to local women to come and see the wonders and goodness of Islam. This was a PR campaign of sorts with the hope of recruiting a few converts. (Article, "Jihad Comes to Smalltown, USA" – *World Net Daily*, April 19, 2005)

Posing as a local resident, Laura showed up an hour early at the mosque only to be told by the men that she should return later. She asked if she could wait in the front until the other women arrived. The men said "Okay." She overheard one man telling the others not to worry, she was an American who did not speak Arabic. But she did speak and understand Arabic.

What she overheard among the men was chilling. The men openly spoke about civil disobedience, ranting on about hate and defiance to all the male attendees in the audience. They were clearly haters of America. The imam closed the session by reminding everyone it was their duty as Muslims to continue on the path of Jihad by using either subtle methods, or violence if necessary to support terrorism.

When the men were finished, a Muslim woman took over and welcomed a small group of curious ladies into the mosque. That's when the rhetoric reversed 180 degrees, painting a glowing picture, talking mostly about the similarities between Islam and Christianity, how peaceful and loving Islam is toward women, how Islam is misunderstood and everything about the gentler side of the religion. What was omitted were all the verses in the Quran that speak of the true view of women by Muslims.

Example:

"Sura 2.223 *Your wives are a tilth for you, so go into your tilth when you like and do good beforehand for yourselves*"

If this is a sampling of Islam in a small town, one can only surmise what rhetoric is espoused in larger mosques throughout America.

To be sure, newly converted women of 2013 will be treated quite well and shown only the brighter side of living as a Muslim wife. It is a smart strategy that they be groomed as exemplars for future female converts by painting a rosy picture of Islam.

Second Additional Factor –Power:

There are some people in this world, male and female, who are totally fascinated by power, drawn like proverbial moths to the flame. No doubt, that is why so many in the post-9/11 era are being driven to Islam in America and in Western societies around the world. Power unites. Power creates a sense of euphoria. Power controls emotion. The most powerful create the followers.

What Islam has accomplished throughout the world, mostly via the Muslim Brotherhood, and particularly since the Iranian revolution in 1979, is nothing less than astonishing. Despite all the terrorism and outright murders of 29,000-plus innocent people in dozens of countries since 9/11, plus all the threats and intimidation that has followed, Islam has the leaders of a hundred countries on their knees, including England, France, Spain, Canada and the United States, kowtowing to Islam, lauding Islam as a "religion of peace" and invoking laws to protect Muslims from harassment. Imagine that? Islam is the common denominator for multi-thousands of terror attacks throughout the world and many thousands of innocent deaths, yet we, the victims of Islamic terror, are the ones who must apologize for speaking ill of Islam.

Islam commands a 57-state bloc in the United Nations. And, with 1.5 billion people around the globe, and a rising political and cultural influence in the West, this is the most powerful ideology the world may have ever known.

Power is the ultimate opiate. We've seen what power fanaticism can do to otherwise rational people. In the 20th century alone, we witnessed the frenzied worship of Adolf Hitler, Benito Mussolini and Emperor Hirohito among a citizenry that would otherwise have been considered peace loving, tolerant and rational. Yet, although they knew the leaders and the armies were committing despicable acts against humanity, they turned a blind eye and happily extended a Nazi salute to Hitler and the passing soldiers, awash in the euphoria of sheer power.

Men and women who convert to Islam would not likely admit to the lure of power, because they aren't even aware of it; can't touch it, see it, hear it or smell it. But it is there. It's awesome. And they want to be a part of it. Because it just feels good.

Muslim Enclaves in America:

Earlier, we talked about "No-Go Zones" in France, England and other countries, where Islamists have basically sealed off their communities from the rest of the country, free to ignore national laws by instituting Sharia and living as a separate nation within a nation. It's where police, fire, media and any other representatives of the establishment are intimidated and unwelcome. And, Islamists get away with it.

It's happening in the United States.

Populated mostly with converted inmates released from the American penal system, and their women, at least twenty-two set-aside enclaves (or compounds) exist in rural areas of the United States. These are Islamic-only communities where non-Muslims are unwelcome. Some sources cite as many as 35 enclaves, but that is not confirmed. These enclaves operate under the systems of Sharia, basically ignoring state and federal laws and living as a small nation within a nation. In many of these, it is strongly believed that some terror training camps are active and thriving. Authorities are stupefied, helpless, by their pronouncements that these are religious retreats.

The enclaves are funded as branches of the Muslims of America, Inc., (MOA) a tax-exempt, non-profit organization formed in 1980 by Pakistani cleric, Sheikh Mubarak Ali Gilani, who has been directly linked to Jaamat ul-Fuqra, an organization that seeks to purify Islam through violence. Gilani is the same Muslim leader who, in 2002, journalist Daniel Pearl sought out for interview in Pakistan, before Pearl was kidnapped and beheaded.

Headquartered in New York, Jaamat ul-Fuqra openly recruits through service organizations in America, including the prison systems. Members live in compounds where they agree to abide by laws of Jaamat ul Fuqua, which are considered to be above that of any state or federal authority.

The most famous of these compounds is situated deep in a forest called "Islamberg," in upstate New York near the town of Hancock. Dr. Paul L. Williams, author and columnist for the *Canada Free Press*, visited Islamberg and describes his visit in an article published by *Front Page Magazine* in May of 2007:

"The 70 acre compound is surrounded by No Trespassing signs...A sentry post has been established at the base of the hill (entrance)...An African American man wearing Islamic garb instructs us to turn around saying, 'our community is not open to visitors.' ...In the distance, women can be seen in full burka... Nearly every weekend, neighbors (in Hancock) hear gunfire and small bangs of explosives."

Williams quotes one resident. "We don't dare slow down when we drive by." Another customer at a local diner, unidentified, said, "If you go in there, you better wear body armor. They have armed guards and if they shoot you, no one will find your body."

Copies of these articles are abundant on line for anyone who is curious enough to surf the web.

Holy Islamville, a 34-acre site in York County, South Carolina, was founded in 1983 by Sheikh Gilani as a Muslim enclave. Visitors are allowed by invitation or appointment only. Gunfire has often been heard coming from the compound where between 500 and 1,000 Muslims converge on the community once a month. In 2006, York County Sheriff Bruce Bryant said that Islamville "is not a location we just sit back and ignore." All of the residents at Islamville accept Sheikh Mubarak Ali Gilani as their leader.

A 2006 law enforcement report produced by the Regional Organized Crime Information Center and funded by the US Justice Department, says Gilani is known as an international terrorist. That report claims Gilani is also the leader of seven covert paramilitary training compounds in the United States, and York County is one of them. http://www.barenakedislam.com/2011/05/09/barrage-of-gunfire-heard-coming-from-a-place-called-holy-islamville-south-carolina/20090212_home_grown_jihad/The classified report adds that Gilani has at least 28 other suspected communes in the US all operating under the name Muslims of America. The report states that they have more than 3,000 members spread out across the country. It adds that at least a dozen members have been convicted of terrorist activities including conspiracy to commit murder, fire bombings and gun smuggling.

Where is the Department of Justice? FBI?

Aliville is another Muslim enclave that sits in a very remote and rural area not far from Commerce, Georgia. Non-Muslims are welcome only by invitation.

Additional enclaves have been established in Hyattsville, Maryland; Red House, Virginia; Falls Church, Virginia; Macon, Georgia; Dover, Tennessee; Buena Vista, Colorado; Talihina, Oklahoma; Tulane Country, California; Commerce, California; and Onalaska, Washington. Others are undoubtedly in the planning stages and certain to encircle the national map in a few short years.

All are being formed under the watchful control of Jaamat ul Fuqua. The degree to which firearms and explosives training are taking place is unknown, though enough nearby witnesses have heard significant gunfire at a number of the sites.

But there are no doubts about their orientation. According to Wikipedia, Jamaat ul-Fuqra is a paramilitary organization of mostly African-American Muslims based in Pakistan and the United States. Several ul-Fuqra members have found their way into prison cells for committing violent acts in the US and abroad. While it is not listed as a terror group by the US or the EU, it was listed as a terrorist organization in the 1999 *Patterns of Global Terrorism* report by the US State Department

Since federal and state law enforcement certainly know about these American Islamist "No-Go" zones in America, it begs the question; what is the threshold for US authorities to initiate a full investigation and take action? We sent thousands of troops halfway around the globe over a period of ten years to wage war against these same Jihadi-minded people who are actively engaged in terror training camps aimed at taking down the United States. More than six thousand Americans lost their lives in these wars, not to mentioned thousands more having lost limbs, hearing and eyesight. Yet, it appears the same style of terror camps can openly exist, *unchallenged*, inside the borders of our own nation. And it's not even newsworthy.

It can only be traced to leadership.

From within!

NINE
TARGETING THE YOUTH

"He alone who owns the youth, gains the future."
■ Adolf Hitler

Hitler wasn't stupid. He knew that the children in the early 1930's mesmerized by his power and wonderment would one day grow up to be part of his army of conquest. As though hypnotized, they would follow his lead to the destruction of free societies everywhere. Young idolizers saw everything that was good about Hitler and decried any criticism, defending his actions all the way to the grave. It didn't matter that he was the aggressor, or that he was slaughtering millions in concentration camps because it was important to look the other way and see only the benefits. Thankfully, with the help of many other nations who were willing to make ultimate sacrifices, Hitler did not succeed.

But he could have. He almost did.

The Muslim Brotherhood of Islam is analogous to the Nazi Party of Germany. Though their tactics are different, their goals are basically the same, driven by sheer hatred of people who are not like them, particularly Jews, and feeling superior to the rest of the non-Muslim world in general. Killing innocent people, women, children, disabled, gypsies, Jews, and others is a necessary offshoot in order to reach the finish line: Conquest.

Islam in Europe and America does not target its propaganda campaigns toward the members of AARP. Insignificant old people are set in their ways; war veterans, retired cops, and doting grandparents, fixated with long-term democratic ideologies that cannot be changed or altered. The older folks are in the way, tolerated and disregarded in terms of effecting long-range change. And, they'll be dead in a short time.

The youth are made of soft clay. They can be persuaded, indoctrinated, molded and formed into images of the power base, radical Islam, much like what is being accomplished among young inmates in our prisons.

Some people liken the process to a computer. Babies are born as little computers, empty and devoid of programs, prepared for input, needing only nourishment in order to stay alive and healthy. From early on, starting usually with the parents, the human computers are slowly programmed into a functioning entity. Kids can be programmed to believe and perform anything.

How often have we seen photographs of small children in southern states, *circa* 1930s, wearing robes of the KKK and spouting disgusting epithets toward black people, or even taking part in lynching? They weren't born with hate in their hearts; it was a learned behavior brought about by indoctrination. There are thousands of photos of young boys in the Palestinian regions wearing garb of violent Jihadi, al Qaeda headbands, and toting little guns eager to please their fathers in training to kill Jews and other infidels. In April of 1945, when the Russians were at the Nazi doorstep, German youths still stood in lines being programmed by Hitler in person to love the motherland and hate the rest of the world. That occurred within days before he killed himself. From 1932 on, he had young German men eating out of the palms of his hands, because he had planned it ten years prior.

The most vulnerable period is the formative years and then, young adults who are ready to rebel and leave a mark.

So what are the best targets for the purveyors of radical Islam?

Where the kids are.

Islamic organizations have been very active in attempts to influence public school systems, inch by inch, around the country with Islamic learning as part of the curriculum. This is done in the name of teaching "multi-cultural tolerance and awareness." While the separation of church and state doctrine is acknowledged all over, and certainly applies to Christianity and Judaism, it seems that exceptions have been made in the name of Islam. Why has this happened? Who, in leadership, has allowed it?

Infiltrating the sensitive issue of mind-bending children and young adults requires five elements:

1. Parental ignorance
2. Manipulating the mind-set of adults
3. Media assistance
4. Subtle Islamic propaganda in K-12 schools
5. Establishing a power base inside universities and colleges

Parental Ignorance:

Most parents know nothing and care little about radical Islam and their intentions, because they think it's only a problem somewhere far away in Afghanistan or Saudi Arabia. They see it as just another religion and think that it will never affect their kids or their grandkids. Parents in general are basically numb to the idea that anything can infiltrate schools and universities where their children can fall prey to stealth propaganda. They send their kids off to school, trust the system and work at their jobs. They have no idea that the enemy is already inside our territorial lines, working with subtlety at molding mind-sets. Our children are in the crosshairs of the radical Islamic propaganda machine, and we have no idea.

This is what radical Islam is counting on, ignorance in the home, ignorance in the schools and ignorance in the government institutions that regulate school curriculum enabling them to exert stealth influence, so gradual that it's hardly noticed. As long as America remains asleep, or continues looking the other way, the enemy will have powerful impact on the thinking process of our children.

Most parents are already burdened with enough to think about in their daily lives, between jobs, schools, the economy, behavioral issues and so much more. So why should this be an "issue" added to the list? They don't see it, smell it, feel it, or touch it. It's not a part of their lives. Not yet.

But they must be alert and diligent, because they are part of the first line of defense. Parents control the formative years of their children. They are the only ones who can monitor and make a difference in what and how the public schools systems teach their kids. If the propaganda machine is in play and the parents don't notice, radical Islam wins. We lose.

It's primarily the parents who can object and demand adherence to the policies of separating church from state in the public classrooms, because in many places, our governments are not doing that. Conveniently, Islam apologists will claim that the intrusion of Islam into the classroom is for teaching "culture" not religion. But where is that line drawn, in any religion, including Christianity?

Some will say that teachers are primarily responsible, but that's pie-in-the-sky. Teachers have jobs to keep, rules to follow and work hard every day in the classroom and at home. They are not motivated or equipped to begin monitoring skewed facts in the textbooks they are assigned to issue. In addition, it is likely that the majority of teachers are not fully versed in the truth and details about the emergence of Islam as a power force during the last 1,400 years.

Textbooks:

The situation is so serious and pervasive that Islamic scholar and author, Robert Spencer, devotes two full chapters in his book, *Stealth Jihad,* to the infiltration of Islamic propaganda into our public schools and universities. In it, he cites numerous examples of textbook manipulations of history, presenting a rosy picture of Islamic culture and society and a not-so-rosy picture of Christian and Jewish history. A study released in 2008 by the American Textbook Council (ATC), an independent textbook research organization, found that ten of the most widely used middle and high school social studies books "present an incomplete and confected view of Islam that misrepresents its foundations and challenges international security." The report found that these books abridge the presentations of Islam while denigrating or downplaying Christianity in Western civilization. Basically, the books are a source of altered truths and propaganda in regards to Islam.

Spencer cites a textbook, *History Alive! The Medieval World and Beyond,* which defines "Jihad" to students as a struggle in resisting evil. It presents nothing about Jihad being the basis for Holy War, or war against the "unbelievers." (Unbelievers are persons who are not Muslim) As we all know, truth is often convoluted, not by what's taught, but by what's not taught. The book also presents text that the prophet Mohammed taught "equality" among people. Anyone who has studied Islam knows that is categorically untrue.

Quran Sura, Verse 5:51: *"O you who believe! Do not take the Jews and the Christians for friends; they are friends of each other; and whoever amongst you takes them for a friend, then surely he is one of them; surely Allah does not guide the unjust people."*

Quran Sura Verse 2.65: *"And ye know of those of you who broke the Sabbath, how We said unto them: Be ye apes, despised and hated."* (Re: Jews)

Equality? I think not. Conspicuous by its absence in the books are certain omissions in the history of Islamic societies where a special tax called Dhimmitude had been imposed specifically upon non-Muslims, plus other restrictions such as being forbidden to build any religious institutions other than Islam, or proselytizing any religion other than Islam. Violations of these edicts resulted in prison or death. The authors of the books were very careful to include and omit information as the purveyors of Islam would have them.

There have been protests in numerous venues around the nation by parents and by the ACT organization, striving to monitor text-book inaccuracies and sheer propaganda designed to manipulate the mind-sets of America's children. The Fountain Valley School Board in Orange County, California, was challenged in 2010 for textbooks that "sanitized" Islamic history, such as the 2006 edition of Hough-ton-Mifflin Harcourt's *World History: Medieval to Early Modern Times.* Protesters claimed the array of inaccuracies were particularly egregious because budget shortfalls would negate the school board's abilities to buy new textbooks for years to come, thus kids would continue to be infused with glowing and sanitized versions of Islamic history and religious content.

Textbook Alert is a textbook watchdog organization run by Doctor Sandra Alfonsi. Its purpose is to review textbooks of government, history and religion for truth and accuracy. In the case of the textbook in California, here are a few examples extracted from the Textbook Alert findings:

Page 61: "Jews, Christians and Muslims also recognize many of the same prophets. Muhammad taught that prophets such as Abraham, Moses and Jesus had lived in earlier times."

Truth: "Judaism and Christianity do not regard Abraham, Moses or Jesus as prophets."

Page 61: "Muhammad respected Jews and Christians as "people of the Book" because their holy books taught many of the same ideas that Muhammad taught."

Truth: "The Quran refers to Christians and Jews as "apes," "pigs," "dogs" and "worse than cattle." (Suras 2:64; 5:59-60; 7:159-166; 7:176; 25:44.) This, according to what Muslims regard as the word of Allah as revealed to Muhammad, is their belief about the true essence of Jews and Christians.

Page 83: "Muslims generally practice religious tolerance, or acceptance, with regard to people they conquered. In other words, the Muslims did not ban all religions other than Islam in their lands. Jews and Christians in particular kept many of their rights, since they shared some beliefs with Muslims."

Truth: Historically, in Islamic majority nations, non-Muslims are offered conversion to Islam, with only two other alternatives: Death or "protection" provided they pay Dhimmitude. Non-Muslims endure public and private humiliation and are severely restricted in religious and civil rights.

What is also disturbing in this and most other Islamic references within textbooks is that the term "Jihad" is defined merely as a struggle, whether an inner struggle to obey God or a struggle to defend the Islamic community. It fails to extend that definition to terrorism and rampant murder, justified by Holy War against infidels, even though the infidels aren't aware they have been deemed an enemy such as victims of 9/11. Nor do the history books accurately reflect the truth about Islamic expansionism, presenting an image of peace and voluntary compliance, rather than the rampant murdering, plundering and enslavement that succeeded in the conquests of North Africa and the Iberian peninsula during the 7th and 8th centuries.

A feisty debate was recently waged by parents and the ACT for America local chapter from Brevard County, Florida, in protest against textbooks grossly slanted in favor of glamorizing the history of Islam with little or no mention of the history of Judaism or Christianity. (ACLU – Where are you?) A Prentice-Hall publication titled, *World History,* which (according to the local daily, *Florida Today*) is used in fifty percent of ninth grade classrooms, was found to devote 36 pages of the book to Islam and only three paragraphs to Christianity. One commentator claimed the book referred to Mohammed as a "messenger of God." In some classrooms, kids were prompted to read verses from the Quran.

Brevard County leaders responded by adding a supplemental guide to accompany the Prentice-Hall books rather than re-ordering new history books.

Similar struggles are taking place in most other states, including a very vocal Texas constituency that has been active in fighting pro-Islamic bias in their textbooks.

Methodology:

How can all this happen? Readers must be shaking their heads asking, if there is such a division between church and state, and Christian proselytizing is forbidden in public schools, how can all this be allowed

In February of 2013, female students in a geography class at Lumberton High School, Texas, were asked by the teacher to dress in burka-like Islamic garb, which were provided. The students were assigned to write an essay based on a newspaper story that the troubles in Egypt were the fault of Democracy and not the Muslim Brotherhood.

Some parents were outraged when they heard about this, saying they were not aware of those teachings until one woman saw the photograph of her daughter wearing a burka on Facebook. One parent told Fox News, "Christian kids who want to pray must do it outside of school hours, yet Islam is being taught to our kids during school hours." Numerous parents complained in this instance, though the school tried to defend the policy as teaching world cultures and belief systems. State Senator Dan Patrick, Chairman of the Senate Education Committee, intervened and the policy was placed under scrutiny.

Without doubt, influence was exerted behind closed doors. This is only one Islamic drop in the proverbial bucket. An entire book could be written about these kinds of atrocities throughout the public schools of America.

Parents in Colorado's Rocky Mountain High School were outraged when they learned that a "multicultural group" was encouraged to recite the Pledge of Allegiance over loud speakers, in Arabic, changing the text to "One Nation Under Allah."

Parents in Tampa have protested the school system inviting a Muslim representative from CAIR to speak to high school students. Dozens of people appeared at the Hillsborough County School Board reminding them that CAIR had been cited by the FBI as an unindicted co-conspirator helping to fund Hamas. The same objections by parents have been recorded in Georgia and Texas.

Karen Holgate, co-author of the book *From Crayons to Condoms*, was interviewed by *Front Page Magazine* in 2008, in which she spoke about the influences of Islam in American classrooms and the absence of other religious exposure.

We've all heard stories about teachers and students not being allowed to pray in schools or bring their Bibles to school. But unfortunately, when it comes to Islam there is a new standard. As the stories in From Crayons to Condoms show, Islam is not always being taught just as a comparative religion class but actually involves students in

Islamic religious rituals. One teacher reported that while she was substitute teaching she was instructed to leave the classroom for an hour while another school employee came to the classroom to lead the students in their prayers to Allah. Certainly the ACLU would file a lawsuit if a public school led children in prayers to God.

In September of 2013, a group of freshmen students from Hendersonville High School in Tennessee, were assigned to attend field trips studying world religions in places of worship, minus churches and synagogues. Of course, that included visiting a mosque where each kid was provided a copy of the Quran. One child who opted out of the trip was given a work sheet stating how Muslims treated their conquered people better than the United States treats minorities.

In Cobb County, Georgia, 2008, according to *Stealth Jihad,* a Channel 2 news reporter spoke to a student's father whose daughter brought home paperwork about Islam that claimed there was nothing wrong with having multiple wives. The assignment was given to seventh graders of Campbell Middle School. The students also had assignments to write about a Muslim woman who advocated wearing a burka and thought good of being one of several wives. The school district officials said they would review the complaint.

In 2010, parents of middle school students in Morgan County, Georgia, were outraged upon learning their kids were told to write 125 words as though going to Mecca, during the Islamic pilgrimage to the Hajj.

Each year, under the guise of diversity and cultural awareness, public schools in Minnesota close for two days so that teachers can attend special training. That includes informing teachers on how to teach about the history and virtues of Islam. Let's not forget that Minnesota's congressman, Keith Ellison, is one of two Muslims in the US Congress.

On the 12th anniversary of 9/11, Boston's Concorde Carlisle High School authorized the recitation of a Muslim poem over the intercom in place of the pledge of allegiance.

September 2010, in Wellesley, Massachusetts, during a middle schools social studies trip to a local mosque, children were indoctrinated with a plethora of sanitized pro-Islam, anti-American propaganda while asked to pray alongside Muslims. Someone used a smart phone to video the event, which anyone can access on the Internet.

CAIR has been actively working in the forefront and behind the scenes to force public schools to provide time and space for Islamic prayer on school time and property. They have succeeded in places like Dearborn, Michigan, and Riverdale, Maryland. Author Pam Geller writes about this extensively in her book, *Stop the Islamization of America: A Practical Guide to the Resistance.*

These examples are merely a smidgen of what we know that is going on all over the country. It signals a specific purpose and destination for our Islamist invaders, one that will grow as the Islamist population grows. Propagandize the kids!

There are over 50 million kids in our public schools today. If Islam manages to sway two percent of that number, they will have succeeded in their goals by reaching one million unsuspecting American children on the cusp of adulthood.

How can this be allowed? We may never know what goes on behind closed doors, but as an investigator who has dealt with undercurrents of corruption in my career, I can only conclude that money talks. Islam and the Muslim Brotherhood are awash in unlimited monetary supplies by which to influence, bribe, intimidate or otherwise get their way whenever and wherever the opportunity prevails. All it takes are people who would be so inclined to accept money for favors under the so-called "radar." While plenty of Americans would not succumb to these temptations, there are plenty who will, especially when the lure is plentiful. What they count on, is how much will slip through unnoticed.

This is particularly ripe in the political arena where Islamists, through their enormous list of influential lobbyists, can sway schoolboard agendas and generate changes in textbook content in order to mold the minds of young people into thinking Islam is the ultimate religion of peace. They portray it as a great and wonderful religion that is misunderstood and wrongly vilified by older biased adults. At the very least, the intimidation factor must certainly play a major role in the decisions of liberal-minded school officials. Nobody these days wants to "offend" Muslims.

Ten year-old kids grow into young teens and then college students, and within a decade, their minds are manipulated by propaganda intended to enhance Islam's future army of followers.

Vladimir Lenin once said, "Give me four years to teach the children and the seed I have sown will never be uprooted."

Colleges and universities:

The following was reported in *The Clarion Project* in May of 2013:

In 1988, an FBI informant inside the US Muslim Brotherhood network warned that it had a front called the International Institute of Islamic Thought (IIIT). The IIIT leadership, the source reported, said they were in the first of six phases to "institute the Islamic Revolution in the United States." Their current objective was to 'peacefully get inside the United States government and also American universities.' And they have. *The source warned that the Muslim Brotherhood in America has unlimited funds and has "set up political action front groups with no traceable ties to the IIIT or its various Muslim groups." The source's identification of IIIT as a front in a 1991 Muslim Brotherhood Memo where the Brotherhood lists IIIT as number 28 of 'our organizations and the organizations of our friends," working toward the Brotherhood's self-defined goal, which it says is a grand jihad."*

A holy war waged against non-Muslims on behalf of Islam considered to be a religious duty; also, a personal struggle in devotion to Islam in eliminating and destroying the Western civilization from within.

The IIIT has offices and affiliates in the UK, Belgium, Egypt, Pakistan, Saudi Arabia, Lebanon, Jordan, Bosnia, Bangladesh, Morocco, Nigeria, Indonesia, India and Brunei. In September of 2012, the top leadership of IIIT met with Mohammed Morsi of the

Muslim Brotherhood as Morsi welcomed the organization to Egypt's schools of higher learning.

In the US, the IIIT has exerted influence and camaraderie with such schools as:

- George Mason University, a recipient of $1.5 million donation from IIIT. A special dinner was held at the school hosted by the university president.
- Hartford Seminary received $1 million from IIIT to help include Muslim clerics for chaplaincy positions in the military, prisons, hospitals and universities.

The IIIT also has special relationships with such schools as Nazareth College, Shenandoah University, Huron University College, Binghamton University, University of Delaware, American University, University of Maryland, Manhattanville College, Georgetown University, University of Virginia and Middle Tennessee State University.

In 2006, while researching and writing my book *Militant Islam in America*, I mentioned a number of schools of higher learning that were the recipients of huge donations by wealthy Muslims across the ocean. Here's an update:

In 2005, Saudi Prince Al-Waleed Bin Talal bin Abdulaziz Al Saud, endowed Harvard and Georgetown Universities with $20 million each, to further Islamic studies. Georgetown also received $325 thousand from CAIR.

Another $20 million was donated by Saudis to the Mid-East Studies Center at the University of Arkansas. Another $5 million to Berkley plus $11 million to Cornell University. Add $1 million to Princeton and $5 million to Rutgers.

As far back as 1976, $1 million was given by the Saudis to the University of Southern California. Those Saudis must really want us all to get a good education.

One can only imagine the multi-million dollar totals if we had access to full disclosure.

This financial influence is not limited only to American schools. According to *Arutz Sheva*, an Israeli news source, eight universities in the United Kingdom, including Oxford and Cambridge, have been the recipients of 233 million pounds sterling since 1995. ($373 US dollars) There are seventeen federally funded centers on American college campuses devoted solely to Middle-Eastern studies, most of which support pro-Islamist, anti-Israeli ideas. In 2011, according to the same report, 70 percent of political science lectures at Oxford have been "implacably hostile" to the West and Israel.

What are we supposed to glean from this generosity? Are we supposed to believe that the Wahhabis of Saudi Arabia, one of the strictest and fundamentalist sources of radical Islam in the world, are only interested in seeing that American youths get a good education?

Money is power. Money buys influence. Influence tips the scales of honesty, fairness and independence. Money buys corruption. The Islamists want something in return. What could they possibly want from our colleges and universities?

Answer: Islamist propaganda. And they are getting it.

As repayment for the favors, universities on the take from Islamist groups will hire more professors of Islamist persuasion than they would otherwise. A disproportionate number of hired Islamist professors infiltrate classrooms and off-campus activities in order to spread the positives about Islam and the negatives about their so-called enemies, Israel and the United States. After all, those young, fertile, impressionable minds are easy to manipulate.

These universities will also capitulate to Islamist demands for such things as installing foot baths for prayer service, as they've done at Michigan, Harvard and Minnesota. College. Serving Halal food in special campus stations has been established in the University of Chicago. Halal foods are also served at a number of other colleges, such as Columbia, Harvard and Georgetown. New rules and schedules for swimming pools and recreation centers have been amended to accommodate Muslim women to be separated from men, to comply with Sharia, which was done at Harvard.

In 2016, according to Young America's Foundation (YAF), 53 percent of commencement speakers at one hundred American colleges were considered of "liberal" persuasion, while 14 percent were conservative and 29 percent riding the fence. Celebrity speakers have often hit stone walls if they dared to address the topic of radical Islam, as in the case of Aayan Hirsi Ali, Somali-born intellectual woman and author, who has lived the life of female subjugation from within. Ms. Ali was invited in 2014 to speak at Brandeis University, then disinvited after pressures and protests erupted. The Muslim Students Association (MSA) has been successful in labeling anyone who speaks of radical Islam as Islamophobic, including Ms. Ali, reform Muslim Asra Nomani, Robert Spencer, Sam Harris and liberal comic, Bill Maher. In 2015, Duke University openly sided with the radical student association against Ms. Nomani.

Regardless of standard political views, it's a known fact that liberals are more inclined to accommodate Islamists as part of the national landscape than are conservatives. The Islamists know that very well. Thus, the school hierarchy, who select the speakers, also knows that. Any way you look, the Islamists get their way.

In 2013, Professor Ghassan Zakaria of San Diego State University presented his Arabic 101 map of the Middle-East that noticeably omitted the existence of Israel. In its place was "Palestine." (source: *Freedom Outpost*, Sept. 13, 2013)

Another professor at Stanford Law School was asked about Hamas to which he replied, "The Hamas perspective is directed at achieving Palestinian self-determination challenging Israel. But I have no evidence that it includes an anti-Semitic perspective."

In 2010, Florida Atlantic University professor Bassem Alhalabi was arrested for assaulting a reporter in Tallahassee in two separate attacks on the reporter and a cameraman. The reporter, Joe Kaufman – a writer exposing Islamist infiltration in the state – was in Tallahassee to give a report about terrorist ties to CAIR. A year later, Alhalabi pled guilty and was reinstated into his position at FAU. In 2003, the same professor was found guilty by the Department of Commerce for illegally shipping a military-grade, thermal imaging device to Syria, a known sponsor of terrorism. He kept his job.

In 2003, Professor Sami Al Arian, from the University of South Florida in Tampa, was indicted for seventeen counts of various charges, from funding Palestinian Jihad, to extortion, perjury, murder, and giving aid to an outlawed group. Al Arian was an outspoken figure on campus, spewing his venom toward Israel and hatred toward U. S. policies in the Middle-East. At the same time, he had garnered influence in the Bush White House where he was an honored guest in 2001. At a Cleveland mosque in the 1990s, al Arian was quoted, "Let's damn America, let's damn Israel, let's damn their allies until death." Al Arian was tried and acquitted of half the charges in 2005. He is still in custody facing legal issues.

In his book *The Professors*, David Horowitz identifies over one hundred academics in America who are on campus for the expressed purpose of exerting influence and support of Communism and Islamic Revolution.

There is no way to tally the true number of radical Islamists occupying classrooms on the payroll, not to teach, but to extol the virtues of Islam and the evils of America. As long as the money flows over and under the radar into university coffers, we are powerless to stop it. One day, when these same students become our representatives in the upper levels of government, we will look back and realize how well the entire process was planned and executed.

<u>The Muslim Students of America (MSA):</u>

The MSA is a powerful presence on the campuses of more than 200 colleges and universities in the United States. It is another one of those thirty-one organizations spawned by the Muslim Brotherhood in order to carry out a mission of Jihad within the upper level learning institutes.

The MSA literature and talking points would have us believe they are nothing more than a college fraternity with men and women of like interests, mainly religious, no more than a social, spiritual and education-minded group of students.

Tell that to Israeli Ambassador Michael Oren who was invited to the University of California, Irvine, in 2010 to speak to the student body. Ten Islamist students were pre-rehearsed to disrupt the ambassador's talk by standing, one by one, and shouting prepared texts in order to subvert the speaker. Each of the MSA students were escorted out of the room as the interruptions continued, defaming Israel and lauding Palestinian causes. Eventually, ten students were found guilty in court of conspiring to disrupt a speech. Representatives of the Muslim group accused the accusers and the court system of "Islamophobia," a term coined by the Muslim Brotherhood and now used globally to combat critics of radical Islam.

Later on, Erick Stakelbeck, a CBN News analyst who reported this incident, was a keynote speaker at Florida State University on behalf of Christians United for Israel. As Florida Congressman Steve Southerland went to the podium, a group of 10 to 12 Muslim and leftist students stood and walked in front of him in a straight line, each wearing masking tape over their mouths and shirts that were inscribed "Justice for Palestine." After being escorted out, the kids continued shouting and chanting leftist slogans.

There isn't a book big enough to chronicle the impact that the Muslim Brotherhood and its sub-organizations have had on the infrastructure of America, including the educational systems.

The MSA Pledge of Allegiance:

In 2011, someone apparently infiltrated a meeting of the MSA at UCLA and made a stealth video of the leader, Amir Abdel Malik, as he led the group in a pledge of allegiance, not a pledge to the United States, but a pledge very similar and derived from the motto of the Muslim Brotherhood:

Allah is my Lord; Islam is my life; the Quran is my guide; the Sunna is my practice; Jihad is my spirit; righteousness is my character; Paradise is my goal; I enjoin what is right; I forbid what is wrong; I will fight against oppression*; and I will die to establish Islam.*

Access URL:
http://www.youtube.com/watch?v=xy3MGIPLevM&feature=player_embedded

Note:

Huma Abedin, a devout Muslim, was raised from age two to eighteen in Wahhabi Saudi Arabia. She has served as a trusted aide to Hillary Clinton in the White House, in the Senate and in the State Department and now as her loyal campaign aide. She was an executive board member of the MSA while attending George Washington University. Abedin's parents and brother are closely associated with the Muslim Brotherhood and Sisterhood.

TEN
MEDIA AND THE PROPAGANDA MACHINE

"Tell a lie big enough, and keep repeating it, people will eventually come to believe it."

■ Joseph Goebbels, Nazi propagandist

In January of 2013, former Vice-President Al Gore sold his failed television news station, Current TV, to Al Jazeera for approximately $500 million. This was a major coup for the Islamist propaganda machine and an act bordering on treason on the part of the vice-president, especially if you consider that the Muslim Brotherhood is our declared enemy.

Mr. Gore had a choice. Conservative talk show host, Glenn Beck (an American) and his entourage was also in the bidding, equally eligible. While we surely know that political differences exist between Mr. Gore and Mr. Beck, it would seem hugely more important for Mr. Gore to favor an American entity over an anti-American entity. Al Gore cannot be that stupid not to know the basic DNA of Al Jazeera.

Al Jazeera is an Arab (Islamic) news giant based in Qatar, now with enormous reach into homes, businesses and gullible minds all over North America by which to present the Islamic agenda. Meanwhile, it portrays itself as neutral, moderate and balanced. Thus, we should never lose sight of the Prophet Mohammed's decree: "War is deceit." At the same time, we should not forget the Muslim Brotherhood's manifesto declaring war on America in which they promise to bury us "*from within*." The two paradigms are intrinsically connected.

The strategies outlined in the Muslim Brotherhood's, "The Project," spells out the plan for western conquest from within. Here are four of those twenty-one strategies that apply:

- Avoid open alliances with known terrorist organizations and individuals to maintain the appearance of 'moderation.'
- Put into place a watchdog system for monitoring Western media to warn Muslims of international plots fomented against them.
- Instrumentally use existing Western institutions until they can be converted and put into the service of Islam.
- Use deception to mask the intended goals of Islamic actions as long as it does not conflict with Sharia Law.

Installing Al Jazeera into America's news media institutions is like giving license to TASS, the news system for the cold war USSR to operate in the United States. Back in the 1950s, 60s and 70s, the Soviet Union's Communist leadership had promised to bury our country from within, and a big part of that strategy was steeped in propaganda. At least our leaders of that period weren't so utterly stupid or naïve to offer the enemy the very tools they needed on a silver platter. All it takes is money and greed on one side and ignorance or greed on the other .

Knowledgeable authorities on the Middle-East, including Americans and many secular Muslims, are well aware that the Al Jazeera Network is the propaganda arm of the Muslim Brotherhood. Al Jazeera had been strongly supportive of the so-called "Arab Spring" of 2011, which we all have learned was a power play implemented and carried out by the Muslim Brotherhood. Since then, as the Egyptian uprising against Mohammed Morsi exposed the Muslim Brotherhood to the world as an Islamist extremist organization, the Al Jazeera Network tried to distance itself from the association. But it was a futile effort. Al Jazeera is born of the Muslim Brotherhood and became rooted in the United States to propagandize for Islam, to portray Islam as "moderate" and harmless, as just a religion and nothing to be concerned about. In other words, to lie. Or worse yet, to fool those who are easily fooled.

The good news is that Al Jazeera failed in the United States. After two and a half years of floundering news shows, the Islamic-based network could not attract an American audience to compete with the existing news giants. Miniscule ratings doomed the network, which went out of business on April 30, 2016. The people spoke. No doubt, a significant portion of the population had gotten wind that Al Jazeera was connected at the hip with the Muslim Brotherhood.

The bad news is that we had a so-called American statesman, AL Gore, who, despite knowing the sordid roots of the Al Jazeera organization, sold out to our would-be enemy, instead of selling to a fellow, albeit conservative, American.

Robert Dreyfuss, who reports for *The Nation,* an on-line news source, wrote in July of 2013, after the Egyptian uprising against Morsi and the Brotherhood:

Al Jazeera, the Qatar-based, Qatar-founded and Qatar-controlled mouthpiece for one of the Arab kleptocracies of the Persian Gulf, has suffered mass resignations. Twenty-two journalists who worked for Al Jazeera quit in protest after being told by their Qatari masters to support the Muslim Brotherhood.

In his article, Dreyfuss cites journalist Abdel Latif Fouad El-Menawy, head of the *Egypt News Center* under ex-president Hosni Mubarak, who said that Al-Jazeera was a "propaganda channel" for the Muslim Brotherhood. "Al Jazeera turned itself into a channel for the Muslim Brotherhood group," el-Menawy told Al Arabiya of *Gulf News.* As most know, Mubarak had outlawed the Muslim Brotherhood as a major threat to peace, freedom and prosperity in Egypt because it was clearly known as a hardline, fundamentalist, terror-supporting organization.

According to *The Gulf News,* Anchor Karem Mahmoud said that Al Jazeera was explicitly ordered to support the Brotherhood. He added that the management had instructed each staff member to favor the Muslim Brotherhood. "There are instructions to us to telecast certain news," he said.

In June of 2013, the new Egyptian government now run by the military, which once again outlawed the Muslim Brotherhood, shut down the Al Jazeera office in Cairo. If the Egyptians consider the Muslim Brotherhood and Al Jazeera a major threat to the peace and prosperity of their country, then why did our government leaders embrace them?

Which brings us to an Islamic cleric named Yusuf al-Qaradawi, Egyptian-born author, scholar and a close ally of Al Jazeera. Qaradawi hosted a regular show on Al Jazeera which, translated to English, is called "Shariah to Life." The show, according to Wikipedia, has an estimated audience of 60 million viewers world-wide. And, according to the same source, Qaradawi has had a long and close relationship with the Muslim Brotherhood and has turned down offers to sit in leadership roles.

Al-Qaradawi's views are considered so radical, that his visas have been turned down by countries like the United Kingdom and France. He was recently barred from entering Kuwait. In January or 2009, during a sermon on Al Jazeera concerning the Gaza War, he prayed as follows (transcribed by MEMRI):

Oh Allah, take the Jews, the treacherous aggressors... Oh Allah, they have spread much tyranny and corruption in the land. Pour Your wrath upon them, oh our God. Lie in wait for them. Oh Allah, You annihilated the people of Thamud (Sodom) at the hand of a tyrant, and You annihilated the people of 'Aad with a fierce, icy gale, and You destroyed the Pharaoh and his soldiers – Oh Allah, take this oppressive, Jewish Zionist band of people... do not spare a single one of them... count their numbers, and kill them, down to the very last one.

In a later statement on Al Jazeera, while speaking about Hitler, he said the Holocaust was divine punishment for the Jews. In the past, he also has expressed support for suicide bombers, particularly by Palestinians. It was on his authority that women have been deployed to carry them out. He has often been interviewed as an honored guest on Al Jazeera. So the picture is clear—that is to anyone who is conscious—that there is a symbiotic relationship between Qaradawi and the Al Jazeera Network.

Wikipedia reports that Al Jazeera has been banned by other nations because of a number of reasons: inciting hatred, biased reporting and association with the Muslim Brotherhood. Those countries include Algeria, Bahrain, China, Iraq and Israel.

But not the USA.

Qatar had been a substantial donor to Bill Clinton's charitable foundations, including up to $5 million dollars in 2008, along with other Islamic nations including Kuwait and Oman. In 2012, Clinton garnered $12 million from Qatar to help rebuild Haiti from its devastating earthquake of 2010. Seems admirable enough. There are two ways to view this generosity:

1. Clinton is an effective fund raiser for which the unfortunate, destitute people of the world, can benefit. We should all be appreciative of any assistance that is provided to the poor and desperate people of Haiti.

2. What is the *quid pro quo*? These kinds of gifts aren't given solely for humanitarian causes. This author has been around too long to believe such generosity is always meant for the glory of charity. Qatar will collect its due favors when the time is right. And having bought Al Jazeera from under Glenn Beck might have been one of those times. Remember, it was Al Gore who served as Bill Clinton's Vice-President.

The bottom line is that radical Islam is winning the war on all fronts. Its sights are set on the long range, not the short range. Sending $12 million to Haiti for Bill Clinton's clout is a drop in the proverbial bucket in the spectrum of twenty or thirty years of stealth Jihad. It is only speculation that Bill Clinton's connection had anything to do with the Al Jazeera purchase. Readers can connect the dots as we move along.

American Media:

Those of us who stay tuned to the happenings within our country are well aware of the deep political chasm among media giants. Broadcast media, outside of commentary, is ideologically supposed to be non-partisan, but those days are long gone. In major television broadcast news there is one conservative channel (FOX) and one slightly to the left (CNN) and the remainder are notably liberal, so much so, that any criticism of President Obama may be met with vigorous discourse. And, along with blind support of Barack Obama comes the support of his policies and attitudes toward Islam in the United States.

Talk radio is a whole new ball game with conservatives dominating the air waves by individually secured sponsors. It includes such personalities as Sean Hannity, Rush Limbaugh, Glenn Beck, Laura Ingram, Michael Savage, Mark Levin and others. Very few liberal talk shows have been successful on the air waves. Why listeners choose conservatism over liberalism in radio is up for speculation. The conclusion of this author is that mass listeners of talk radio for informational purposes are generally more educated, aware and politically informed than the masses of liberal counterparts.

How does media affect Islamic propaganda? By behaving as an acolyte to the president, very liberal newscasters and commentators vicariously advance the Islamic agenda. It is that simple. When we hear about Obama's outreach to Muslims, his friendships, and his Islamic workers in key government positions, commentary by people on MSNBC or CNN will blather everything that is good and righteous about the president while failing to mention the worrisome aspects. President Obama can have any number of Islamists employed as advisors in the Department of Homeland Security, Justice Department, State Department or even the White House, and no one will utter a peep about the possibility that this may be compromising our national security.

The media has become a major player in the political field. Left wing = Democrat. Right wing = Republican. Most network and cable television news affiliates lean left. Only one news channel leans right wing, though it is the highest rated of all the other channels combined (FOX). From there, the talking points and propaganda emerges.

There is no better example than the Benghazi fiasco of October 2012, when four American were killed at the Libyan consulate. This was one of the most tragic and corrupt incidents in the history of American government and the failings of its leadership. For months, FOX News and a Republican-based congress demanded answers such as:

- Why was the consulate under-staffed for security when the dangers were obvious and grievous?
- Why was the consulate not only denied extra security, and why was the existing security downsized?
- Why was there no attempt, in a period of eight hours of the attack, by American forces to intervene and rescue?
- Why did the President go to bed the night it was happening? And why did he leave Washington the next day to attend a Las Vegas fund raiser with the bodies still warm and the embers still burning in Benghazi?
- Why did the administration, primarily the President and his Secretary of State, lie to the American people by announcing it was the result of a demonstration protesting an amateur anti-Islam video, when they knew otherwise?

American heroes died that night, including the ambassador, when something went terribly wrong. Clearly, the President and his Secretary of State lied and covered up the truth, whatever that is. As this book is written, the administration will still not release the twenty-five or more surviving American witnesses to that attack needed for testimony to the House Investigation Committee. It would also pose a legal hazard to those witnesses. Federal State Department employees who were required to sign a non-disclosure agreement could be subject to harsh punishments if they testify in the investigation. The administration will not waive those restrictions.

Stations like MSNBC, CNN, CBS and ABC spin news claiming this to be mere politics, over-played as a Republican fight against the Democrats, ignoring facts and demanding no answers. It's treated like a sex scandal that will dissipate in time. Sadly, they prevailed. Fox News has been tenacious at getting to the truth, though not always unsuccessful. The President calls it politics and sloughs off all criticism like Teflon. The leftist slant in television news is alarming, and it plays into the propaganda plan of the Muslim Brotherhood. They win, we lose.

Whatever led up to, and whatever went wrong in Benghazi has the President's fingerprints all over the crime scene, which, incidentally was never examined until two-three weeks later by the FBI, long enough to ensure full contamination and decimation.

Obama Media - All in the Family:

The American news consumers do not have the foggiest idea of how much is being spoon-fed to them by media in terms of partisan politics, or how much is being ignored, hidden, avoided and deliberately omitted. It is all about mind-manipulation, on all sides.

During the election campaign of 2008, the major networks set aside their standard mantra about being balanced and unbiased. Instead, they blatantly advocated for one candidate over the other, blindly anxious to see the first black person take over the Oval Office while ignoring the personal and professional past records (or absence thereof) for that candidate, Barack Obama. Here we had a candidate with almost no achievements or track records in politics, who voted "present" nearly every time while in the Illinois State Senate – presumably to avoid establishing a voting record – and who hit the deck running for president the day he was elected to the US Senate. Previously, he was an associate in a small Chicago law firm for three years with no significant achievements as an attorney, and held no other regular job other than "community organizer" which is a legitimizing term for a political fund raiser. He went to college, became a community organizer, ascended to state senator and then a US Senator, during which he had an insignificant voting record. His greatest assets were 1) being black and 2) being a dynamic speaker. His origins of birth, citizenship, religion, financial records and the non-disclosure of his college records, have all been questioned by authorities throughout the nation, while being ignored by all the major news networks but one.

His opponent, Senator John McCain, was an American from birth without question of divided loyalties, a national war hero, a former POW who has already served twenty-five years in the United States congress (House and Senate) with a remarkable record of being a

Republican "moderate." This was like pitting George Washington himself against the bugle boy. Yet, the bugle boy won.

This could never have happened without the complicity of a biased American mainstream media.

Amazingly, at the start of the Obama vs. McCain campaigns, candidates planned a journey to Europe to bolster their images abroad and show how interconnected they were to our allies and friends across the sea. The major news anchors of ABC, NBC and CBS – Katie Couric, Charlie Gibson and Brian Williams –traveled with Obama covering every moment, every word and every nuance of the Democrat candidate, while being granted daily interviews and shooting video and commentary back to the United States that portrayed Obama in the most favorable of light.

No anchors traveled with John McCain, the war hero.

In August of 2013, this author researched and posted an eye-opening blog titled, *"Obama and Media: All in The Family."* This is only a microcosm of influence the Obama camp has engineered over network and cable television, save the Fox News Channel.

At that time, David Rhodes was the president of CBS. Benjamin Rhodes, his brother, is the National Security Advisor for strategic communication and a speech writer for the President. He wrote Obama's famous Cairo speech in 2009 as well as many of the talking points following the Benghazi fiasco.

Ben Sherwood is the president of ABC News. His sister, Elizabeth Sherwood-Randall, was actively employed as special National Security Advisor to President Obama and Senior Coordinator for Defense Policy. She is now Deputy Secretary of Energy.

Claire Shipman, ABC News contributor, is married to Jay Carney, the former White House Press Secretary.

Virginia Mosely, Senior Executive and Bureau Chief with CNN (formerly eighteen years with ABC) is married to Tom Nides who, until February of 2013, was Deputy Secretary of State for Management Resources under Hillary Clinton.

Ari Shapiro, until 2014 was the White House correspondent for NPR. Michael Gottlieb, her husband, served as Assistant White House counsel for Barack Obama for four years.

And so the story goes. Is it any wonder that news materiel is filtered, massaged, manipulated and interpreted to portray a special image for one side of the political spectrum?

One cable network (FOX) unapologetically leans to the right. Thank goodness for one. If not for FOX News, we might as well have a state-run news system like Russia or China.

How does all this pertain to the Islamic infiltration? If the reader has not figured it out by now, the following chapters will bring it all together.

Banning "Islam" in Terrorism:

Incredulously, the Obama Administration has banned the mere mention of Islam in training courses and manuals for FBI, ATF, Border Patrol, ICE, or any other law enforcement entity in the federal government, including the military. This, while 99 percent of organized terrorism throughout the world is rooted in Islamic radicalism. What could possibly be the motive of the President?

They win; we lose.

Even in the despicable horror in Fort Hood, 2009, when an Islamic officer in our own military randomly shot 41 people, killing 14, the Obama Administration refused to allow the incident to be labeled an attack of "Islamic Terror," labeling it instead as "workplace violence."

Since 2009, the White House, under Barack Obama, has consistently downplayed the role of Muslims in terror incidents and calls the perpetrators "extremists" without reference to Islam. This attitude has bled into the training systems on the federal level. No one knows this better than Steven Emerson, an author and expert on radical Islam and the head of the Investigative Project on Terrorism that monitors a network of Islamic groups that are associated with the Muslim Brotherhood. Quoted in an article for the *Washington Times* in April of 2013, Emerson said:

"Numerous experts on Islamic terrorism, like myself, and I, had given 143 lectures at the FBI and CIA were banned from speaking to any US government counterterrorism conferences. Instead, these agencies were ordered to invite Muslim Brotherhood front groups."

In October 2011, 57 Islamic groups wrote a letter to John O. Brennan, now CIA Director, then President Obama's Chief Counterterrorism Adviser. (How intimidating would that be?) Citing news reports, the groups complained of... "biased, false and highly offensive training materials about Muslims and Islam" inside the federal government's instructional halls. The organizations' letter demanded that biased trainers be disciplined, that all instructors undergo retraining and that materials deemed offensive by Muslim activists be purged.

The White House issued an edict to scrub all law enforcement, intelligence and military teachings on Islam. The FBI had to discard many pages of information that warned about the threat from the Muslim Brotherhood.

John Guandolo, a former FBI counterterrorism agent, spent years studying the global Muslim Brotherhood movement and its links to American Islamic groups. The political left now has branded Mr. Guandolo an "Islamophobe." Mr. Guandolo told the *Washington Times*:

"There is no strategy. At FBI headquarters, it is a daily fire drill. The threats come in, and they run around to deal with them and run them down. But because none of it can have anything to do with the Muslim Brotherhood movement in the US or Islam, they never address the root cause and common investigative realities."

Steve Emerson claims that all slide presentations on Islamic extremism must now be first submitted and screened by a special Justice Department panel.

Islamophobia:

This is the term coined to describe anyone who exhibits concerns about the rise of Islam, terrorism, subjugation, Jihad or any organization and its members. It has evolved into the most dreaded adjective assigned to people, like the author of this book, second only to the "N" word. Just about every scholar, expert, teacher or ex-Muslim who speaks out has been dubbed an "Islamophobe."

Let us remember the tenets of effective propaganda, taught to us by the experts like Hitler and Goebbels, that if you repeat something often enough, even if it is not true, people will begin to believe it. Thus, the Islamic propagandists and American leftists use and abuse the term to the fullest, which does have an impact on the gullible people who cannot or will not see how they are being manipulated. Remember, labeling anyone who has concerns about the rise of radical Islam in America is now an "Islamophobe."

Guilty!

But maybe not. Definitions vary from source to source, mostly citing fear or hatred of Islam. A more detailed definition would be the "irrational fear or hatred of Islam." For that, this author would plead *not guilty*, simply because fear and hatred of *radical* Islam is not irrational at all; it is born of intense and wide-ranging study over a period of twelve years, as I tried to learn all there is to know about this dominant ideology. That, plus bearing witness to what is going on all over the world.

Nevertheless, it is a term freely exercised by apologists for radical Islam in making people like me–and thousands of other authors, experts and intellectuals about the subject–out to be the bad guy, and not the Jihadists.

The term "Islamophobia" was first coined in the early 1990's by the International Institute for Islamic Thought – the IIIT – a front group of the Muslim Brotherhood. Abdur-Rahman Muhammad, a former Imam who was with the IIIT at that time, has since evolved as a "moderate," distancing himself from the radical groups. He revealed the origins of the term and its intent.

"This loathsome term is nothing more than a thought-terminating cliché conceived in the bowels of Muslim think tanks for the purpose of beating down critics. Islamophobia was a term designed as a weapon to advance a totalitarian cause by stigmatizing critics and silencing them."

In October 2010, CAIR announced that it was forming a new "Islamophobia" department that would produce an annual report tracking *"trends in rhetorical attacks on Islam and Muslims and... offer accurate and balanced information to be used in the struggle for tolerance and mutual understanding."*

It is all part of the propaganda effort designed to demonize people who want to protect America from those who would Islamize this great nation, inch by inch. It works. Sympathizers often side with the Islamists and spew the very hatred they condemn, toward people like the author of this book who has no other motive other than create awareness about the threat our children will be living under in years to come.

The propagandists are succeeding in every direction we turn – in the schools and universities, in the military, in the federal law enforcement agencies, in the media, and in the very government we elect to serve the people.

A glaring example of ignorance within the mainstream media occurred when former Speaker of the House Newt Gingrich was being interviewed by CNN anchor, Wolf Blitzer, during the 2012 presidential campaign. Gingrich was complimenting the bold stand against radical Islam by Congresswoman Michelle Bachman. He had barely touched on the subject of a Brotherhood-connected Arab working for our government when Blitzer exploded at him to defend Hillary Clinton's top aide, Huma Abedin. It is well known among terrorism experts that Abedin's mother, brother and father have all been connected to the Muslim Brotherhood. Abedin, as mentioned earlier, had been imbedded in the MSA, a Muslim Brotherhood offshoot. Blitzer changed the interview into a blast, citing the woman as an advocate, not an independent journalist. In fact, Huma Abedin has embedded the stamp of the Muslim Brotherhood during her adult life. The CNN anchor jumped all over Gingrich insisting that Abedin is a "wonderful woman with no connections to the Muslim Brotherhood." Even the more experienced of journalists on television can be duped.

Blitzer is a respected journalist considered “moderate” in today’s political environment. Yet, without considering the glaring facts about this woman’s clear connections to the Muslim Brotherhood, he, in truth, was blindly defending the President and Secretary of State Hillary Clinton who has hired and embraced a likely mole within the highest ranks of government.

ELEVEN
SHARIA COMES TO AMERICA

As mentioned in previous chapters, there are several nations in Europe that have lost control of their legal systems by acquiescing to Muslim populations, permitting "No-Go" zones" or Islamic-only enclave neighborhoods in which non-Muslims are not welcome and denizens are basically free to form their own government, presumably Sharia-based. That includes government authorities, police, fire, or military personnel.

Numerous articles and reports have been issued substantiating the existence of these burgeoning, non-assimilating societies within societies. The Gatestone Institute, a non-profit think tank and international policy council, released a report in January 2015, citing a myriad of sources that clearly outline the infiltration of unfriendly Islamic communities throughout Europe that are growing into a prominent security dilemma for national governments. The terrorist attack by Islamists in Paris in November of 2015 where 130 people were murdered, brought some of these enclave problems to light, not only in France, but other countries like Belgium where one of the perpetrators was found to be in hiding.

Neighborhoods throughout England have signs posted declaring areas protected by Islamic Law, with cautions about entering. Police officers do not patrol these neighborhoods, and if they must, they arrive in multiple units for protection. Basically, non-assimilating Muslims are taking over parts of these nations by implementing Sharia Law, though it may—and often does—conflict with the laws of the land.

Imagine Miami, Chicago or New York City in ten years, where large dense neighborhoods consisting of Muslims-only completely disregard American law—federal, state or local—and basically establish their own nation within a nation by virtue of bold intimidation. It only bodes more apprehension for what is to come in the United States 30 and 50 and 100 years from now, and how our great-grandchildren may never know the freedoms we have enjoyed as Americans.

People of these communities continue to accept welfare, health care and other entitlements, though they refuse to obey the prevailing laws of the land in deference to Sharia. While the state of New York may deem it illegal to be married to more than one person, Sharia allows a Muslim man to keep four wives. In state law, he can claim one wife, but within his Islamic compound, he is married to four women with rights of husbandry, including the right to beat a wife for failing to comply with his wishes.

In Chapter Eight, we learned about the 22 or more enclaves that have been formed in the United States in which non-Muslims, including authorities, are unwelcome. It is not inconceivable that with population growth and unchecked immigration, we could see a huge increase in those communities multiplying in every state. What then?

We saw what happened in 1993 when President Clinton's new Attorney General authorized federal agents to seize the Waco compound known as Branch Davidians. Nearly 100 members of a religious cult led by David Koresh were living in their own godly world, which was unwelcome to outsiders, operating independently of state and federal laws. It was also learned that the compound was storing a huge cache of weapons–including 305 firearms and many assault rifles–that led the ATF to obtain a search warrant. A 51-day stand-off led to multiple shoot-outs and eventually an enormous fire that killed 76 Branch Davidians, including many children and a number of federal agents. The actions of the government were heavily criticized. It served as the motive for Timothy McVeigh to bomb the Oklahoma City Courthouse in 1995.

Imagine the chaos if authorities in England, France or Germany set out to force anarchists to comply with existing state laws and to abandon their Sharia systems. Worse yet, imagine what would happen if the state of New York or the FBI invaded Islamberg, Waco style, with intent to investigate reports of terrorist training, polygamy, and other violations of the law. Knowing that the compound is heavily armed, it would likely incite a mini-war.

At the same time, we should consider what will evolve in coming years if authorities never investigate the compounds. The proverbial tail is increasingly wagging the dog.

Here are a few examples of Sharia as practiced in predominant Muslim countries:

- A husband may beat his wife if she refuses his command or refuses sex
- A woman who claims to be raped must produce four witnesses who are males to corroborate. If she fails, and she is married, she is guilty of adultery, punishable by death by stoning
- Girls can be married off at any age, with consummation of the marriage allowed at age nine
- The testimony of a woman in court is worth half the value of a man
- A woman inherits half what a man inherits
- A husband may divorce a woman by saying "I divorce you," three times
- A man may engage in temporary marriage for the purpose of sex
- A Muslim who leaves Islam (apostasy) carries the death penalty
- Homosexual conduct is punishable by death
- Non-Muslims are not equal to Muslims under the law. They are forbidden to marry Muslim women, display wine or pork, recite scriptures or openly celebrate religious holidays

American Law for American Courts (ALAC):

The foot is in the door.

In June of 2009, a New Jersey trial judge in a domestic abuse case issued a ruling that gave greater weight to Sharia over the laws of the state. It did not go well for a woman who was routinely and repeatedly raped and beaten by her ex-husband who claimed it was his right as a Muslim. Seeking a restraining order to prevent him from raping and beating her, the Moroccan woman provided photographs and medical records showing severe injuries all over her body at the hands of the husband. He told her it was his right to do anything he wanted, she had to obey. An Imam testified to the rights of the husband.

The judge found that the criminal acts were proven but, nonetheless, denied the woman's request for a restraining order, stating the husband was acting in a manner he felt was consistent with the laws of his religion.

Of course, this judge knew better, that a religious precept does not supersede state or federal laws. Neither is the judge a Muslim. So, it begs the question; why did this judge knowingly violate his oath of office–to uphold the laws of the state–and issue an absurd ruling that was not only legally flawed, but placed the physical welfare of an abused woman in jeopardy? We may never know. The answer leads to speculation, which we will leave to the reader.

A New Jersey appellate court overturned the decision a year later. However, the case sounded the alarm to conservative-minded Americans that Islamic priorities were starting to creep into our legal system.

TWELVE
THE GRAND PLAN

I cherished my friendship with Doctor Joseph H. Davis. He was also one of the most renowned medical examiners in the history of the United States, serving Miami-Dade County for 40 years as the guru for forensic investigation and a consultant to hundreds of other police and forensic jurisdictions in the US and around the world. Doctor Davis once said to me, "Marshall, don't get side tracked. Always follow where the evidence takes you."

That evidence has been made crystal clear, in regards to the pending conquest of America by the Islamist powers. The previous chapters have given us a glimpse at that evidence. It should not be ignored it.

Yet, while the Muslim Brotherhood's "Explanatory Memorandum" has been made public, and other documents like "The Project" have revealed the secret war plan for infiltration and conquering America *from within*, our government—including politicians on both sides of the aisle—continues to ignore them as though they do not exist at all. Our protectors are forever sidetracked and driven by political motives, and never do they focus in on the absolute hard evidence that stands before us, evidence that the enemy is winning the war of propaganda and the war of infiltration. Every politician—whether Democrat or Republican—wwho truly cares about this nation, should heed the words of Doctor Davis.

But they will not, because the media and the political community is stuck on the "religion" of Islam, while ignoring the "politics" of Islam. Religion, as we know, is off limits to criticism. And as long as we pursue the mantra of political correctness, our enemies will ultimately get their way. That is part of the plan.

The Plan:

There is no arguing the point: The goal is conquest. That is not conjecture. That is not a guess. That is not bias. That is a hard, cold fact. It is as factual as Hitler's Nazi machine was in the 1930s.

Every invasion of another country with sights on conquest, particularly in the modern age, has required an in-depth plan with strategies and tactics laid out long in advance of the actual implementation. To do so militarily involves weapons technology, delivery systems, troop management, battlefield support and so on. A stealth invasion involves much more, particularly if the target country is the United States.

Stealth conquest takes much longer because the conquerors must employ a widespread system of psychology and deceit. Considering the current wave of conquest was reignited in 1980, the enemy is in its fourth decade. The invaders must have great patience and focus in order to guide the plan through to fruition. Many, or most, of those initiators and planners know they will probably never see the end result. But when Allah intervenes and assures the believers (Muslims) that they will, in fact, witness the conquest by Islam from a vantage point in eternal paradise, there is no reason to be impatient. It's the end result that matters.

Stealth conquest first requires that the invaders are in tune, psychologically and physically, with the society they wish to conquer. They must know America's weaknesses and strengths, the cultures, the languages, the infrastructure, the political arena, social weaknesses, crime and punishment systems, economic matters, and much more. For blending in, they must start building a population base that is indigenous or natural born, so that the Ikhwan (brothers) are part of the internal society and cannot be recognized as "foreigners," thereby owning the same rights as any American citizen, including the right to vote and hold office. Thus we have seen the proliferation of birth rates, conversions and mass immigration, legal, and illegal.

The successes of Islamist infiltration is no accident. The inch-by-inch gains of Fundamentalist Islam here and abroad is part of a long range plan hatched years ago by the higher echelon of mullahs and Jihadists. The documents revealed in this book are part of a grandiose plan and set of rules to follow for the Ikhwan and Muslims in general. We know their intent and how they will go about carrying out the plan. Yet, our media and our government and the governments of Europe, sit on their hands, confused and beleaguered by the compulsion to respect a "religion."

Origins of the Plan:

Where and when did it all begin? In truth, it began in the 7th century with Mohammed and his conquests through the Arabian Peninsula. Following his death in 632 A.D. after he had urged his followers to spread Islam and conquer the world, Islamist armies invaded and conquered the Middle-East, Southern Asia, North Africa and part of Europe. America did not exist then. Neither did modern technology or the ocean of wealth now at the offering for the Islamists.

In the 20th century, the Ottoman Empire based in Turkey collapsed after the losses in World War I. Islam no longer had a caliphate, which spurred the formation of the Muslim Brotherhood. As pointed out in previous chapters, the great threat to the Western Hemisphere did not manifest until the Ayatollah Khomeini assumed control of Iran (Persia) in 1979 and the westernized rule of the Shah came to an abrupt halt. The seizure of American hostages for 444 days revealed the United States to be a paper tiger under the leadership of President Jimmy Carter. The new Islamist regime in Iran sparked the nascent rise of terrorism around the world, which, coupled with the Muslim Brotherhood, gradually increased until this very day.

Christian Lebanon, which had been the only non-Muslim nation in the Middle-East other than Israel, was conquered by the radical Islamists, to the point of murdering Christians in their communities like Nazis to Jews, causing thousands to live underground. Today,

Lebanon is an Islamist state ruled by a terror organization known as Hezbollah. The Iranian revolution set off the chain reaction of Islamist power throughout the world, emboldened by terror, fear, unlimited financial reserves and effective intimidation of western powers.

That began sometime in 1980-1981.

I have often wondered how the war plans were concocted behind closed doors. For the Ikhwan hierarchy, it would consist of top mullahs within the Muslim Brotherhood swearing loyalty and secrecy to one another, much the same as La Cosa Nostra swears Omerta. Minions, at the risk of death, can never violate that oath. For a Muslim, that would mean he would never reach the gates of Paradise. Nothing could be worse.

This would not evolve after one simple meeting. These plans are complex and multi-lateral within the fundamentalist Islamic movement. The Brotherhood would have to reach out to key Islamists all over the world, from Chechnya to India, from Pakistan to Indonesia, from Africa and to all the Middle-East nations in order to coordinate strategic terror and stealth invasion of Western societies. The mere existence of the documents, "Explanatory Memorandum" and "The Project," found hidden in America and in Switzerland, tells us that the communications have been far-reaching, intended for specific personnel only. It is not much different than top-secret classified war documents of WWII or any other conflict, except that the Ikhwan (brothers) are based in nearly 100 counties throughout the world.

A Mosaic - Deploying the Plan:

This author cannot affirm the following to be true. However, based on the hard evidence recorded in this book, it would be more than plausible to assume that the actions, deeds, motives and plots initiated by the Muslim Brotherhood have been deployed. It is beyond a reasonable guess. It is a matter of assembling the picture from a myriad of painted tiles that, individually, reveal nothing. Again, when assembled, they create a clear picture.

Serving 30 years in a career largely comprised of evil and deceitful people, the author—like most career cops—has developed familiarity with the methods of nefarious and powerful organizations. It has provided a better-than-average comprehension of crime syndicates and the stealth behavior of people who are so driven by dogma, they have no conscience. Thus, we introduce the mosaic. You, the reader, may determine if it is fiction, or not.

Starting around 1980 emboldened by the success of the Iranian revolution, the Muslim Brotherhood assumed the task of formulating long-range plans for conquest of the West. How would they go about such a humongous task? What would be the order of priorities? How could acolytes of the Muslim Brotherhood lull people into believing they are "tolerant" and "peace loving" while at the same time, infiltrating and seizing control of European and North American nations without the people even realizing it?

First. –Islamist conquerors have incredible patience. They know that time is on their side while enabling them to keep the long-range objectives in sight. Beliefs would be unified among all Islamists, driven by their undying loyalty to the Prophet Mohammed. Those beliefs would be absolute, that striving for conquest in the name of Allah would render all Jihadists the ultimate reward of eternal life in Paradise. Therefore, the many millions of Jihadists who participate or assist in the conquest would likely not witness the end result during life on earth. It would be witnessed after death within the glory of God. This is the fervent belief of suicide bombers and their devoted families, that a new and better life awaits them if they die for Allah.

Death in the name of Jihad is our greatest wish, is recited at Muslim Student Association meetings throughout America. Radical Muslims are programmed from birth and predisposed to serving Allah, and if that means dying, it is considered a great service to God.

There is no time frame. All that matters is the end result.

Second. – Numbers matter. In 1980 there were very few Muslims living in Europe and America. At most, the United States had approximately 400 mosques, and as noted in chapter six, that number has increased by nearly 700 percent in just 35 years.

If Islamists were to establish a power base in these countries, the population of Muslims in Europe and America must grow by huge numbers via soft immigration policies, illegal entries, conversions and significant birth rates. The babies of immigrants would become American and European citizens, as would the babies of their babies. Conceivably, a married couple settling in the US could have seven children. A generation later, those seven kids would parent a total of 45-50 kids. If each Muslim child formed a family of seven or more children, those two settlers will have spawned 350 new Muslims living in this country, any one of which could be future Jihadists, or senators, or even, a president.

Settling a half million Muslims in America, from the Middle-East, Africa, Asia and other Muslim nations, would multiply the numbers 10 times over in a matter of two generations. They would eventually become voters with power at the polls, and later, viable for holding public office, even in Congress and other high positions. And as the numbers increase over the decades, the United States Constitution would ultimately cede to the tenets of the Quran and Sharia law. No amount of Democrat or Republican resistance could stop it.

Meanwhile, such Muslims must realize that their purpose is not to assimilate or become westernized. Rather they must maintain a mindset of Jihad at all times (as outlined in "The Project.")

Third. – Jihadists would require unlimited cash flow, into the trillions. Even though many of the Islamist nations are often at each others throats, i.e., Shiites versus Sunnis, they all agree on one solid goal: Mohammed's death wish – for Islam to rule the world. That pursuit has never waned. Since 1980, it has accelerated with great successes.

Iran, Libya, Saudi Arabia and Iraq are awash with the glut of oil. It is the yoke with which they hold other nations of the world at their behest, because those nations must import oil to provide energy in their societies, in Europe, South America, China, and even the United States. The money is best used, not for charity or arms and war materials, but for buying influence. Americans would have no idea, or would they be aware, just how much oil money has bought influence from politicians, corporations, banks, media, colleges, courts, law enforcement other government agencies on the federal and state levels throughout America. When Islamist nations are on the same page with the same purpose, it is not difficult to transfer billions of dollars under the radar to selected destinations in order to serve the cause of Jihad. Money would not even have to change hands. In the 21st century, huge funds can easily be transferred from one bank to another in most any country.

Let's be clear. We are talking about stealth bribery and payoffs. If Islam has learned nothing else about the Western culture, they came to know that Americans are selfish and short-sighted, particularly the power brokers. Americans think mostly of the "now" and not the "later." Greed prevails everywhere, and the mullahs of radical Islam are only too happy to oblige. No persons and no organizations are immune. This can manifest in the political arena by buying the influence of politicians or the media by influencing how, what and when news is slanted, included or omitted according to the needs of the briber.

Bribery is nothing new to Islam or to America for that matter. Money talks, especially big money. Bribery does not always have to take place in the form of cash favors. It can be used in support of political campaigns, media propaganda (al Jazeera), or education for selected college kids, hospital wings, presidential libraries, charities dear to the hearts of politicians or material items like cars, boats, travel and sex, lots of sex.

The original Muslim settlements in Europe all expanded due, in part, to national laziness and greed among the indigenous people. Moroccans, Algerians, Turks and Egyptians were willing to work in menial domestic labor jobs for far less money than employers would have had to pay Europeans. That became a successful arm of the Jihad campaign. After 40 years, those Muslim families and operatives have evolved into power blocs, most of whom do not, and will not, assimilate as Europeans. Thus, Europeans are destined to become the minority – in Europe.

Now, the big bonus has arrived in the form of mass refugees fleeing Syria and Iraq, with other indigenous Muslims from other countries joining the movement. As of now, the projected total is some three million, but that can expand as the next 10 years pass.

Americans are spoiled, greedy and gullible as well. Mullahs may launch a massive campaign of accusing people who utter any negative comments about Muslims, calling them Islamophobes, racists and bigots, insulting and demonizing them into virtual hiding. Muslims would ride piggyback on the anti-racist mantra borne from black-oriented movements from which white people will tap dance around every accusation of racism.

Corrupt deals are made in back rooms and then sanitized for public consumption as legal and justified policy and process. Americans rarely know the truth. They are easily manipulated by deception. Major policy makers in the upper ranks of the Muslim Brotherhood would establish solid networks for unlimited funding on a large scale, pro-rationed according to target issues and importance, including Senators and Congressmen and media moguls. They would be ready to dispense multi-billions of dollars if it were possible to install one of their own, disguised as a Christian, into the most powerful position on Earth—The United States presidency.

Mass Immigration:

Earlier, we talked about the gradual infiltration of North America, via immigration, birth rates, financial institutions, colleges and so forth. That was then. This is now.

The migration explosion has only just begun. What would be better, for Jihadists, than to overwhelm Western nations with calculated mega-surges in non-assimilating Muslim people to the point where the new population becomes so large that they eventually assume power with numbers? For free nations like England, France, Spain, and even the United States, that would alter the political spectrum, including schools, law enforcement, economic priorities and ultimately, the US Constitution that is blatantly incompatible with Sharia.

As this book is written, nearly three million "refugees" are storming into Europe and North America to escape the scourge of ISIS and other terror operations in the Middle-East and Africa. Almost 800,000 have invaded Germany alone, mainly because the government there has extended open arms in the name of humanity. Other masses of Islamic immigrants will spread throughout that continent, certain to alter the cultural, religious and political landscape for all time. Almost 50,000 asylum seekers reached Greece in the single month of July in 2015. All nations in Europe are in a quandary dealing with the enormous impact this will have.

It ain't over yet.

One wonders if this was not part of the overall strategy; to create havoc and chaos in the Middle East, engage in war and terrorism on all fronts, and cause the indigenous people to flee by the millions into the land of infidels. After all, they did promise conquest *from within.*

In a *World Net Daily* article in September 2015, reporter Leo Hohmann cites a statement by the Hungarian Foreign Minister in which he predicted as many as 35 million Muslim migrants may eventually flood Europe as part of a historic population shift. While a large portion of those numbers may be good and decent people, we can only speculate what percentage will be riding that wave on a Jihad mission. In other words, thousands of Islamist warriors will be among the new population growth.

The United States is part of the immigration bandwagon as the *Bloombergview.com* reports how national security officials in the Obama Administration will consider raising the limit from 70,000 Syrian migrants in FY15/16, to 85,000 next fiscal year, and then 100,000 more in 17/18. This does not address the 40 percent of all illegal aliens that come to America by overstaying visas, thousands of whom are from fundamentalist Islamic countries. President Obama is expected to sign off on all immigration issues while still in office. Again, will we ever know what percentage of these "refugees" are actually coming here to do us harm?

The author wonders if this was not part of the overall plan when he vowed, just prior to his first election in 2008, "We are five days away from fundamentally transforming the United States of America."

Forever in the crosshairs of international Jihad, the United States is the top prize as clearly stated over the years by radical sources like Iran (Death to America) and the Muslim Brotherhood. So what has our government done to ward off this nascent threat? We have basically aided and abetted our future enemies. They told us so. And we did not believe them.

THIRTEEN
THE COMMANDER IN CHIEF

If all went well, the head mullahs could achieve utopia if Islam could assume control of the most powerful political position on planet Earth, the presidency of the United States. Without a president's power, Islamists might gradually gain support in congressional seats, perhaps even the courts. That would take a very long time and entail many conflicts with the Executive Branch of the government. But to have an ally, or a future Caliph, in the White House would be the ultimate coup. It is definitely conceivable if the Ikhwan (Brothers) are careful, cunning and cleverly deceitful. How could they possibly go about achieving that end? How could they pull the proverbial wool over the eyes of the American populace and the media by installing a stealth Jihadist in the Oval Office?

It is unthinkable.

This could not take place with short-range thinking. In the 1980s and 90s, America would not yet be primed. With tentacles of power and loyalty reaching all over the world, it would be incumbent upon the Muslim Brotherhood to begin a search for potential candidates at a young age and to cultivate those persons for political power in the United States before the end of the century, and then, hopefully, election in 20 or 30 years when he is in his 40s or 50s.

In order to achieve that end, the Brotherhood would require the following:

- The primary candidate must be a male.
- As the search and recruitment begins in the early 1980s the candidates should be in their 20s or early 30s in order to allow time for cultivation and preparation.

- The search would likely entail several exceptional young men from which to select. In the event the primary candidate dies or fails the mission, an understudy must be ready to assume the primary role so that the mission is not stalled.
- The candidate must be Muslim with a full understanding of Islamic ideals, religious tenets and goals, but disguised as a non-Muslim to the general populace.
- The candidate must know and understand his purpose and never violate his loyalty to Islam and his allegiance to Allah.
- The candidate, by necessity, would be required to violate many laws of Islam and the Quran, but to be forgiven since they are deemed acts of Taqiyya for the noble purpose of establishing Islam.
- It would be best to recruit a young man from the ranks of academia, with no significant employment record from which to expose or measure his work ethic, controversial ideals or personal life. His attachment to Islam must be low-key and disassociated with the candidate for public consumption.
- The candidate must be home-grown and not from the Middle-East or any Islamic Asian nation. He must be highly intelligent, ideally a black or mulatto, in order to draw from the ultra-liberal side of American politics and media, including mass voting blocs such as black Americans, other minorities, low income people seeking entitlements, immigrants and criminals.
- The candidate should be a media magnet. Mainstream journalists would likely be thirsting for a spectacular story in politics, a departure from the stiff, stereotypical white male model for the presidency. This would provide a distraction from personal scrutiny, luring media into a state of euphoric sensationalism for which they would provide undying support for the candidate in later years, regardless of any negative connotations. A black president will have the luxury of a built-in defense for questionable actions, which then provides greater leeway in effecting change in the path of Islam. Any criticism of him can be countered with accusations of racism.
- He must be discreet and play down his Islamic connections as he works toward his scholastic degrees.

- He must enroll as a false Christian in order to publicly identify with the majority religion and to facilitate his election in office. All these deceptions and violations of Qur'anic Islam are forgiven.
- He must be a convincing and eloquent public speaker.
- He should marry and have children, presenting the appearance of an average American family man.
- Like all other presidential hopefuls in the modern era, he should write and publish at least one autobiography, or perhaps two, even if the candidate has no remarkable background. All future presidents of the last fifty years have published books about their lives before running for office. It is the norm. The content should be carefully structured in order to portray himself as a liberal young man, admitting to misbehavior as a youngster, but minimizing his Muslim roots as anything that guides his purpose. If he has no eventful background, he can write about family conflicts or racial strife. But he must author a book or at the very least, publish a book naming him as the author.
- The candidate must have ample credentials, with graduate degrees of higher learning equal to that of other presidents. Funding is not an issue.
- Once completing graduate school, the candidate should be grounded in a political environment that will gradually assemble a following, first in the local and state level, then national. The primary focus will be on amassing financial appropriations and assembling voters within the liberal and mass sectors from the lower class.
- He should join and become active in the Democratic Party, which is the major political body closest to socialist ideals, and the most tolerant of Islam as an accepted religious community in the United States.
- While in political office, whether state or national, he should try to avoid establishing a legislative voting record, left or right. All attempts should be made to appear as a centrist, or center-

left, but not an extremist. His appeal must reach out to the Independents, women, minorities, youths and central voter blocs.

- Once elected to the presidency, the candidate should make efforts to follow Marxist socialist doctrines (distribution of wealth) as a governing ideology because it will ultimately place centralized power in the hands of the president. America will soon be ready to follow the course set by Europe and Russia as socialist forms of government. As more power is exerted over the citizenry by government, the threat of resistance will be diminished. That will set the stage for Islam to march over Christianity and Judaism, and the American Constitution, as conquerors did in the third decade of the millennium.
- All efforts should be made to establish Democratic Party control over the entire Congress in order to provide the new president unobstructed power to advance an agenda suitable to socialists, and eventually, Islam.
- While in office, the new president must use his power and authority to downplay Islam's relationship to terrorism and thwart all intelligence/surveillance investigations of Muslims throughout America. Islam must be seen as harmless, religious, and Americanized, casting blame only with extremists, i.e., al-Qaeda and ISIS, as the sole, isolated threat to Western democracy and peace.
- As president, depending on the level of support he gains from Congress and the Supreme Court, he should set goals for transferring the power of the people to the power of the government.
- He should stablish an unshakable rapport with the mainstream media that will act in his behalf as a loyal extension of his administration by promoting the new president and withholding critical commentary whenever possible.
- He should nationalize health care and strive toward a single payer system so that all health care services are under the control of the government, including doctors, health care facilities and insurance companies.

- He should use taxpayer funds to bail out major corporations that go bankrupt, thereby establishing power over the free market in those businesses.

- He must aim to legitimize aliens—legal and illegal—to inflate the future voting blocs for the Democratic Party. Included among them, should be Muslims from Africa, Asia and the Middle East who immigrate via visas, then remain to establish residency, legal or illegal. Hispanics from Mexico and Central America can simply stream over the border with impunity and then find refuge in any of nearly two hundred sanctuary cities in the US. All these aliens and their children are guaranteed to be future Democrats.

- His goal should be to lure blocs and minorities, i.e. Latinos, Blacks, Arabs and Asians, including women and homosexuals, as Democrat-exclusive voters.

- It will important to demonize any Republicans who present serious electable qualities, to and including the public ravaging of their personal lives, whether valid or invalid.

- He must covertly assist the Muslim Brotherhood in attaining power throughout Middle-East nations, including Egypt, Tunisia, Libya, Yemen, Syria and Iraq.

- He should diminish European nations as allies of the United States, and vice-versa.

- While verbally claiming to be an ally of Israel (to secure Jewish support,) he should covertly aid and abet efforts of Palestinians and other Arab nations in setting the groundwork for the ultimate destruction of the Jewish state. He must advocate for Israel's borders to be returned to pre-1967 lines. These goals can be achieved vicariously by supporting all efforts of the Muslim Brotherhood, including takeovers of Muslim nations and working with the Iranians to provide them a path for developing nuclear capacity.

- The American people should be disarmed. Efforts should be made to weaken Second Amendment rights by using examples of gun violence as justification for rallying the American people to demand harsh federal gun control measures. Americans, in general, should be manipulated into thinking that the big problem in terror attacks is the lack of gun control, not Islam.

- He should work to diminish American military might, using the economy and budget cuts as imperatives while appointing loyal novice officers at command levels who will perform as obedient acolytes. He must dispose of any command officers who pose a threat to the security of the mission.
- He must support and subtly enhance a deep chasm in race relations, manipulating media and leftist organizations to espouse outrage and hatred in protests (civil disharmony) in major cities throughout America. He will couple that by disarming police, not literally, but figuratively so that officers become impotent in the maintenance of order.
- He must appoint judges to all federal courts who will covertly support the encroachment of Sharia in order that it is accepted as compatible with the American system of justice. Criticism or resistance to appointing Islamists into government and judicial positions would be countered with vigorous assertions of religious intolerance.
- He must target the youth in schools and universities for brainwashing and developing allies in the Jihad struggle toward establishing social justice and eventually, Islamic law. This can be further enhanced by Islamist sources contributing huge donations to major colleges and universities in America, which then translates to subservience to Islamic demands. With that, colleges will hire left-leaning or Islamist professors who can then influence the thinking of American youth.
- No matter what distractions or obstacles are presented in the course of the presidency, the Muslim president must never lose sight of his primary mission.
- The president must employ Taqiyya, 24 hours a day, 365 days a year. This would require him to be the consummate actor, portraying who he *is not* in order to achieve the final objectives. He will falsely claim loyalty to America. He will falsely identify himself as a Christian. Without revealing his Islamic attachment, he will

defend and espouse love for Islam to the United Nations and the world in general. Meanwhile he will never associate terror with Islam, no matter the evidence. Instead, he will simply refer to them as "extremists."

During a speech at the United Nations, two weeks after four Americans were killed at the American compound in Benghazi, Libya, President Obama told the audience, "The future must not belong to those who slander the Prophet of Islam."

FOURTEEN
BARACK HUSSEIN OBAMA

As the author of this book, considering its sensitivities, it is important to be unambiguous.

After years of study about world affairs, the national economy and the rise of radical Islam here and abroad, plus the advent of Barack Hussein Obama as our commander-in-chief, his history and his conduct and rhetoric in office, I have assembled the mosaic from all those tiles we discussed earlier from which a picture has become crystal clear.

Here are my conclusions:

- Obama is a dedicated neo-Marxist and a Muslim obsessed with a mission to Islamize the North American continent.
- Obama is, without doubt, an ally of (or membered with) the Muslim Brotherhood
- Obama is a stealth enemy of Israel who has the ability to oversee its destruction while posing as a sympathetic friend.
- Much of the rise of ISIS, Muslim Brotherhood and turmoil within the Islamic world has been designed and intended to divide. The disasters following the pull-out from Iraq was not only predictable, they were planned and deliberate.
- Obama's principal goal is to oversee the downfall of capitalism in America, replaced with socialism whereby the state exerts total control over the populace and eventually interwoven with Sharia law.
- Much like V.I. Lenin who referred to low-level revolutionaries as "useful idiots," Obama will continue to strive toward assembling masses to the polls like stooges

because they are rewarded monetarily or afforded special accommodations, or both.

- I believe this quest will ultimately result in repealing all or parts of the Constitution, amended with, or replaced by Sharia Law.
- Because burgeoning power and money will become a formidable lure, the press will further be controlled by the government, much like TASS in the Soviet Union and the newspapers in Saudi Arabia and Pakistan.
- Free speech and religious freedom will be monitored and curtailed.
- Obama's promise of a fundamental transformation of America will go down as one of the greatest successes of anyone's political career.
- In the next 20 years, and beyond, there will be as much anti-Semitic hatred and activity toward Jews as there were during the Nazi regime. Christians will not be far behind. Even as a growing minority, Muslims will dominate society.
- Obama will go down in Islamic history as one of the great prophets of Islam, having set the stage for conquest, as outlined by the Muslim Brotherhood.
- The long range plan is to establish a caliphate in North America in which, Mr. Obama will likely emerge as the Caliph, if he's still living.

* * *

Progress:

Barack Obama took charge of the White House and became our commander-in-chief slightly over seven years after radical Islamists killed nearly 3,000 people on American soil, September 11, 2001, only seven years from the time the enemy declared its war on the United States, in the name of Islam.

President George W. Bush may have seemed to be a man of action, initiating wars against radical Islam in foreign lands like Afghanistan and Iraq. Meanwhile, the president naively cozied up to Saudi and other Arab powers despite knowing that many of the 9/11 terrorists were Saudis, and disregarding the roots of Osama bin Laden that were mired in Saudi Arabia and the Muslim Brotherhood. Bush openly and continually portrayed Islam as a religion of peace, giving solace to those who might be our enemy, while also molding complacent attitudes among the American populace and the media, ensuring us all that the bad guys were on the other side of the world when, in fact, they were forming a power base in the United States.

In 2008, despite the overt hatred of fundamentalist Islamists toward America, we elected a new president who uses an Islamic name, who was marinated in Islam for more than three years from ages 7 to 10, whose father and stepfather were Muslim and whose religion was listed as "Islam" in his Indonesian school where he was also a citizen. From there, after returning to Hawaii where he lived with his grandparents starting at age ten, he was mentored throughout his teen years by one of the most notorious Communist intellectuals in the United States through whom he established a future array of close contacts in politics, including Communist, Vernon Jarrett and his daughter-in-law, Valerie Jarrett.

Are we nuts?

If we checked out police officer applicants as sloppily as we vetted Barack Obama, the Mafia and the drug lords would be running state and local governments, cops would routinely be on the take, criminals would run wild, people would be bolted in their houses and jails would be empty.

This was like electing Tojo to run the White House seven years after Pearl Harbor.

The mainstream media was so blatantly blinded by charisma, oratory skill and—more than anything—racial identity, that they not only failed to vet his background, they avoided it at all costs. Beyond that, they attached racism labels to those who would challenge his identity, his motives or his veracity, to the point that the most well-meaning of journalists and politicians grew paranoid of openly daring to question.

It is inconceivable that the American people could be so easily duped to elect a virtual neophyte into the Oval Office, devoid of any notable accomplishments, who had never followed a career path nor established a clear political track record, whose childhood and early manhood was immersed in Islam and Marxism, the two ideologies that have often sworn to destroy American democracy.

Islamists of the Muslim Brotherhood should be congratulated as utter geniuses. They have won every chess game and every move from 1980 to the present and we are well on our way toward seeing the nascent growth of an Islamic society begin to dominate the political arena. (The one chess move that went awry was Egypt ousting the Muslim Brotherhood in 2013.)

The prior chapter titled, "The Plan," suggested the complex scheme by which the Muslim Brotherhood set out to coordinate and direct the Jihad with the purpose of eventual conquest over the Western nations of Europe and the North American continent. That long-range plan, initiated around 1980, certainly targeted the eventual surrender of the presidency in which the chosen candidate would have eight years, or more, to arrange for the submission to Islam before the year 2020.

This chapter could be a book of its own. Though hundreds of samplings exist of Obama's sheer corruption, deceit, anti-American motives and at best, incompetence, we will harness the material facts that most importantly pertain to his role in advancing the mission of Islamist domination while at the same time portraying himself otherwise.

With that in mind, let's examine the progress.

<u>The Birth of Barack Obama:</u>

This is a topic of which most people have become sick and tired. It was hammered into oblivion to the point that even the most conservative of pundits were glad to see it put to rest and move on, even though the issue was never truly resolved in many people's minds.

Why should the birthplace issue of Barack Obama be so important? Even if he was born in Kenya, who cares? Well, there is a Constitutional question of Obama's eligibility that could pose a major stumbling block. He did have an American mother, though not an American father.

The real truth may never be known. We do know that, beginning in his 2008 campaign, an enormous amount of money was expended in efforts by the Obama camp—millions of dollars—to field a barrage of legal challenges, all dismissed in court based on standing and other procedural grounds, but none dismissed on merit. If there was nothing to hide, why embark on a charade? Why hire lawyers? Why would any presidential candidate, ever, be resistant to producing a valid birth certificate, not to mention fighting it in court proceedings?

Obama's team continued to defend legal challenges for three years until suddenly, out of nowhere in April of 2011, Obama produced an alleged Hawaiian document as if to say, "Oh, is this what you were looking for?"

Three years overdue, this document settled the storm. Though many (including this author) still have doubts, the mainstream media wanted to let the matter rest. The right-leaning media was intimidated into accepting the document and to move on. It became a nuisance issue. Any further questions about Obama's birth origins would dub the doubters as fools or racist maniacs. But rhetoric does not settle the issue.

As Doctor Joseph Davis had taught me, it is a matter of following the road where the evidence takes you. That evidence is convincing enough to this author to believe Barack Obama is foreign-born, thereby ineligible to hold the office of president.

Amongst the evidence one highly perplexing item says it all. In 1991, Barack Obama's first book, *Dreams From My Father* was published with an author-bio pamphlet produced by literary agency, Acton & Dystel. For sixteen years, until he began his run for president, that pamphlet stated, "Barack Obama, the first African American president of the Harvard Law Review, was born in Kenya and raised in Indonesia and Hawaii."

Ask any author, agent or publisher; book authors are the source for providing personal bio information to their publishers and agents. Therefore it is normal to conclude that this information was provided by Barack Obama, the book author. As brilliant as he may be, this Constitutional lawyer failed to remember that if he had his sights set on the presidency, he could not be born in another country. As though an afterthought in 2007, two months after he announced his run for the presidency, someone must have alerted him that the book leaf data could cause him problems. After sixteen years, the information was changed to read that Obama was born in Hawaii. Hmm.

The birth certificate that he produced in 2011 is still believed by many to be counterfeit for a number of reasons. Anyone can Google the question and find scores of graphics experts who pored over the document concluding that it was computer generated with various overlays, inconsistent numbering fonts and printing flaws. Further, the forgers overlooked a number of other gotchas, such as:

- The birth certificate states Obama's father's race as "African," which, in 1961, was not listed in the census data as a race. Rather, the citing should have been "Negro."
- The questioned birth certificate also shows Barack Obama Sr. as being born in Kenya, East Africa. Not possible. Kenya was not established as a country until 1963, two years after Barack Jr. was born.
- Add to that, the listed birth venue is Kapiolani Maternity and Gynecological Hospital. Not possible, because that name was not established until 1978 when two hospitals merged, 17 years after his birth.

So, it is clear that many of these afterthoughts were injected into the birth certificate issue; his book leaf, the hospital name, the father's race and nation of birth, as a ruse to put the question to rest, despite the falsehoods. And it worked.

What is the significance in regards to this book? In truth, it matters not at this point, other than to highlight what lengths this man and his team will go to obfuscate truth. It is not so much an issue of eligibility as it is pure unadulterated dishonesty.

Early Childhood:

There are a myriad of questions and inconsistencies concerning young Barack Obama, where he was born, where and how he was raised from birth to manhood and his political and religious orientation growing up. For the purposes of this book, we will confine our focus to those elements that had a profound impact on his outlook and how those attitudes eventually molded a future president that, in turn, has molded a nation.

It is important to acknowledge the one person who probably had more influence on Barack Obama Jr. than any other human being, his mentor Frank Marshall Davis, a well-known, avowed card-carrying Communist. A devout activist from the 1940s through the 1970s while in the surveillance crosshairs of the FBI, some folks think that Frank Marshall Davis only knew young Barack from age ten and older, but that is not actually true. Long before Barack Jr. was born, Frank Marshall Davis—poet and photographer—was close friends with Mr. Stanley Dunham whose daughter, Stanley Anne Dunham, posed for pictures for Davis. She would ultimately become Barack's mother. Frank Marshall Davis actually hailed from Chicago and had many close political and journalistic ties there.

Filmmaker, Joel Gilbert, produced a 90 minute documentary in 2012 in which he claims having conducted two years of exhaustive research in determining the truth about Obama's beginnings. Titled, *Dreams From My Real Father*, Gilbert goes into great detail based on literature, photographs, interviews and records dealing with Frank Marshall Davis and Stanley Anne Dunham. From on his findings, Gilbert asserts that Davis is the true biological father of our president, and that the wedding between Barack Obama Sr., and Anne was a sham arranged by Anne's father to protect Davis, his friend and a married man with kids. Obama Sr., while visiting Hawaii on an education visa from Kenya, agreed to a clandestine wedding with Anne in exchange for benefits he would receive while married to an American citizen, including admission to Harvard for doctoral studies. They never cohabitated.

Within a couple of weeks after Barack Obama's birth, she took the baby and moved to Seattle where she lived and attended college for two years before returning to Hawaii. There, she formally executed the divorce from Barack Obama Sr., who then was living in Africa with another wife. Two years later, she met an Indonesian graduate student at the University of Hawaii named Lolo Soetoro, another Muslim man who she married. In 1967, when Barack was six, he moved with his mother and new stepfather to Indonesia where he became a citizen renamed Barry Soetoro. He was also enrolled in school with his religion listed as Islam.

In September of 2012, noted author, intellectual and expert on Islamic affairs, Daniel Pipes, published a comprehensive article for the *Middle East Forum* in which he cited numerous sources confirming that young Obama attended Koranic studies, mosques, engaged in prayers and even wore Muslim garb. The article cites a number of people who testified to these facts, though Mr. Obama has always denied ever being a Muslim.

Note: In a *New York Times* Op-Ed by Nicolas D. Kristof on May 3, 2007, Obama is quoted describing the Muslim call to prayer as "one of the prettiest sounds on earth at sunset."

Regardless, Obama was returned to Hawaii at age ten while his mother remained in Indonesia. Still using the adopted name, Barry Soetoro, the boy was not among the stereotypically poor, disadvantage black kids of that era that some folks think. Rather, he attended a private school at the behest of his grandfather, Stanley

Dunham. Obama's grandparents were regular attendees at a Unitarian Church, an all-inclusive religion that hosts a blend of former Jews, Christians, atheists and others who departed from traditional religions. The grandfather worked for the CIA recruiting foreigners from around the world to help serve as liaisons for the agency in foreign lands, which is how he met Barack Obama Sr. when he first traveled to Hawaii on a student visa.

It was during the next eight years, starting at age 10, and encouraged by Mr. Dunham, young Obama established that very close, mentoring relationship with Frank Marshall Davis. And if it was true that–according to Joel Gilbert's two-year research study–Frank Marshall Davis was the truly the biological father of Barack, and the boy knew that, he might have been awash in a near-familial relationship as well.

As gleaned from Obama's own biography, Davis had a profound impact on the young boy, particularly during his very impressionable years. Davis was known to hold hostile feelings toward whites in general and hated the capitalist system of government. It is not unreasonable to assume that Obama spent countless days, weeks and years being mentored by this strong-minded intellectual whose mission in Chicago and Hawaii was to lure more minorities into the Communist Party. Davis' writings, lectures and obsessions were locked into promoting Communism in the fight against bigotry, oppression and prejudice in the black communities of America.

One can only speculate about the extent to which this man had influenced the mind and heart of this mixed race child, but it was surely profound.

Davis was not only a Party member, but a focus of attention by the FBI for nearly twenty years. This rapport oozes throughout Obama's memoir, *Dreams From My Father,* where he is mentioned with respect and affection as "Frank" more than twenty times. In 1995, his first year as an Illinois State Senator, Obama gave a speech about his new book, in which he openly revealed "Frank" as being Davis.

Film maker Joel Gilbert's assertion that Davis was Barack Obama's real father may seem whacko theory to some folks, but when viewer pays close attention to the connected dots and all the surrounding circumstances of Obama's childhood, it is certainly feasible. Then, there are the physical features. As can be seen in photographs, the facial likeness of Barack Obama Jr to Frank Marshall Davis is remarkable, far more so than with Barack Obama Sr.

There is no evidence that Obama Sr. and Anne Dunham ever lived together as man and wife. Neither did Obama Sr. ever have any relationship with the future president. But Frank Marshall Davis surely did. It is important to know these things, because young Barack Obama had been immersed in the ideologies of Islam and Communism for many years leading up to college.

College and Islam:

Barack Obama's school records at all three of his college institutions have not been released and at his direction, they may not be released or open to scrutiny. The concern is certainly not about grades, because nobody would care. Because these records remain closed, we are not privileged to know what courses he chose to take and by whom his college courses were financed. Also, the American people are prevented from access to identification records such as passports or birth certificates, both of which have been seriously questioned, and for good reason.

It is mind-boggling that any presidential candidate would stonewall release of school records unless there was something to hide. Obama is not the first president to do so. G.W. Bush also refused to release school records, though Bush's American roots or financial status was never in doubt. In the case of this president, a myriad of questions remain unanswered that are pertinent to his identity, his legal qualifications as president and most importantly, his truthfulness.

It has been alleged that Obama received an affirmative action scholarship to Occidental College in Southern California. Pundits have speculated in a myriad of publications suggesting that he may have been awarded a foreign student scholarship because his citizenship in Indonesia was still valid. But we do not know these basic things about our president and he has not been forthcoming to clarify.

According to *Wikipedia*, in 2012, Donald Trump offered Barack Obama a gift of five million dollars to go to his designated charity if he would open his college transcripts and passport records. As of 2016, Trump is still waiting for an answer.

Occidental is a private, liberal arts institution based in Los Angeles. In today's dollars, tuition alone is approximately $50,000 a year, not including dorm fees and other expenses. We have no record of Obama holding any jobs or saving money. It is possible that Obama's grandfather helped with the tuition, or some other supportive person, but we do not know.

While residing on campus, Barack Obama chose to room with two students who were Pakistani Muslims, Muhammad Hasan Chandoo and Wahid Hamid. In this case, religion is significant, as much as it would be if and when strict Hassidic Jews choose to room together. In the case of race during the 70's and 80's, blacks and whites rarely cohabited. In our multicultural society, we think nothing of Catholics, Protestants or agnostics sharing the same room. But it is different with devout Muslims, whose culture and religious mandates are bound to special dietary laws, prayer duties (five times a day) and other rituals of life. While there may be exceptions, Muslims will rarely share living quarters with anyone other than Muslims.

In 1981, Obama went on vacation. No, not Europe or Africa, or the Far-East or even Canada. Obama travelled to chaotic Pakistan with Hasan Chandoo staying three weeks with friends in Karachi. At the time, Pakistan—which is 95% Muslim—was in political turmoil and under travel restrictions that excluded American and European non-Muslim tourists.

Questions have arisen over the years concerning what passport Obama must have used, but those issues have consistently been excused and swept under the proverbial rug by media protectorates. It is not impossible, but unlikely that he travelled with a US passport. Until we see college records, we will never know. Most significant, is that this young, handsome half-black American man preferred his vacation time in some strife-torn Islamic country, as opposed to any other part of the world. Islam was obviously a major part of his life, as we have chronicled here.

We may never know to what degree Obama was indoctrinated in the Islamic religion, but as he traveled through life, Islamic friendships were plentiful, more so than with mainstream Americans. As we have seen throughout his presidency, Obama is highly sensitive to any denigration of Islam, making speeches around the world praising and protecting the religion as if it were a personal obsession, regardless of international terrorism and Jihad.

Somewhere in his life, Obama dropped the adopted name of Barry Soetoro and reassumed his birth name. We can only assume that the adoption was nullified and that he somehow resumed being a citizen of the United States. Nevertheless, Obama's future life indicates a strong alliance with Islamic personalities, some of whom were known to have hostile feelings toward the United States.

Columbia University:

We do not know how or why Barack Obama ended up in New York City, transferring to this prestigious and very expensive Ivy League university in 1981. Nevertheless, it's interesting to note that his roommate in New York was another Muslim fellow named Sohale Siddiqi, or "Sadik" as Obama affectionately referred to him in his book *Dreams From My Father.*

Again, as history reflects, Barack Obama was quite comfortable amid the Islamic community, though we have no specific records that specifically identify him as a believer in Islamism. And, it is rare that an Islamic person will agree to be a roommate with a non-Muslim, for reasons aforementioned.

Muslims (therefore, Islam) continued to play a significant role in Obama's personal and social world. One of his closest associates starting from the Columbia years in the 1980s, was professor Rashid Khalid, a well-known activist and advocate of Palestinian causes, not to mention a strong adversary of Israel. This friendship was formed, developed and nurtured during the time Obama also established his relationship with Bill Ayres, former leader of the hate group, Weather Underground, which had been responsible for a number of domestic bombings. According to numerous sources, Khalid and Ayers were best of friends thereby forming the social, educational and cultural nexus with the future president.

Naturally, as in the case with his roommates in two colleges, the Islamic relationships are not limited only to that inner circle. Those relationships would have entailed an expansion of relationship in the social and political arenas.

In 2003, then Illinois State Senator Barack Obama attended a gala dinner held in honor of the esteemed professor, in which he gave a speech lavishing praise upon Khalidi, who was accused by many as being an apologist for terrorists, and who had been an advocate and spokesman for the PLO leader, Yasser Arafat. Other speakers took to the podium to praise Khalidi and the PLO and to denigrate Israel, to enthusiastic applause.

No one knows for sure to what degree Obama first established his friendship with Texas-based Muslim cleric, and hater of America, Khalid al-Mansour. According to *Newsmax* reports published in September and December 2008, al-Mansour, a radical African-American Muslim convert, was a former advisor to radical Black Panthers, Bobby Seale and Huey Newton, plus an educator, lawyer, and outspoken enemy of Israel. After graduating from Columbia in 1983, Obama resettled in Chicago to embark upon his now famous position as a "community organizer." Later in that decade, it appears that al-Mansour would have a significant impact upon Obama's future. (It is hard to fathom that a future president of the United States had such strong associations within anti-American, activist circles.)

These revelations came from Percy Sutton, the former president of Manhattan Borough, who was interviewed on a New York City cable television program in March of 2008. In his talking points (accessible on You Tube), Sutton—a respected, black New York City administrator—spoke about being contacted 20 years earlier by Khalid al-Mansour, who claimed to be a good friend of young Barack Obama. According to Sutton, al-Mansour was a close advisor to Prince Al Waleed Bin Talal of Saudi Arabia. The prince was interested in helping Barack Obama enter law school at Harvard, to which al Mansour acted as a go-between in soliciting Percy Sutton's support by writing a letter to Harvard University to recommend Obama.

Why?

As we all know, after five years living in Chicago as a community organizer, Obama entered law school at Harvard in 1988, finishing in 1991.

Chicago:

One might wonder what drew the future president to the city of Chicago as a permanent residence.

If we connect the dots, the answer is simple: Frank Marshall Davis. While we know that Davis lived in Hawaii for a good portion of his life, he also had frequent connections and lodgings in Chicago where he worked ardently for the Communist Party in various facets, including the publication of *The Chicago Star*, which was known as a strong supporter of the Communist movement.

Davis was a very close associate of Vernon Jarrett, a politico operative in Chicago and a writer like Davis, also with ties to the CPUSA (Communist Party). In fact, Jarrett was an active Communist. He also worked as a reporter for the *Chicago Sun Times*. There is a plethora of data on the information highway, either in books or on-line courses, plus several reports by *Judicial Watch* that was gleaned from FOIA-obtained (Freedom of Information Act) FBI files, that reveal these nefarious connections that led to Obama becoming a significant figure among Chicago left-wing power brokers.

Paul Kengor authored a powerful, well-researched book titled *The Communist* which chronicles the maze of Communist associations connected to Davis and Obama.

One of Vernon Jarrett's close associates in Chicago was James Bowman, a medical doctor, who had moved to Iran in 1956 to work as a teacher. That year, he and his wife, Barbara, had a baby whom they named, Valerie Bowman. The family moved back to Chicago in 1963. Twenty years later, she would marry her long-time childhood friend, William Robert Jarrett, son of Vernon Jarrett, though the marriage only lasted five years. This baby would one day become the most powerful woman in the history of the United States government as Chief Assistant to the President: Valerie Jarrett.

During Obama's first year as president, Valerie Jarrett was instrumental in lauding and hiring Van Jones to be the Green Jobs Czar for the administration's White House. Van Jones was well known as a civil rights activist, but more so, he was a diehard Marxist who believed in distribution of wealth. He did not last long because of the controversies, but it certainly revealed where Valerie Jarrett's heart lied, and the president's.

The Relevance of Communism:

Though Islam is a 1,400 year-old religion, and Western civilizations had periods of skirmishes here and there, as in the Barbary Coast, 18th century, it never posed a major threat to Europe and the Americas until the latter part of the 20th century, particularly more so in the early stages of the 21st century.

Communism, on the other hand, rose as a dominant threat before WWII and since has been omnipresent both from within and out. The Soviet Union, dubbed the Evil Empire by President Reagan, has often seen its leaders vow to bury the United States, while espionage and skullduggery prevailed between America and behind the Iron

Curtain. The Cold War nearly erupted into a hot war in 1962 when the Soviet Union planted its missiles in Cuba aimed at the US only to be backed down and quelled by President Kennedy.

Regardless of how evil the empire had been, it sure mustered a lot of left-wing support in the United States, particularly after the boondoggle of senate hearings headed by Senator Joseph McCarthy in the early 1950s. McCarthy's zeal backfired, and the true victim was the country itself, for there certainly were influential people in America then who supported the Communist movement, but McCarthy went about the probe more as a witch hunt than a solid investigation. Anyone who dares to attach the term "Communist" to a citizen or politician in today's world is usually stained by being branded a McCarthyite.

Paul Kengor's book and others including Michelle Malkin's *Culture of Corruption* and Aaron Klein's *The Manchurian Candidate*, address the details of communist connections to which Obama had been allied with over his early years. The reader may wonder, what this has to do with Islam and Obama's alignment with radical forces hell-bent on Islamic conquest.

Good question. In a nutshell, the ideologies enhance one another. At least, they do for Obama's purposes toward instilling Islam as a ruling government in the distant future.

Both systems rely on fear and intimidation of the masses in order to exist. Both can be ruthless and savage when it comes to maintaining control. Both systems rely on government controlling laws and rules while stripping individuals of the basic rights and freedoms Americans hold dear: speech—assembly, religion, press, and petition. Both unabashedly use deceit and propaganda to further power. As proven by the accounts of history, these governments are omnipresent and omnipotent. When fully in power, they represent the opposite of individual liberty. The press has been and is fully controlled by the government in countries like the Russia, China, Pakistan, Cuba, Saudi Arabia and many more.

That's the nutshell. When introducing Barack Obama to the equation we can see how well one system has been used to achieve objectives of the other. To Barack Obama, it will be easier to dispatch extreme left Socialists (or closet communists) to whittle away the Constitution, because much of our political system today has already tilted to the left. We see bits and pieces of that happening, chipping away at Second Amendment rights, free speech rights and unlimited use of the executive order system to enact new laws (as in Obamacare), or disregard other laws (as in illegal immigration) and support anarchism in the form of manufacturing anti-police sentiment, as in the cases of the New York City, Ferguson and Baltimore protest demonstrations, including the infamous Trayvon Martin case.

There are plenty of far-left Socialists in elected office. A fine line exists between a far leftist and an ideological Communist, neither of which is identified by holding a membership card, but they are here nonetheless. Retired Army Lieutenant Colonel Allen West boldly declared in 2012—after serving a short stint as a US Congressman—at least 80 members of the House of Representatives were Communists. Of course, he was basing that allegation on their political ideologies, not Party membership. When that news was published, Colonel West was predictably accused of McCarthyism.

Meanwhile, Obama has enjoyed undying support of Socialist and Democrat party loyalists in employing the power of the pen—regardless of law—to enlarge the army of pro-entitlement voters and to seed America with illegal immigrants who will be on track in future years to become supporters of extreme leftist views. Among those, the Muslim population will explode and in a matter of time become the foremost religious, cultural and financially powerful entity in America's future.

With that, we will see more and more Islamists running for public office in extreme liberal areas, claiming to be "moderate" while they owe their loyalty to Allah and the oil-rich caliphate in order to seek and hold power.

It will be an America that our ancestors would not recognize.

The Christian Conversion:

If and when Obama consulted with his closest advisors to form a list of his most important preparatory elements before embarking on a future campaign for president, they surely must have discussed religion. In doing so, they would have noted how American presidents are often vetted by voters based on religious orientation, and that non-Christians of these times had little or no chance of succeeding to the White House.

Knowing that Christians made up nearly three-fourths of the American population, conversion to Christianity—or the appearance thereof—would be essential for an aspiring president.

Folks might be shocked to learn that a man whose entire family and associated history was intrinsically aligned to atheism, including mentor Frank Marshall Davis, could suddenly be a Christian. Add to that, Islamic indoctrination when Obama was a child, ages 7-10, leaving fond memories in Indonesia, plus having a father and stepfather who both were Muslims. Obama makes no apologies for his undying passion and admiration for Islam for which he unfailingly comes to its defense in every instance. Other than the political motive, it would be mysterious that someone whose history was mired with Islamists and Communists, suddenly–out of nowhere–would adopt Christianity as his new religion in 1988, a faith totally outside the realm of all his mentors, family members, college friends, role models and even, domestic terrorists with whom he established an alliance. Christianity? One must wonder about the epiphany.

Let's play a game called *Conspiracy Theory.*

Somewhere in his early adult life, through his contacts with Frank Marshall Davis, Vernon Jarrett, Valerie Jarrett and many others, including prominent and wealthy Muslims with whom he associated during his five-year residency between Columbia and Harvard, Obama was clearly on track for bigger and better things other than being a community organizer. Thanks to Frank Marshall Davis, and later associates, he had the connections, he had the skills and he had the ideology that fit within the far-left scheme of things. He was assembling the dossier. Having a president sympathetic to Islam would be a coup for Muslim societies and governments around the world. This might explain why a Saudi prince would be involved in funding some or all of Obama's law school education at Harvard. He was very bright, handsome, mixed race, and charismatic with outstanding natural oratory skills—a perfect candidate for future positions of power and influence. His friends were movers and shakers in the realm of left-wing Illinois politics.

It is a simple fact that atheists, agnostics and Muslims could not get elected in a state-wide or district election in Illinois, or most anywhere in the US at that time. It was almost as rare for a Jewish candidate to get elected, except in specific states where prominent Jewish populations exist, such as New York, Florida. As with most presidents of past years, it was important to officially identify as Christian. To be a president, you gotta be a Christian, even if you must fake it.

If he personally identified as anything else – atheist, Muslim or other – he'd simply lie. No big deal. After all, that's what politicians are noted for. If he was a Muslim, he could resort to *Taqiyya,* i.e., forgiveness for lying in order to advance Islam.

Obama did not hook up with a typical America-loving, Christian-loving congregation. Far from it. Fraudulent or not, he began attending the nearly all-black, infamous Trinity Christian Church in 1988, headed by the fire-breathing Reverend Jeremiah Wright. Wright was noted for his anti-American radical theology, and his damning speeches from the pulpit that included references to "chickens coming home to roost" about the 9/11 terror attack that killed nearly 3,000 people. He also was seen on video shouting "God Damn America" in one sermon. How Christian is that?

For nearly eighteen years, Barack Obama attended these hate-filled services, and served the church in many fashions including financial support when not in the pews. This was not the Christian church symbolic of Christ's teachings. After all, the bedrock upon which Christ prevailed was the element of love—to love everyone, including your enemies. Reverend Wright—Obama's favored preacher—was no teacher of love. But it was a church of political convenience that allowed Obama to expediently identify himself as Christian without having to practice.

This is the same church that often welcomed special visits by Minister Louis Farrakhan, leader of the Nation of Islam, famous for his barrages of hate rhetoric, particularly as it related to Jews. Indeed, Barack Obama partnered with Farrakhan in helping to organize the Million Man March on Washington, D.C. in 1995.

So, is Barack Obama truly a believer in Christianity? We shall see.

Community Organizer:

Between 1983 and 1988, before entering Harvard Law, Barack Obama had designated his job as being a "community organizer," which is ill-defined as a specific work ethic or a particular sources of income. Regardless there is substance to the term that, according to *Wikipedia*, means:

A goal of community organizing is to generate durable power for an organization representing the community, allowing it to influence key decision-makers on a range of issues over time. In the ideal, for example, this can get community organizing groups a place at the table before important decisions are made. Community organizers work with and develop new local leaders, facilitating coalitions and assisting in the development of campaigns.

In essence, Barack Obama spent the five years after graduating from Columbia, networking and building a base for a future career in politics. "Community organizing" could be more accurately described as assembling a political base, i.e., registering voters.

The Marriage:

Though it seems to translate to sheer imagery, being married and with a family is another popular and essential element for a presidential candidate. Doing so secured his place within mainstream America, and thus, more palatable for people to be seen as a president. Other than one man, James Buchanan, who preceded Lincoln in 1857, we have never elected an unmarried president. First ladies, especially in the 20th and 21st centuries, are an integral element in the election process, particularly when women comprise a majority of the electorate. Potential first ladies are scrutinized as though we are electing a co-president.

Barack Obama and Michelle Robinson met in 1989, when she was employed as an attorney in a Chicago law firm, and Barack was hired on as an associate during summer break from Harvard. They were married in October of 1992, presided over by none other than Reverend Jeremiah Wright. Barack Obama was then thirty-one years of age.

This author can find no other history of romance in Barack Obama's life, from his teen years to meeting Michelle, whereby he dated or was involved with any other women. Despite volumes of biographies, political and historical publications about the current president, there is no mention of any other relationships, other than his immediate family, plus Frank Marshall Davis, and a selection of roommates and other friends derived from his schools and Chicago community work.

This was a pivotal period in Barack Obama's life, particularly following his graduation from Harvard Law School. Not only did he settle down with a wife, he altered his official religion to Christianity, which had never played a role in any part of his life. And, in 1991, he began working on—what else?—an autobiography.

The stage was set.

***Dreams From My Father*:**

By his own admission, Barack Obama spent a lot of his early adult years just hanging around, using drugs and going to schools. He had no compulsive proclivity for writing. His teen years were unremarkable, not accented with any particular accomplishments, either in sports, arts, literature or in any romantic endeavors. The same goes for his twenties. He was charismatic, drawing the attention of professors and other students in general, eventually being elected the president of the Harvard Law Review in 1990.

After graduating in 1991, he began working on an autobiography that would eventually be titled, *Dreams From My Father*. Why would a young man who had yet to make his mark in life, who had yet married or fathered children, or held any remarkable jobs, or had ever served his country or risked his life to save others, or accomplished anything of note, decide to sit down at the ripe old age of thirty-one and write an autobiography?

Because it was part of the political check-off list.

By age 31, I had been a symphony violinist, garnered a number of girlfriends, served in the US Marine Corps Reserves, followed by employment as a Miami-Dade police officer and detective for ten years working many high-profile cases, with five kids and three marriages to my credit while attending night college to earn a bachelor's degree. The last thing on my mind would be to write an autobiography. First, there was too much to do, life was hectic. Second, I was not famous, thus I had no base for marketing a book. Third, I lacked *gravitas*, or the depth of life experience to yet commit my life to print.

Yet, at age 30, Barack Obama would begin penning an autobiography which, in those days, would have little meaning or interest to most readers. He wrote mostly about his life and perceptions as a mixed race child, the relationships with Frank Marshall Davis, his grandparents, the absence of his mother and then his friends in college. A ho-hum story. Yawn. The book ends before his entry into Harvard in 1988.

Amazingly, a literary agency, Acton & Dystel, offered neophyte author Barack Obama an advance of $40,000 and a guarantee to have the book published. Having written fourteen books myself and knowing scores of other authors, that is beyond astonishing. Obama was a mere college kid, not famous, not a draw for readers and, the book, on its merits was totally unremarkable.

There is no coherent answer. But one can conjecture. If a Saudi prince had the clout and financial well to usher Barack Obama into Harvard Law School, the same well could conceivably buy influence in most any venue, including politics and the publishing world. That is, if there was a long-range grand plan.

Imagine, for a moment, persons of influence consulting with Barack Obama in the late 1980s convincing him he could be the first black President of the United States. In doing so, he would have to abide by certain processes and preparations in order to build the foundation for a run. If that was the case, it worked.

Brilliant.

The Illinois State Senate:

After earning a law degree, becoming a Christian, authoring an autobiography and then marrying in a Christian church, the groundwork had been laid. The time had come to make the move into politics, though he had never held steady employment or ran a business. After working in Chicago to assemble voters within the black communities, he was handpicked by Illinois State Senator Alice Palmer to be her successor as she left the office to run on the national stage for US Congress. Obama jumped into the race for state senate.

It should be noted that Congresswoman Alice Palmer, a good friend, was a noted leftist who had written for the Communist Party newspaper, *Peoples Daily World*, and also appeared in the Soviet Union to attend the 27th Congress of the Communist Party in 1986. Obama's political career was actually launched by Ms. Palmer at the home of friend, William Ayres and Bernadine Dorn, well-known anti-American activists and Marxists with a history of domestic violence and terrorism.

Obama also shared a table and worked closely with terrorist, Bill Ayres, on the Board of Directors for the Woods Foundation in Chicago. Ayres had been a leader in the Weather Underground domestic terror organization.

Obama's service in the state senate was unremarkable, likely so because he was waiting for the right time and place to make a move into the national scene. As reported in the *New York Times* in December 2007, Obama made a habit out of taking no stance on important issues, avoiding the yea/nay votes and responding "present" for 129 legislative measures, thus sidestepping to distance himself from left-wing or right-wing voters. For example, in 1999, a bill was introduced that would allow juveniles to be tried as adults in some cases. Though he may have been inclined to vote "yea" to show a tough-on-crime stance, he risked drawing fire from African-Americans, thus the best stance was no stance. "Present" votes could not be held against him.

Obama did make an attempt to run for the US Congress in 2000 that failed. It should be noted that Palestinian Muslim professor, and close friend, Rashid Khalidi, held a fund- raiser for Obama in that race.

The US Senate:

Open door, enter room.

In 2004 Obama jumped into the race for US Senate to fill the newly vacated seat that had been occupied by Senator Carol Mosely Braun. Before being elected onto the national stage, Obama already had lined up a barrage of prominent and not-so-prominent supporters within the Democrat Party and was selected to give the keynote address at the Democratic National convention in July of 2004. Consider, out of all the sitting governors, senators and congressmen in the United States, plus ex-senators, governors and even two ex-presidents, a neophyte with no experience in federal office or state administration was elevated into the national spotlight, not because of any accomplishments—because there were none—but merely on charismatic appeal, oratory magnetism and minority profile. But he certainly had a load of mysterious financial backing.

This community organizer with a law degree first defeated Hillary Rodham Clinton in the Democrat primary, then defeated former war hero, Senator John McCain, long-time lawmaker from Arizona who had served 25 years as a Congressman and Senator with a long list of accomplishments.

But that didn't matter.

The Presidential Campaign:

During his campaign, Obama was endorsed by many radical organizations and questionable personalities, including the American Communist Party in 2008 and in 2012. Then, there was Jeremiah Wright. In a *CBS News* and *National Review On-line* report dated June 2, 2008, it stated:

"Having now left Trinity United Church of Christ, can Barack Obama escape responsibility for his decades-long ties to (radical leftist preachers) Michael Pfleger and Jeremiah Wright? No he cannot. Obama's connections to the radical left politics espoused by Pfleger and Wright are broad and deep. Obama largely approved of their political-theological outlooks."

Obama was endorsed by the radical New Black Panthers in 2008, as well as Jew-hating leader of the Nation of Islam, Louis Farrakhan. In April of 2008, Barack Obama was even endorsed by a leader of Hamas, a known terror group. "We like Mr. Obama," said Ahmed Yousuf, top political advisor in the Gaza Strip on the "John Batchelor Show" on WABC Radio, and to *World Net Daily*. "We hope he will win the elections."

Hamas later retracted that endorsement, likely at the request of the Obama campaign. But, you cannot put the toothpaste back in the tube.

Libyan dictator, Gadhafi, endorsed Obama and referred to him as a Muslim during a speech (available on YouTube) in 2008. The Palestinians set up phone banks in Gaza to support Obama, revealed on Al-Jazeera Television in May 2008.

The President and Islam:

The strategy worked. Barack Obama became a president of these United States with the least credentials of all predecessors, never having run a business or commanded any form of organization, or having served the country in any capacity other than a newly elected US Senator in which he actually did nothing other than prepare for and execute his run for the presidency. He went to college and organized people in communities to be active in the voting process.

The plan, formed sometime in the late 1980s, worked like a charm. Marry, have kids, get a law degree, claim Christianity as his religion, be a Democrat, schmooze the Islamists, Jews, immigrants (legal and illegal), the large bastion of liberals, including blacks and college voters while coddling the left-leaning media and the Hollywood elite.

Although a number of blacks in America, with a background of public service, were intrinsically qualified to be president, like Colin Powell or Condoleezza Rice, America chose a neophyte, a cool dude who could shoot hoops, who admitted frequent drug use i.e., illegal behavior and laziness in his background, and who possessed a history of being sympathetic to the two most threatening ideologies to the American dream: Communism and radical Islamism.

All of the nefarious concerns about his historical ties to anti-American leanings, and his gravitational pull to Communism and Islam were successfully blurred by a doting media that was more mesmerized by style and skin color, which makes a great story, than the absence of concrete personal and professional achievements. As for the media, the mere idea that a person of color stood a chance at altering the course of history by becoming the first black president mattered far more than substance. It was the story that mattered.

Barack Obama's words and actions during his presidency clearly indicate that his love and loyalty is inexplicably in the corner of Islam and the Muslim Brotherhood. No time in his public background has Obama spoken about Christianity with such reverence and defense as does he with Islam. Even as Middle-East churches have been destroyed and Christians have been lined up for executions in Egypt during the Muslim Brotherhood's Arab Spring and later by ISIS, we have heard very little outrage from Obama. But the moment Islam is publicly scorned, for whatever reason, he comes to their defense, publicly admonishing Americans to see Islam in a favorable light. An entire book could be written with such examples of his words and deeds.

It's hard to imagine anyone who is not a Muslim uttering these words. Here are a few samples:

- "The future must not belong to those who slander the Prophet of Islam" (Spoken at the UN following the Benghazi video sham)
- "The sweetest sound I know is the Muslim call to prayer."
- "We will convey our deep appreciation for the Islamic faith, which has done so much over the centuries to shape the world — including in my own country."
- "As a student of history, I also know civilization's debt to Islam."
- "Islam has a proud tradition of tolerance."
- "Islam has always been part of America." (huh?)
- "We will encourage more Americans to study in Muslim communities"

- "America and Islam are not exclusive and need not be in competition. Instead, they overlap, and share common principles of justice and progress, tolerance and the dignity of all human beings."
- "I made clear that America is not – and never will be – at war with Islam." (He sidesteps any reference to Islamic organizations being at war with us, including the Muslim Brotherhood.)
- "Islam is not part of the problem in combating violent extremism – it is an important part of promoting peace."
- "The United States has been enriched by Muslim Americans." (oh, really?)
- "So I have known Islam on three continents before coming to the region where it was first revealed." (Notice: "revealed." That is an Islamic term in this context. He could have said "first born," or "first started." It is "revealed" to Muslims.)
- "In ancient times and in our times, Muslim communities have been at the forefront of innovation and education."
- "Throughout history, Islam has demonstrated through words and deeds the possibilities of religious tolerance and racial equality."
- "I consider it part of my responsibility as President of the United States to fight against negative stereotypes of Islam wherever they appear." (Nearly 2,000 deadly terror attacks are perpetrated by Islamists annually around the globe, including forty-three deadly terror attacks in the US since 9/11.)
- "I also know that Islam has always been a part of America's story." (Certainly true since the 1979 Iranian revolution and then the 9/11 attacks)
- "You're right, John McCain has not talked about my Muslim faith..." (corrected on camera 2008 by George Stephanopoulos, ABC News.) Common sense dictates, that this kind of slip-of-the-tongue would never have been uttered by a non-Muslim.

It was reported in *Israel Today*, May 2010, that Obama visited Egypt shortly after his election in 2009. There, he met with Foreign

Minister Ahmed Aboul Gheit, who revealed that Obama had told him in a private conversation that he was a Muslim.

Critical Appointments in US Government:

- Valerie Jarrett, Iranian-born daughter-in-law of Communist Vernon Jarrett, and close associate of Frank Marshall Davis, has been Obama's closest and most influential advisor in the White House since Day One.
- Huma Abedin, Hillary Clinton's closest confidant for 20 years, worked closely with Clinton during her four years as Secretary of State (as well as Clinton's stint as Senator) which would never have been allowed without the endorsement of the president. Abedin, a devout Muslim, was born in Michigan but raised in Saudi Arabia from ages two to 18, attended George Washington University (GWU) and served as an executive board member of the Muslim Students of America (MSA), a powerful group on many campuses originally formed by the Muslim Brotherhood. Abedin's family, including mother, father and brother, are closely aligned to or are members of the Muslim Brotherhood and Sisterhood. In 2001, the spiritual guide/chaplain of the MSA at GWU was Anwar al-Awlaki, an al-Qaeda operative who ministered some of the 9/11 hijackers.

Never in the history of American politics would someone of Huma Abedin's questionable orientation have been allowed a unique position of trust within the highest of inner circles that could be seen as a threat to national security operations. But who would dare question the first black president or future first female president?

Remember the Muslim Brotherhood mantra: *From Within.*

- Rashad Hussain, an American Muslim attorney, has a history of participating in events hosted by the Muslim Brotherhood, according to columnist Cal Thomas, who wrote for *Townhall.* Hussain has been employed by Obama to serve as special envoy to the Organization of Islamic Cooperation. An Egyptian magazine, *Rose El-Youssef*, writing for the Investigative Project on Terrorism, reported in 2013 that Hussain "maintained close ties with people and groups that comprise the Muslim Brotherhood network in America." Hussain participated in the 2002 Conference of the American Muslim Council (AMC), formerly headed by Abdurrahman Alamoudi, who went to prison for financing terror. The AMC is closely aligned with a number of other Muslim organizations, including CAIR, which is an offshoot of the Muslim Brotherhood.

- Mohamed Elibiary, a devout Muslim, was identified in a report by the *Center for Security Policy* in 2013, citing concerns about his employment under Obama in the Department of Homeland Security (DHS) because of his strong alliance with, and defense of, the Muslim Brotherhood in America. Elibiary has been the focus of congressional and media attention, particularly in light of his association with the radical group Assembly of Muslim Jurists in America and convicted Hamas fund raiser, Shukri Abu Baker. In a report issued by the *Washington Free Beacon*, September 2014, Elibiary had been a senior member of the DHS Security Advisory Council where he worked for four years until he was finally let go, or resigned, amid controversy and media pressure.

Question: Why was he employed inside our security systems to begin with?

- Islamist Salam al-Marayati was selected by Obama in 2012 to represent the United States at the Organization for Security and Cooperation in Europe's annual 10-day Human Rights conference. According to a *Jihad Watch* article, October 2012, authored by Robert Spencer, noted expert on radical Islamic affairs, al-Marayati is a defender of terror groups like Hamas and Hezbollah, and blames Israel for the 9/11 attacks. Obama came under attack from all sides in selecting this man, including from clergy and Jewish leaders.
- Arif Alikhan is a devout Sunni Muslim who was appointed to be Assistant Secretary of Homeland Security in charge of Office Policy in 2009, after serving Los Angeles as the deputy mayor. In 2007, he was instrumental in removing the Muslim Tracking Plan in Los Angeles that basically

handcuffed police from surveillance and investigative activity in and around mosques. In December 2012, Egypt's magazine, *Rose el-Youssef,* identified Alikhan as the founder of the World Islamic Organization, which the magazine identifies as a subsidiary of the Muslim Brotherhood.

- Imam Mohamed Magid was appointed by Obama in 2011 to serve DHS on the Countering Violent Extremism Group where he was authorized to advise and train personnel in federal agencies, including the FBI. He became a regular visitor to the White House and is considered by many to be the most sought-after Muslim authority in the nation. Magid also served on the National Security Council. Magid is president of the Islamic Society of North America (ISNA) a powerful group originally formed by the Muslim Brotherhood.
- John Brennan, Director of CIA since 2013, and Homeland Security Advisor to the president from 2009 to 2013, appears at first blush to be a non-controversial figure. After all, he had served in the CIA in one capacity or another for 25 years, including a stint in the 1990's as Station Chief in Riyadh, Saudi Arabia. Brennan also earned degrees in Middle-East studies and speaks fluent Arabic. So what's the problem?

Strong indications prevail that John Brennan converted to Wahhabi Islam while serving in Saudi Arabia, but that is kept from the general public. Such a revelation would normally exclude anyone from serving in high-ranking government positions therefore it would be important to avoid any personal mention about "religion." While the rumors and conclusions from numerous sources are many, Mr. Brennan has never denied the allegations. (Wahhabism is among the most fundamental and strictest sects of Islam.)

Wayne Madsen, a former naval officer and member of the National Security Council (NSC), is a Washington, D.C. journalist who has appeared in print in numerous high-powered newspapers in America. On his news site, August 11, 2015, Madsen referred to growing evidence indicating that Brennan is, indeed, a Muslim convert. He cites some examples that support the view:

1. When Brennan was sworn in, he refused to place his hand on the Bible, rather, he swore on a copy of the

original Constitution, the version that preceded the Bill of Rights.

2. While at the NSC, Brennan forbid the use of the term "Jihad" and instead, approved of the term "Extremist."
3. Brennan was the highest ranking American ever to be permitted to visit the holy city of Mecca, a privilege traditionally reserved only for pious Muslims.

As Brennan awaited confirmation of the Senate as CIA Director, former FBI Agent and renowned international terrorism expert, John Guandolo, publicly declared that Brennan did convert while in Saudi Arabia and quotes Brennan as saying how much he "marveled at the majesty of the Hajj (Mecca)."

Thirty-four senators voted against Brennan's confirmation, including liberal Democrats Pat Leahy, Jeff Merkley, Barbara Boxer and Bernie Sanders. What did they know that we do not know?

On January 9, 2013, James Lewis wrote for *The American Thinker*, "John Brennan is an open Israel-hater...who hasn't bothered to keep his opinions to himself. He is passionately pro-Muslim."

Numerous quotations and speeches can be retrieved from the Internet in which Mr. Brennan vigorously praises and defends Islam, with the exception, of course, of ISIS which he vehemently asserts is not Islamic. Summed up, we have a CIA director who is either a Muslim, Muslim sympathizer, or otherwise compelled with a predilection to align with Islamic causes, religious and cultural, when our nation should require 100% allegiance to the United States first and foremost.

That is not an accident.

It is inconceivable in time when our national security is at risk, and the free world is fending off incessant barrages of Islamic terror throughout the world by a widespread religious sect that openly declares its intent to destroy America, *from within,* that we would employ a person with so many unanswered questions about divided loyalties, to be in charge of the most sensitive, intelligence gathering agency in the entire United States. It personifies the cliché about the fox guarding the hen house.

FIFTEEN
BARACK OBAMA AND THE MUSLIM BROTHERHOOD

What if… just, what if… the Muslim Brotherhood succeeded in infiltrating the pinnacle of American government, The White House? Could one of its own become the leader of the free world, while holding the power of president of the United States? Translated, that would mean that the declared enemy of America would occupy the very position from which to preside over the destruction of "their miserable house from within, as vowed in the Muslim Brotherhood Explanatory Memorandum of 1991. It would be like Herman Goering becoming Prime Minister of Great Britain before WWII.

It's unthinkable. But not impossible.

People can be easily fooled, especially when they wear blinders. We should bear in mind that the Explanatory Memorandum declaring a "from within" conquest of North America was composed in 1987, and signed off in 1991, the very years that Obama was attending Harvard Law School with the financial support of at least one prominent Saudi Arabian. From there, his blasé life changed dramatically. He wrote his autobiography, got married, earned a graduate degree and converted to Christianity before launching his political career with the assistance of many nefarious characters mentioned earlier in this book, the ones we know about.

Yet, as we review the actions and inactions of Barack Obama during his term starting in 2009, it is not unreasonable for a clear-thinking person to conclude that he is either an ally of the Muslim Brotherhood or, at the worst, imbedded. For political purposes, he may verbalize that he cares about the best interests of the United States, but that is highly doubtful. His veiled disdain for the United States of America was summed up on October 30, 2008, as he was about to sweep the presidential election: "We are five days away from fundamentally transforming the United States of America."

Did anyone ever consider trying to translate that message? What was so terrible that America needed "fundamental transformation?"

And, what is meant by "fundamentally transforming?" We know the answer to that now. He was sending a message to his allies, whoever and wherever they were, that very few people among the naïve truly understood.

This book could cite event after event, speech after speech, actions and inactions that, as the mosaic—once assembled—would compose the picture that would lead any well informed, conscious person to conclude those findings.

Early on, this author considered the possibilities of Obama's alignment with the Brotherhood. I stored those suspicions in the back of my mind during the first three years of Obama's presidency, wondering, preposterous as it sounds, if he could be an ally of the Muslim Brotherhood. It seemed every action and inaction taken by the administration in the Middle-East was to the advantage of the Muslim Brotherhood, almost as though he was doing their bidding.

- The Apologetic pro-Muslim speech in Cairo, 2009
- The incessant public excuses and defenses of radical Islam no matter the evidence that it is responsible for nearly 2,000 deadly terror attacks throughout the world, every year, in at least fifty countries.
- The refusal to cite "radical Islam" as the source of international terror and instead, calling them softer terms such as "extremists," "lone wolves," and the rising ISIS terror group as "a JV team." Refusing to acknowledge the Ft. Hood mass shooting of 41 people (killing 14) by a radical Islamic mole as an act of terrorism, rather calling it "work-place violence."
- Altering all training and orientation to military and federal law enforcement to exclude any mention of Islam as the source of international terror and unrest.
- Pulling the defense missile system from eastern Europe, leaving the region wide open for the Soviets, or radical Islam, to take advantage.
- Overseeing the collapse of relations with Israel by openly supporting the return of 1967 borders in favor of the Palestinians, knowing it would be suicide for Israel. Speeches aside, Obama left no doubts where his heart lay, as well as his loyalty.

- The drawing of a red line to Syria's Assad for public consumption, then ignoring it after the dictator deployed chemical weapons against his own people.
- The pull-out of all troops from Iraq, despite repeated warnings by scores of military and civilian experts citing how it would create a vacuum for radical Islam to swoop in. Could it have been part of the grand plan? After all, history has shown that this action completely destabilized the region and opened the platform for ISIS to expand.
- Early on, despite intelligence to the contrary, Obama played down the threat and referred to ISIS as a "JV team."
- Openly forecasting America's military strategy to the Taliban, and the rest of the world, when and how he would conclude American activities in Afghanistan. That's like the coach of the Packers sending the play-plan to the opposing team before game time.
- Engineering the release of hundreds of dangerous anti-American terrorists from Guantanamo by executive order in order to expedite the closing of the prison camp. This also presents the possibility for ceding Guantanamo back to Cuba before the president leaves office.
- Establishing a new relationship with the Cuban Communist regime, knowing that Hezbollah has set up a terror camp there, just 90 miles from our shores.
- Aiding and abetting the illegal immigration problem from the southern border by which millions come into the United States to establish residency, have untold anchor babies and use taxpayer entitlements for education, welfare, health care and even prisons. Border Patrol unions and border law enforcement leaders have decried the president's policies, which have allowed thousands Other Than Mexican (OTM) immigrants from Middle-East countries to infiltrate the porous border of America.
- Aiding and abetting, even inviting the 2015-2016 mass migration, in biblical proportions, of Muslim refugees into Europe and the United States and refusing to negotiate with other Arab nations to assist and open their doors to migrants. This migration movement of multi-millions of

non-indigenous people, historically known not to assimilate, is destined to alter the cultural fabric of nations for all time. Within the next two generations, it will transform countries like France, Belgium, Sweden and even Great Britain into Sharia-based nations. With Obama's encouragement and endless justifications, the United States will follow suit.
From Within.

The Arab Spring:

While this author had considered the possibility of President Obama being in collusion with the Muslim Brotherhood, I was never fully convinced. All those tiles in the mosaic became crystal clear with the advent of the so-called Arab Spring in 2012. The actions and inactions of the President and his minions, particularly during the revolts in Egypt, Tunisia and Libya, clearly aligned him with the objectives of the Muslim Brotherhood. There is no logical explanation, unless President Obama deems the Muslim Brotherhood a higher priority than the security of the United States and our allies.

The fact remains that the entire Arab Spring was a power play, supported by the United States government, to enable the Muslim Brotherhood to assume power over many Islamic nations in the Middle-East. It almost came to fruition, if not for the determination and will of the Egyptian people to free themselves of suffering under strict fundamentalist Sharia laws.

Egypt:

Let's briefly revisit the facts pertaining to Egypt:

1. Egypt's President Hosni Mubarak had been an ally of the United States for more than 30 years. Egypt adhered strictly to the 1978 Camp David Accords that, along with Jordan, established peace with Israel. It was in the national interest of the United States and Israel to continue supporting the alliance. For America, the role was simple; don't fix what's not broken. But we did. There must have been a motive.
2. Prior to the Arab Spring in 2011 the Muslim Brotherhood was banned in Egypt, because it was considered a destabilizing force with terrorist connections. (Osama bin Laden was groomed within the Muslim Brotherhood, as was his Number 2, Ayman al-Zawahiri.)

3. According to sources cited in Wikipedia as of 2013, six nations have officially declared the Muslim Brotherhood to be a terrorist organization; Russia, Syria, Egypt, Saudi Arabia, Bahrain and the United Arab Emirates (UAE).
4. As disturbances and uprisings broke out in various Arab countries, the United States government inexplicably supported the ouster of America's friend and ally, President Hosni Mubarak. Immediately, the Muslim Brotherhood declared its organization as legal and began the political agenda to assume control of the government. For nearly a year, Egypt was in a state of chaos as the Muslim Brotherhood moved in and assumed power over the country following an election that installed Mohamed Morsi from the Muslim Brotherhood as the new president of Egypt. Morsi immediately named himself as supreme ruler and imposed strict Sharia law throughout the nation, giving himself unlimited powers. This resulted in greater chaos, as the Egyptian people, rejecting Sharia, revolted by the millions.

Photos streamed across the media depicting then Secretary Hillary Clinton, and later, John Kerry, sitting and smiling with Morsi, showing support. Meanwhile, the Muslim Brotherhood supervised the defacing of hundreds of Christian churches that were burned or destroyed as Christian Coptics, protected under Mubarak, under siege ran for their lives. In one town, three nuns were paraded like POWs after burning their Franciscan school. Two guards working on a tour boat owned by Christians were burned alive. Islamist mobs chanted, "Death to Christians," throughout the cities. The stories of death and destruction, particularly to Christians, are endless, yet very little intervention or condemnation of Morsi's new government emanated from the American administration under Obama.

In the ensuing year, the fearful Egyptian people retook control of their country, forming protest mobs by the millions in major cities throughout Egypt, decrying Morsi and the Muslim Brotherhood, and more specifically, carrying hundreds of banners and signs depicting President Obama, Secretary Clinton and Ambassador Ann Patterson as terrorists, haters and conspirators in cahoots with the Brotherhood. Clearly, the Egyptian people faulted the Obama Administration for supporting the Muslim Brotherhood and the overthrow of the Mubarak regime.

Morsi was ousted as the Egyptian military took control of their country. In 2014, the people elected Abdel Fattah El-Sisi, military commander, as their new president.

The entire episode from beginning to end was an embarrassment for President Obama, if not exposure, who had walked lockstep with the Brotherhood, but had underestimated the will of the Egyptian people. While some may say that the Muslim Brotherhood assumed power via elective process, one can argue that the proverbial wool was pulled over the eyes of the populous much like the Nazi party used propaganda and deceit in 1933 that helped elect Hitler into office. But contrary to the German people, the Egyptians quickly realized the hard fascist and dangerous hazards of Sharia being foisted upon them by the Muslim Brotherhood and re-took control, thereby reopening their country to tourism, secularism, tolerance and peace. They once again outlawed the Brotherhood, which was already declared illegal in five other Arab countries.

The Egyptian people grew to despise Barack Obama, Hillary Clinton and Ann Patterson because they were instrumental in helping to support and install the Muslim Brotherhood in their nation. Those who followed the course of events since the take-back in 2013, should notice that the silence from Barack Obama and Hillary Clinton has been deafening. We hear nary a word from the President or anyone in his state department cabinet, especially Hillary Clinton, about their humongous, embarrassing blunder that resonated across the Arab world. And to this day, America's relationship with Egypt remains a blur, rarely addressed even in election campaigns.

The whole effort to expand the power of the Muslim Brotherhood blew up in Obama's face. The strategy, like so many other scandals, was to ignore, deny, allow time to pass and hope the complicit media and people in general would forget. The less he or the media talked about it, the better. Pretend it did not happen and let time, lots of time, heal the wound.

New president, Abdel Fattah el Sisi, established himself as a secular moderate after assuming power in Egypt. This was personified by an amazing New Year's speech he gave to a large assembly of Imams in which he called for a "religious revolution," asking Muslim leaders to support the fight against extremism. To demonstrate his spirit of peaceful coexistence, the new president attended a Christmas mass at a Coptic church in Cairo where he made a short speech imploring national unity.

Not a word from Barack Obama, as the Muslim Brotherhood returned to the underground.

More than any other episode, in this litany of episodes, the Egyptian blunder aligned Barack Obama as an ally with the notorious Muslim Brotherhood, whose infamous documents call for the destruction of the United States.

<u>The Libyan Initiative:</u>

The Muslim Brotherhood also had its sights set on Libya.

Under the premise that Gadhafi is a murderous despot and after numerous street protests by Libyans and Libyan rebels, the United States, along with a number of NATO allies, supported a regime change in the Libyan government in early 2011. A military intervention took place in the wake of the Egyptian-based Arab Spring. Moammar Gadhafi was captured and killed by Libyan rebels and military in October of 2011.

Truth be told, US relations with Libya had actually improved in the years prior to Obama. Gadhafi had strived toward easing economic sanctions from the US by agreeing to implement a plan to eliminate all weapons and materials of mass destruction, starting in 2003, after the US led invasion of Iraq. This was reported as a very complicated intervention, but it all became clear when the Muslim Brotherhood, as in the case of Egypt, turned out to be part of the so-called solution. In hindsight, it would have been more beneficial to the interests of Europe and the US to continue the interaction with Gadhafi whose interests did not include sharing power with the Brotherhood.

This further confirmed the hard truth that northern Africa (Egypt, Libya and Tunisia) was in the crosshairs for conquest by the Muslim Brotherhood, not to mention Syria, Iraq, Gaza, Lebanon, Tunisia and Yemen. The US government, under Obama, supported the plan.

<u>The Benghazi Fiasco</u>:

Volumes of congressional investigative records and other sources have written and disclosed much about the Benghazi attack of September 11, 2012. Some folks are calloused from hearing so much about it, but they should not be because serious crimes were committed, not only by terrorists, but by high-level people within our own government in an effort to mislead, deny, convolute or possibly, obstruct justice.

1) Four Americans were killed in a terror attack, including a US Ambassador
2) The attack was predictable and preventable, but officials did nothing to prevent or prepare the Benghazi compound, to defend it, including the Secretary of State and the President of the United States
3) Benghazi was a timber box on the verge of exploding, forecasted by a number of events in which the Red Cross and the British Consulate were bombarded with threats and attacks, necessitating their departure just weeks and months before the attack on the American compound. The American Benghazi compound had already been attacked on three occasions in the months prior to September, without casualties. Ambassador Stevens' diary, found on the scene, recorded his concerns about a growing al-Qaeda presence in the area and worried about being on their hit list. These assembled facts painted a grim forecast that the terrorists would be attacking–again
4) Everyone in Benghazi knew this, which is why the CIA, State Department. NSI and Ambassador Stevens himself repeatedly begged for increased security at the compound; over 600 times in 2012 as was disclosed during Hillary Clinton's appearance at a congressional hearing in October, 2015. According to her, she never heard, and never knew about them.

Imagine if hundreds of threats against the United States were made known to the CIA, FBI, NSI and other agencies, in which they were asked to provide increased security, and no one bothered to tell the President or the Secretary of State?

Not only was additional security denied and ignored, security at the compound was actually reduced during this period, according to Senator Ron Johnson. Another published story in the *Milwaukee Journal Sentinel* in May of 2014, found this to be true.

It was almost as though, our leadership knew the attack was pending. Worse, it was tantamount to aiding and abetting.

5) The series of attacks on the compound, September 11, 2012, extended over eight hours. During this time, the White House, CIA, State Department and the US military, and all

their leaders, were fully informed in real time what was happening. No military was deployed, or allowed to deploy, to render assistance to the staff or to the ambassador during this time.

In December 2015, *Judicial Watch* released an e-mail (obtained under Freedom of Information) in which the Department of Defense clearly advised it was ready to deploy forces to Benghazi. Never happened.

In 2013, congressional testimony by Gregory Hicks, who was second in command at the American Tripoli Embassy, claimed a show of force by US military during the siege could have prevented much of the carnage especially in the later hours. He added, if there had been a scramble of fighter planes deployed over Benghazi shortly after the attack commenced, "There would not have been a mortar attack on the annex in the morning because the Libyans would have split." Basically, according to Hicks, at least two of the four Americans killed would be alive today.

Some defenders of the President and the Secretary of State assert that the military rescue effort could not have arrived in time. But who knew? Who could have predicted the length of the attack? In real time, the assault could have gone on for eight hours, twenty-four hours, or even days. The bottom line? The leadership within the United States did nothing–before, during and after the attack–other than lie to the American people.

6) As the attack carried on, our national leader, the president went AWOL. A *Washington Post* column in May of 2014, by Marc Thiessen spells out the diary system for a president in which all his activities, visitors, calls, and movements are meticulously recorded for every second of every day, ostensibly available to media scrutiny. Not this time. According to Thiessen, 20 months after the Benghazi attack, the diary for those eight hours was still being withheld from media, unreleased.

We do know that a single phone call was made from the President to Hillary Clinton at approximately 10 p.m., roughly six hours into the attack. That was their only contact that night. Shortly after that call, while the attacks were still happening, and before Americans Tyrone Woods and Glen Doherty were yet killed, Hillary issued a bizarre statement to the press in which she linked the attacks in Benghazi to an inflammatory anti-Muslim video that had been posted on the Internet.

Here is the irony. The President is known to have only one conversation with the Secretary of State in the entire evening (during a crisis!). Within that hour, she issued a statement, unsupported by any evidence. defining the attack as a "spontaneous protest" over an anti-Muslim video that had been posted on the Internet. Thus, it is logical to conclude:

a) The Secretary of State could not have known this while the siege was still being carried out, and while no one in the line of communications ever advised of such a "spontaneous demonstration" that night. How would she have known?
b) Hillary Clinton's talking points, via the press release, was likely spurred by the president during the phone conversation just prior to the release. In other words, he told her to adhere to that story. Those were her marching orders.
c) Hillary Clinton was stuck. She knew this was a false statement, but simply followed the lead of her president.
d) The "spontaneous protest" talking points (untruths) carried on through the casket-laden services attended by Obama and Hillary Clinton three days later at Andrews AFB, as she told the parents of the dead American heroes that the fault lay with an anti-Muslim video, a lie. Years later, Hillary denied these remarks and has inferred that the family members were lying.

7) During the testimony of Hillary Clinton to the Congressional Committee in October of 2015, three e-mails were issued by her on the evening of, and later the next day, all three of which clearly revealed that the offensive anti-Muslim video story had nothing–zero–to do with the attack, and that she knew she was lying when she was lying.

On the night of the attack, she sent an e-mail to her daughter, Chelsea, that stated, "Two of our officers were killed in Benghazi by an al Qaeda-like group."

She also concluded, "I fear more of the same tomorrow."

The next day, she sent an e-mail to the Egyptian prime minister, Hesham Qandil, in which she wrote: "We know that the attack in

Libya had nothing to do with the film. It was a planned attack, not a protest."

She sent a third e-mail to the Libyan President, Mohammed Magariaf, while the battle still raged, stating this was a "gun battle...which I understand Ansar al-Sharia is claiming responsibility."

The Secretary of State was mired in a pool of mendacity, forced upon her by the president to spread as the official talking point. But at the same time, not realizing she would one day be investigated, she actually told the truth in three e-mails during that night and the following morning that unequivocally refutes her public statement the evening of the attack. Not only that, it refutes her ensuing statements and those of UN Ambassador Susan Rice who, curiously, was selected to appear on five network news shows to propagate the lie while Hillary avoided media and embarked on round-the-world diplomacy tours for the next three months.

When you can't stand the heat, get out of the kitchen.

Assembling the Tiles:

To sum this up, we connect all the matching tiles to give us a clear picture and a coherent conclusion. Throughout this book, the focus has been to disclose and convey enough facts to help readers realize how radical Islam is on a global mission of conquest, that its leaders have a detailed plan that is moving forward with great success and effectiveness. The primary concentration for conquest is in Western Democracies throughout Europe and North America. The enemy has emphasized its objectives, that racial Islam would achieve goals, not by a standard war, but a war *from within,* by infiltrating all aspects of government, religious and educational institutions, infrastructure, finance, politics and corruption. Yes, violence occasionally plays a role in the scheme, as well, because it is effective at the core of critical intimidation.

We have also suggested that certain people in the hierarchy of the United States government have, by design or ignorance, been part of a stealth plan to aid and abet the enemy while presenting a public image otherwise, an image that is rapidly fading among people who are willing to open their minds and hearts, who are conscious and aware of the skullduggery that has taken place, and will continue to take place unless we are willing to make drastic changes in how we approach this deadly threat.

The umbrella organization behind global Jihad is the Muslim Brotherhood. It does not matter if the terrorists or financiers are from Iraq, Egypt, France or Libya; they are everywhere pulling the strings, including those of propaganda and deceit.

Though backed by the Obama Administration, efforts to install the Muslim Brotherhood in Egypt failed, thanks to the uprisings of outraged citizens of Egypt. But that is their only failure. The Jihadi infiltration of Western civilization is proceeding well. In ten years, the political and cultural landscape of America will be subjected to major overhauls as are the civilizations of Europe, all of which leans toward Islam as the common denominator.

All we have to do is step back and look at the progress of Radical Islam and the Brotherhood in recent years, particularly in the Middle-East and in Western nations of Europe and North America. Much of that progress could not have been achieved without the complicity and incompetency of the Obama Administration.

The picture becomes brilliantly clear as we highlight the most significant of these milestones and see them as assembling tiles of the mosaic:

- President Obama called for Israel to withdraw back to 1967 boundaries, despite overwhelming evidence that such a move would be suicide for the Jewish state. This falls directly into the plan of the Muslim Brotherhood. Relations between the US government and the Israeli government have never been worse.
- From 2005 through 2014, Israel has come under random attack by 18,454 rockets and mortars, causing five million people to live in constant fear of death and destruction and resulting in little outrage has come from the Obama Administration.
- President Obama ordered US troops fully withdrawn from Iraq at the end of 2011, defying the advice and warnings of military experts, including Generals Lloyd Austin, David Petraeus, Admiral Mike Mullen and his own Secretary of Defense, Robert Gates, that a vacuum would be created for al Qaeda-related groups to seize control. Obama disregarded the experts. Indeed, the withdrawal ultimately provided the stage for ISIS to assemble, invade and establish an Islamist state.

- ISIS seized control of land in Eastern Syria and Western Iraq that led to an on-going war that, according to the Arab League and United Nations, estimates at least 400,000 have been killed. US Army General Jack Keane, who helped lead the 1967 surge in Iraq, had publicly stated the withdrawal would "jeopardize the stable political situation in Iraq." He was right. Our greatest military minds tell us that none of these horrors would have occurred if 20 to 25 thousand US troops had remained.
- ISIS has embarked on tactics of enslavement, rape, public torture and murders of Syrian and Iraqi citizens, for a myriad of reasons – homosexuality, Christian faith, Kurdish, suspected enemies, etc. Over 700,000 of the 1.1 million Christians living in Syria have been displaced. Thousands of homosexuals have been thrown from buildings, drowned, set on fire or hung in the streets. Beheadings, especially on video, became commonplace. Young girls from Iraq's Yazidi religious minority were held captive and raped. The horrors continue.
- Despite the unstable situation and a resurgent Taliban, Obama ordered mass withdrawals of US troops from Afghanistan, forecasting and telling the world–including our enemies–the precise date, time and method. As of July 2016, approximately 10,000 troops remain, while Obama ordered only 5,500 non-combat troops, a negligible force, to remain after he leaves office. Knowing when and how the US will be departing Afghanistan was undoubtedly music to the ears of the Taliban.
- Four months after President Obama publicly propagandized in 2014 how Yemen was a "model worth emulating" in our fight against the "war on terror," the US backed government collapsed and handed over the reins of government to Houthi rebels, who then faced a rising al Qaeda force that has basically taken over the country. The leader of al Qaeda in the Arabian Peninsula is none other than Ibrahim al Qosi, a Sudanese-born terrorist who was released from Guantanamo in 2012. Radical Islam wins again.
- Since 1979, Iran has unapologetically been one of America's greatest enemies. Yet, to the disbelief of American diplomats, an array of experts and military brass, plus millions

of Americans, and while thousands of Iranian subjects openly cried "Death To America," President Obama led an effort to form a deal with the Iranian government that calls for a ten-year delay for Iran to make a nuclear bomb, with caveats for American monitoring and inspections. In exchange, the United States must lift sanctions that translate into releasing $150 billion in assets back to Iran. This country is considered by most experts as the leading sponsor of terror in the entire world. This was a huge victory for anti-Americanism and pro-Islamic objectives. Even if Iran complies with all requirements, which is highly doubtful, that country will still have a nuclear bomb in nine more years.

Radical Islam scores another victory.

- Had we not interfered with the Libyan situation, Moammar Gadhafi would likely still be the prevailing dictator and no major threat to America. The US-backed uprising resulted in the killing of Gadhafi and takeover by the Muslim Brotherhood, during which the Benghazi attack took place. As of today, ISIS claims a significant presence in major cities throughout Libya. According to numerous sources, ISIS is recruiting fighters from the poor nations of Africa, including Chad, Mali and Sudan, offering generous salaries. In essence, they have taken root as a result of the vacuum left by the actions (and inactions) of the US government. Radical Islam wins again.
- According to several American and British sources, including the *Blinq Express* in Great Britain, ISIS and its affiliates are now significantly present in several countries in the Middle-East, Africa and Asia. Besides Syria and Iraq, they include, Egypt, Libya, Nigeria, Algeria, Morocco, Mali, Saudi Arabia, Yemen, Afghanistan, Pakistan and Yemen.
- Boko Haram, another notorious terror group that is based in Nigeria and Cameroon, announced its allegiance to ISIS in 2015. This comes after six years of terror activity in North Africa, including mass kidnappings of young women and mass murders of Christians and other non-Muslims. Altogether, nearly 2.3 million refugees have been displaced.
- The cancerous growth of ISIS is metastasizing in the United States, as the FBI director announced in November of 2015

that his organization is pursuing at least 900 terror suspects rooted in all 50 states.

- The rampage of the ISIS/Syrian/Iraqi war created a refugee crisis of Syrians, Iraqis, Afghans and others desperate to leave the squalor of camps and to seek aid from Western nations. The same is happening with refugees from North Africa, climbing overcrowded en masse into crude Mediterranean boats in order to reach the shores of Greece, Italy, Germany and other Western countries. According to the BBC, more than one million Syrian/Iraqi/Afghan refugees swarmed into Europe in 2015, a number that will eventually alter the cultures and economies of Europe everywhere. According to a report in Wikipedia, 58% of those refugees have been men, with 17% women, and 25% children. The European Union (EU) expects three million more refugees by the end of 2017 which, in part, weighed heavily on the July 2016 British referendum in which 52 percent of voters elected to leave the EU.

The cultural and economic impact of the refugee crisis is immeasurable. European countries are already struggling with crumbling economies, and with the advent of millions more people who need food, clothing, health care, living quarters, and more, the results for Germany, Belgium, France, Greece and others, is catastrophic. That does not even mention the bane of street crime and rapes committed by foreign Muslims that has already created an atmosphere of paranoia in countries like Sweden, Norway and Germany.

The population projections do not yet address the long-range effect of Muslim birth rates, emigration by indigenous Europeans and multiple families, all of which will ensure the future for a burgeoning Islamic population and an already declining European population. Considering London is now being led by a Muslim mayor. Scores of Sharia zones exist throughout the UK, plus the "no-go" zones of France and Belgium. Europe is destined to be a far different culture than what we have known for centuries. It has only just begun.

Among the millions of desperate refugees, the majority of which are young men, it is without doubt that a significant percentage of these people will bring with them a non-assimilating Jihad mentality, determined to establish Islam as the only religion and Sharia as the only law, as prescribed by the Muslim Brotherhood. They are coming with a mission. That's not speculation; that is a certainty.

The *From Within* movement is shifting into high gear.

- As this book is written, President Obama is striving to bring 10,000 refugees into the United States in 2016, most of whom are unable to be vetted in terms of radical orientation and Jihad mentality. Secretary of State John Kerry announced that the ceiling for 2017 will be 100,000 refugees. Without doubt, a portion of those arriving in our shores will be Jihad-indoctrinated terrorists on a mission.

Including Europe, we are talking in the multi millions.

The Trojan Horse is arriving—Bold and Deadly.

* * *

Authors Sam Solomon and E. Al Maqdisi published a book in 2009 titled *Modern Day Trojan Horse: Al-Hijra, The Islamic Doctrine of Immigration*. In it, they discuss the *Al-Hijra* Program:

1. Islamic Terrorists, including ISIS, Taliban, Al Shabaab, Boko Haram, and Al Nusra, massacre people and generate refugees.

2. The Muslim-Controlled UN Refugee Resettlement program "hand selects" the "refugees," rejecting Christians and accepting Muslims.

3. The United Nations Relief and Rehab organization sends Muslim "refugees" to various non-Muslim host countries.

4. The "refugees" refuse to assimilate, create "No-Go" zones, multiply exponentially and demand imposition of their *Sharia* law, and *Voila*!

5. The non-Muslim host country becomes part of the Caliphate!

This book was published over seven years ago. The Muslim Brotherhood's written plans were laid out in 1981 and in 1991. And, here we are.

SIXTEEN
CONCLUSIONS

The Nazis tried to destroy the United States and failed. The Imperial Japanese tried to destroy the United States and failed. The USSR promised to bury the United States and failed. The Communist Party, using the deceitful lure of entitlements via socialism has attempted to bring down our great nation through political upheaval and stealth infiltration. They have all made progress, but still have a long way to go. Guns, tanks, planes and bombs could never bring down the greatest power in the history of the world. Despite our enemies, we remain the most generous and benevolent, the most free and self-determined people that ever existed on planet Earth.

But not for long.

Radical Islam is not failing. The enemy is at our doorstep, pounding the battering ram, while we gradually open the politically correct gates in surrender. In the name of religion, they are closer to incapacitating the United States than any enemy in history, because they are smarter and stronger than all our prior foes. They not only have the weaponry, the tactics and the strategy, they have the power in sheer numbers, plus unlimited resources and the instillation of blind fanaticism that breed killers who gladly kill themselves by the thousands to achieve the pleasure of killing us. They are the masters of deceit without conscience because they hold no allegiance to any hosting society; they hold allegiance to Allah and Allah only. Although they may live in Saudi Arabia, Iran, Pakistan, India, Australia, England, Russia, or the US, their nation is one and only one, and it is ruled by their God. It does not matter what sector of the globe they inhabit.

This enemy has ardently studied the weaknesses of Western civilization, knowing we have become war-weary, willing to accept destruction if it means no more dead and wounded soldiers. Meanwhile, we are utterly naïve, willing to see only goodness in our enemy while ignoring the evil that stares us in the face. We elect leaders who fall into the trap of our enemies, allowing them access to our internal government operations. Our leaders are motivated too often by greed, too easily corrupted by material wealth and power. Financial rewards are all too available under the radar from enemies who purport to be our friends. Evil doers succeed in getting what they want because too many of our leaders and information guides (press) are stupid, blind and greedy.

It does not matter if we are liberals or conservatives, Democrats or Republicans, men or women, we are human being s who seek love and reject hate. When we pursue love so desperately, we wear blinders, unwilling to see what is in front of our very noses – an enemy willing to die, to kill us all while we stand by, aglow in denial. Meanwhile, leaders blather about such things as global warming and gun control to create a diversion from the crisis we face.

Worst of all, the enemy is smarter than we are. Much smarter. They have the brains, the discipline, the plan and the passion to execute that plan. We have been outsmarted much like Mohammed Ali played rope-a-dope with George Foreman, pretending to be weak, until his opponent became weary, and then he went in for the kill. As a people, we are weary, we are lazy and we are ignorant – a perfect storm.

The leadership within the Muslim Brotherhood managed to infiltrate the very government we cherish and they hate. They did exactly what they promised in the Explanatory Memorandum and other documents and decrees, which is to conquer by destroying America, not with guns and war, but *from within*. It is as clear as the noon sun on a cloudless day.

After reading this book, the conclusions will not surprise anyone. Yes, they are "opinions" based on the cumulative array of evidence, actions, inactions and circumstances that have taken place since the horror of 9/11 and more specifically, since the rise of Barack Obama's reign in the Oval Office. If ever a victim nation handed over the government keys to an enemy power, it happened on January 20, 2009, when Barack Hussein Obama was sworn in as President of the United States.

Why?

- When Barack Obama vowed to fundamentally transform America in 2008, it has become obvious that he was talking about neo-Marxism and Islam as the two primary influences from which to enact change while using the definitive tactic called "deceit."(Taqiyya)

- It is naïve to believe Barack Obama discarded Communism as a fervent objective for America considering his cozy history with so many Marxists, as well as a number of communist-leaning advisors he has invited into the bowels of government since his election, even if they were not card-carrying members of the party. It's in front of our noses. Our media, our extreme leftist officials, and our citizenry simply let it all unfold without challenge.
- The Muslim Brotherhood's quest for Islamization of the free world has been successfully engineered while aided with the power of the presidency by adhering to the false narrative that Islam is only a religion, thereby protected under various freedom laws in Europe and North America. In fact, Islamic fundamentalism is a fascist political ideology with its own set of laws that are not compatible with the US Constitution. Claiming to be only a religion is an obfuscation of truth, meant to fool those who are easily fooled.
- Barack Obama is a stealth Muslim, allied with the Muslim Brotherhood in carefully and slowly carrying out their plan of conquest/conversion. His public identification as a Christian has been a deceptive ploy of Taqiyya in order to access and exercise power.
- Every action and inaction pertaining to Islamic infiltration and the goals of the Muslim Brotherhood have been aided and supported by Barack Obama.
- Obama's Middle-East policies and actions have been calculated for the benefit of the Muslim Brotherhood objectives, including the short-lived rise of the Brotherhood in Egypt from which the people rebelled and then ousted the new regime.
- United States military generals and the Secretary of Defense warned Obama that the pull-out of all troops from Iraq would cause a vacuum in which violent radical Islamists could assume control. He pulled out the troops, despite that risk. He had to know that this would happen because everyone else knew it. He also had to know the long-range

outcome of a genocidal war by terrorist organizations would be the spread of Islam to the Western World.

- It cannot be mere coincidence that the waves of refugees from Syria/Iraq happen to be flooding into Europe and the United States. This has occurred with the support of the President, regardless of the threat of increased terrorism it would also bring alterations of the cultural landscape, customs, religion and language. Neither has President Obama made any attempt with Arab nations to absorb some or all of the refugee migrants as an alternative. In all probability, this was planned years ago.
- Obama is the dream president for our adversaries. He and his minions have weakened the military might of the United States to critical shortages of personnel and equipment, leaving our country vulnerable to any potential war enemies, including Iran, North Korea, Russia, or the array of radical Islamic terror groups.
- Obama has aided and abetted our fiercest declared enemy, Iran, in negotiating an agreement that returns $150 billion to their coffers while they chant "Death to America." Again, we aid and abet our adversaries.
- The policy of open borders and Obama's blatant refusal to enforce immigration laws has emboldened the liberal wing of politics that claims this is all an act of humanity. In truth, the immigrants, no matter their origins, are being used as pawns of conquest as the president has carefully and cleverly expanded future voting blocs of indigents to weigh heavily in favor of entitlement government, i.e. socialism, which then, increases government control over the people. It all translates to votes and power.
- Considering immigration and sanctuary cities, the president has endorsed the breaking of laws with impunity in order to further his long-range agenda, a clear violation of his oath of office.
- The president recklessly disregards the danger to the future economy by allowing the national debt to double within an eight-year period, from $10 trillion to $20 trillion, from which we may never recover. Financial experts agree that

the outcome will eventually result in ruinous taxation, runaway inflation and eventual financial collapse. America will be economically weakened on the international stage.

- Obama has taken unofficial control over national news media giants, minus FOX, by employing the closest of mogul relatives in the administration to garner support and favor which in turn, alters the mind-set of fans and viewers. In turn, whether inadvertent or by design, our enemies have greater access to the inner workings of our government, including national security issues.
- Unless he commits a violent felony on national television, no amount of "high crimes and misdemeanors" would ever result in an act of impeachment against Barack Obama, and he knows it. To be blunt, his source of immunity is skin color. Such an act by Congress would trigger national uprisings within the African American and liberal communities nationwide, regardless of the violations. Basically, Barack Obama is unimpeachable.

*   *   *

One must acknowledge the genius of it all. The plan has been concocted, executed and carried out to near perfection while our mass media, which manipulates thinking, gushed over the new black president without daring to look beneath a single pore. Hundreds of intellectuals and educators with years of expertise in this arena implored America to wake up, to read books, to study the obvious, to stop denying and realize their country is being overrun, inch-by-inch, day-by-day, by an organizational ideology whose insidious game plans are well known and documented. Nevertheless, the people, particularly on the far left, choose to look the other way, much to our peril....

The enemy has wisely counted on American stupidity to advance their agenda. Early on, the Obama Administration went about exploding the entitlement parade by upping food stamps, cell phones, housing, and other benefits not only to American poor, but aliens as well, legal and illegal. Offering free everything to people who will not, or cannot work, results in amassing millions of votes from folks who do not have a clue, or do they care, about government, democracy or self-determination, other than to access services, food and goods for free. These are the people who care only about the here and now, not giving a damn about tomorrow, next year or the next generation.

Barack Obama has basically done nothing for blacks in America, other than release thousands of convicts from prison and coddle the New Black Panthers who feloniously intimidated white voters at the polls (2008) with impunity. Black communities are just as poor as the day Obama took office. The unemployment rate for young black men is at an all-timer high. Inner city violent crime is soaring out of control. Illegitimate babies are born every day by the thousands, with 77 percent of them growing up without fathers, leaving mothers to raise kids alone while sucking on taxpayers for survival. Older babies eventually become the caretakers and role models for the younger siblings, no matter their drug habits or criminal tendencies. Family mores are developed in the streets. Having a black president–*this* black president–accomplished nothing for blacks other than the ability to boast about his presidency.

Barack Obama has no interest in helping blacks in America. His only interest is in using them to advance his agenda.

Meanwhile, the Muslim Brotherhood goal line looms closer, thanks to ignorant voting blocs and brilliant campaign strategies on the part of our enemies. Sharia Islam is heading our way and by the time they actually root in, it may be too late. Unless there is a drastic change, very drastic, America will have lost identity as the home of the brave and the land of the free. The Constitution, unless appropriately amended, will be reduced to shreds, replaced by the Quran and a Sharia system of laws. Human rights, Constitutional rights and basic rights, will be relegated to a laughing matter. America, as we know it, will be nothing more than an era in history, much like we view ancient Rome or Greece. And if radical Islam has its way, by the 22nd century America will not even be recorded in any book, any archive or any museum. The radical Islamic holocaust will make the Nazi era look like a street fight.

This is the mosaic. The tiles, as this is assembled, form the picture and tell the undeniable story. This may not present sworn court testimony from which to cite. We may not have produced hard evidence that our president and his minions are, in reality, our enemy. However, there is something in the law called inference, from which the trier of fact is permitted to reach conclusions from known facts, facts that can only lead to one reasonable conclusion. This author may be seen by some as a right-wing crack pot. That's fine. But my conscience is clear, my conclusions are defensible and, sadly, critical. I have no doubts.

I base these conclusions just as I would assemble evidence and data in the hundreds of major crimes I investigated during thirty years with a major police agency. Sometimes, we absolutely knew the truth, but did not have that smoking gun, thus, the inability to prosecute, "beyond and to the exclusion of any reasonable doubt." But we still knew.

My regret would be if I had failed to share these points of view, because that would be like having failed my country. The matter is grave. Now is the time for Americans to make a difference. Not next month, not next year, not in ten years. We have nearly arrived at the point where it is too late.

I love this country. I love the people within. I love what our founders provided us from which we still prosper and live free 240 years later. As certain as this book has been written, I know that America has indeed been conquered, just as the enemy promised, *From Within!*

SEVENTEEN
WHAT CAN WE DO?

1. Read, Learn, and Be Aware.

The greatest asset for Jihadists is public ignorance. Most Americans do not really know what is going on and they don't want to know. Part of Jihadists grand plan includes many methods of propaganda by which to fool well-meaning people.

The most liberal of Americans tend to point out that the great majority of Muslims are peaceful. That may be true, but it does not matter. Those who are not peaceful cloak themselves in the costumes of peace, if only to gain our trust. And, as we learned in 1930's Germany, the violent minority will ultimately control the peaceful masses.

Read as many books and articles as possible on these topics, written by bona fide authorities and scholars. Listen for the truth, no matter the political parties and leanings.

2. It is better to be a living Islamophobe than a dead ignoramus. Be Islamophobic and do not worry about the label. The term was invented by the Muslim Brotherhood in order to capitalize on the labeling trends that commonly censure people, i.e. racists, misogynists, sexists, etc. I wrote this book because I am unapologetically Islamophobic. The Jihadists, who are ALL Islamic, scare the hell out of me.
3. Promote good relations and more prominence by Islamic followers who identify as "reform" Muslims. There is hope for peaceful coexistence if a growing number of Muslims would admit that the Quran is imperfect and that many of the hateful or violent verses should not be followed, much like we no longer follow wrongful verses in the Old Testament.

4. Hold politicians, colleges, schools, banks and other institutions accountable for all the money they are accepting from hard-core radical Islamic countries. These are a source of bribery to those who will sell their souls for riches.
5. Vote smart. Think outside the box, political parties be damned. All of our cherished resources are at risk if radical Islam gains more of a powerful foothold in the American government. The single most important issue in the voting booth must be immigration, legal and illegal, in order to limit or temporarily stop immigration from Muslim countries known to harbor fundamentalists. That would include a temporary ban on issuing visas until we can design a better method for vetting individuals with less risk to Americans.
6. Women must wake up. While women's organizations wave banners about government influence over birth control, a greater threat looms that will make those political issues utterly inane. Women's rights, in many respects, are at serious risk if Islam gains control of the free world. In many predominantly Islamic nations, women are treated as useful property, much like owning a camel. Husbands may beat their wives, as proscribed in the Quran. (Suras 4:34, 38:44)
7. Airport security: Stop wasting time with grannies in wheelchairs and obvious non-threats. Like Israel, profile, profile and profile, especially those who appear to come from the Middle-East or other Muslim-based countries. Secure baggage handlers and airline maintenance by tightening standards for hiring.
8. Pass more laws that better secure our nation's borders and fully enforce them as a national security issue. Beef up Border Patrol, ICE, and National Guard to act as the protectorates of American sovereignty.
9. Allow our federal and state law enforcement and intelligence agencies to monitor selected mosques that are suspected of

promoting anti-American hatred or support the Jihad movement. Assembling intelligence is essential to national security.

10. Stop treating Islam as though it was only a religion and accept the fact that it is also a government ideology. As long as Islam promotes the doctrines of Sharia and strives toward establishing laws in conflict with the US Constitution, it should be declared as dangerous to America as is the Ku Klux Klan, only its population is 1.5 billion people greater.)
11. Congress should declare radical Islam and the Muslim Brotherhood (and their off-shoot organizations) as an enemy of the United States, because they have declared war against the United States. Enact wartime restrictions to enemy representatives and personnel within the US. Terrorists and Islamic combat prisoners should be detained indefinitely at Guantanamo where vital intelligence can be garnered through effective interrogation methods.

In any conflict, the playing field must be level. A war cannot be won when the enemy is permitted greater advantages in weaponry and tactics. That's like giving one football team helmets and shoulder pads, and tee shirts and beanies to the other team.

12. Beef up all branches of the military to adequate numbers so that soldiers are not required to deploy four, five and six times to combat zones around the world. Replace old planes and ships with modern equipment. Political correctness in training should be halted immediately. If we do not appropriate adequate funds now for national security, it will be too late in five or ten more years.
13. Reach out to the youth to reestablish a sense of patriotism that once existed in America.
14. Readers of this book, and all Americans, should learn, know and study the Muslim Brotherhood manifestos known as "The Explanatory Memorandum for the Muslim Brotherhood in North America," and "The Project," both of which are provided at the end of this book as <u>Addendum One</u> and

Addendum Two. In doing so, folks will see how well the enemy has planned this war, then compare it to the stark realities of today to see the progress. Hopefully, Americans will realize this is not a fiction movie, it is not a right-wing conspiracy and it is not a product of imagination. It is as real as cancer, metastasizing around the world, especially into the land of the free.

We owe it to our children and grandchildren.

THE END

ADDENDUM 1.

An Explanatory Memorandum On the General Strategic Goal for the Group In North America
May, 22, 1991

Contents:

Northeast Intelligence Network
Investigating threats to our homeland
www.HomelandSecurityUS.comBate #ISE-SWI 1B1010000414

In the name of God, the Beneficent, the Merciful, Thanks be to God, Lord of the Two Worlds

And Blessed are the Pious

The beloved brother/The General Masul, may God keep him

The beloved brother/secretary of the Shura Council, may God keep him

The beloved brothers/Members of the Shura Council, may God keep them.

God's peace, mercy and blessings be upon you. To proceed,

I ask Almighty God that you, your families and those whom you love around you are in the best of conditions, pleasing to God, glorified His name be. I send this letter of mine to you hoping that it would seize your attention and receive your good care as you are the people of responsibility and those to whom trust is given. Between your hands is an "Explanatory Memorandum" which I put effort in writing down so that it is not locked in the chest and the mind, and so that I can share with you a portion of the responsibility in leading the Group in this country.

What might have encouraged me to submit the memorandum in this time in particular is my feeling of a "glimpse of hope" and the beginning of good tidings which bring the good news that we have embarked on a new stage of Islamic activism stages in this continent.

The papers which are between your hands are not abundant extravagance, imaginations or hallucinations which passed in the mind of one of your brothers, but they are rather hopes, ambitions and challenges that I hope that you share some or most of which with me. I do not claim their infallibility or absolute correctness, but they are an attempt which requires study, outlook, detailing and rooting from you.

My request to my brothers is to read the memorandum and to write what they wanted of comments and corrections, keeping in mind that what is between your hands is not strange or a new submission without a root, but rather an attempt to interpret and explain some of what came in the long-term plan which we approved and adopted in our council and our conference in the year (1987).

So, my honorable brother, do not rush to throw these papers away due to your many occupations and worries, All what I'm asking of you is to read them and to comment on them hoping that we might continue together the project of our plan and our Islamic work in this part of the world. Should you do that, I would be thankful and grateful to you.

I also ask my honorable brother, the Secretary of the Council, to add the subject of the memorandum on the Council agenda in its coming meeting. May God reward you good and keep you for His Daw'a.

Your brother, Mohammad Akram

In the name of God, the Beneficent, the Merciful Thanks be to God, Lord of the Two Worlds And Blessed are the Pious.

Subject: A project for an explanatory memorandum for the General Strategic goal for the Group in North America mentioned in the long-term plan

<u>One: The Memorandum is derived from:</u>

1 - The general strategic goal of the Group in America which was approved by the Shura Council and the Organizational Conference

for the year (I987) is "Enablement of Islam in North America, meaning: establishing an effective and a stable Islamic Movement led by the Muslim Brotherhood which adopts Muslims' causes domestically and globally, and which works to expand the observant Muslim base, aims at unifying and directing Muslims' efforts, presents Islam as a civilization alternative, and supports the global Islamic State wherever it is".

2- The priority that is approved by the Shura Council for the work of the Group in its current and former session which is "Settlement."

3- The positive development with the brothers in the Islamic Circle in an attempt to reach a unity of merger.

4- The constant need for thinking and future planning, an attempt to read it and working to "shape" the present to comply and suit the needs and challenges of the future.

5- The paper of his eminence, the General Masul, may God keep him, which he recently sent to the members of the Council.

<u>Two: An Introduction to the Explanatory Memorandum:</u>

- In order to begin with the explanation, we must "summon" the following question and place it in front of our eyes as its relationship is important and necessary with the strategic goal and the explanation project we are embarking on. The question we are facing is: "How do you like to see the Islam Movement in North America in ten years?", or "taking along" the following sentence when planning and working, "Islamic Work in North America in the year (2000): A Strategic Vision". Also, we must summon and take along "elements" of the general strategic goal of the Group in North America and I will intentionally repeat them in numbers. They are:

I- Establishing an effective and stable Islamic Movement led by the Muslim Brotherhood.

2- Adopting Muslims' causes domestically and globally.

3- Expanding the observant Muslim base.

4- Unifying and directing Muslim's efforts.

5- Presenting Islam as a civilization alternative

6- Supporting the establishment of the global Islamic State wherever it is.

- It must be stressed that it has become clear and emphatically known that all is in agreement that we must "settle" or "enable" Islam and its Movement in this part of the world.

- Therefore, a joint understanding of the meaning of settlement or enablement must be adopted, through which and on whose basis we explain the general strategic goal with its six elements for the Group in North America.

Three: The Concept of Settlement:

This term was mentioned in the Group's "dictionary" and documents with various meanings in spite of the fact that everyone meant one thing with it. We believe that the understanding of the essence is the same and we will attempt here to give the word and its "meanings" a practical explanation with a practical Movement tone, and not a philosophical linguistic explanation, while stressing that this explanation of ours is not complete until our explanation of "the process" of settlement itself is understood which is mentioned in the following paragraph. We briefly say the following:

Settlement: "That Islam and its Movement become a part of the homeland it lives in".

Establishment: "That Islam turns into firmly-rooted organizations on whose basis civilization, structure and testimony are built".

Stability: "That Islam is stable in the land on which its people move".

Enablement: "That Islam is enabled within the souls, minds and the lives of the people of the country in which it moves".

Rooting: "That Islam is resident and not a passing thing, or rooted "entrenched" in the soil of the spot where it moves and not a strange plant to it".

Four: The Process of Settlement:

- In order for Islam and its Movement to become "a part of the homeland" in which it lives, "stable" in its land, "rooted" in the spirits and minds of its people, "enabled" in the live of its society and has firmly-established "organizations" on which the Islamic structure is built and with which the testimony of civilization is achieved, the Movement must plan and struggle to obtain "the keys" and the tools of this process in carry out this grand mission as a "Civilization Jihadist" responsibility which lies on the shoulders of Muslims and—on top of them—the Muslim Brotherhood in this country. Among these keys and tools are the following:

1- **Adopting the concept of settlement and understanding its practical meanings:**

The Explanatory Memorandum focused on the Movement and the realistic dimension of the process of settlement and its practical meanings without paying attention to the difference in understanding between the resident and the non-resident, or who is the settled and the non-settled and we believe that what was mentioned in the long-term plan in that regards suffices.

2- **Making a fundamental shift in our thinking and mentality in order to suit the challenges of the settlement mission.**

What is meant with the shift—which is a positive expression - is responding to the grand challenges of the settlement issues. We believe that any transforming response begins with the method of thinking and its center, the brain, first. In order to clarify what is meant with the shift as a key to qualify us to enter the field of settlement, we say very briefly that the following must be accomplished:

- A shift from the partial thinking mentality to the comprehensive thinking mentality,
- A shift from the "amputated" partial thinking mentality to the "continuous" comprehensive mentality.
- A shift from the mentality of caution and reservation to the mentality of risk and controlled liberation.
- A shift from the mentality of the elite Movement to the mentality of the popular Movement
- A shift from the mentality of preaching and guidance to the mentality of building and testimony
- A shift from the single opinion mentality to the multiple opinion mentality.
- A shift from the collision mentality to the absorption mentality.
- A shift from the individual mentality to the team mentality.

- A shift from the anticipation mentality to the initiative mentality.

- A shift from the hesitation mentality to the decisiveness mentality.

- A shift from the principles mentality to the programs mentality.

- A shift from the abstract ideas mentality the true organizations mentality [This is the core point and the essence of the memorandum].

3- **Understanding the historical stages in which the Islamic Ikhwani activism went through in this country:**

The writer of the memorandum believes that understanding and comprehending the historical stages of the Islamic activism which was led and being led by the Muslim Brotherhood in this continent is a very important key in working towards settlement, through which the Group observes its march, the direction of its movement and the curves and turns of its road. We will suffice here with mentioning the title for each of these stages [The title expresses the prevalent characteristic of the stage] [Details maybe mentioned in another future study]. Most likely, the stages are:

A- The stage of searching for self and determining the identity.

B- The stage of inner build-up and tightening the organization.

C- The stage of mosques and the Islamic centers.

D- The stage of building the Islamic organizations—the first phase.

E- The stage of building the Islamic schools - the first phase.

F- The stage of thinking about the overt Islamic Movement - the first phase.

G- The stage of openness to the other Islamic movements and attempting to reach a formula for dealing with them—the first phase.

H- The stage of reviving and establishing the Islamic organizations - the second phase. We believe that the Group is embarking on this stage in its second phase as it has to open the door and enter as it did the first time.

4- **Understanding the role of the Muslim Brother in North America:**

The process of settlement is a "Civilization-Jihadist Process" with all the word means. The Ikhwan must understand that their work in America is a kind of grand Jihad in eliminating and destroying the Western civilization from within and "sabotaging" its miserable house by their hands and the hands of the believers so that it is eliminated and God's religion is made victorious over all other religions. Without this level of understanding, we are not up to this challenge and have not prepared ourselves for Jihad yet. It is a Muslim's destiny to perform Jihad and work wherever he is and wherever he lands until the final hour comes, and there is no escape from that destiny except for those who chose to slack. But, would the slackers and the Mujahedeen be equal.

5- **Understanding that we cannot perform the settlement mission by ourselves or away from people:**

A mission as significant and as huge as the settlement mission needs magnificent and exhausting efforts. With their capabilities, human, financial and scientific resources, the Ikhwan will not be able to carry out this mission alone or away from people and he who believes that is wrong, and God knows best. As for the role of the Ikhwan, it is the initiative, pioneering, leadership, raising the banner and pushing people in that direction. They are then to work to employ, direct and unify Muslims' efforts and powers for this process. In order to do that, we must possess a mastery of the art of "coalitions", the art of "absorption" and the principles of "cooperation".

6- **The necessity of achieving a union and balanced gradual merger between private work**

and public work:

We believe that what was written about this subject is many and is enough. But, it needs a time and a practical frame so that what is needed is achieved in a gradual and a balanced way that is compatible with the process of settlement.

7- **The conviction that the success of the settlement of Islam and its Movement in this country is a success to the global**

Islamic Movement and a true support for the sought-after state, God willing:

There is a conviction—with which this memorandum disagrees—that our focus in attempting to settle Islam in this country will lead to negligence in our duty towards the global Islamic Movement in supporting its project to establish the state. We believe that the reply is in two segments: One - The success of the Movement in America in establishing an observant Islamic base with power and effectiveness will be the best support and aid to the global Movement project. And the second - is the global Movement has not succeeded yet in "distributing roles" to its branches, stating what is needed from them as one of the participants or contributors to the project to establish the global Islamic state. The day this happens, the children of the American Ikhwani branch will have far-reaching impact and positions that make the ancestors proud.

8- **Absorbing Muslims and winning them with all of their factions and colors in America and Canada for the settlement project, and making it their cause, future and the basis of their Islamic life in this part of the world:**

This issues requires from us to learn "the art of dealing with the others," as people are different and people in many colors. We need to adopt the principle which says, "Take from people... the best they have", their best specializations, experiences, arts, energies and abilities. By people here we mean those within or without the ranks of individuals and organizations. The policy of "taking" should be with what achieves the strategic goal and the settlement process. But the big challenge in front of us is: how to connect them all in "the orbit" of our plan and "the circle" of our Movement in order to achieve "the core" of our interest. To me, there is no choice for us other than alliance and mutual understanding of those who desire from our religion and those who agree from our belief in work. And the U.S. Islamic arena is full of those waiting—the pioneers.

What matters is bringing people to the level of comprehension of the challenge that is facing us as Muslims in this country, conviction of our settlement project, and understanding the benefit of agreement, cooperation and alliance. At that time, if we ask for money, a lot of it would come, and if we ask for men, they would come in lines. What matters is that our plan is "the criterion and the balance" in our relationship with others. Here, two points must be noted. The first one we need to comprehend and understand the balance of the Islamic powers in the U.S. arena [and this might be the subject of a future study]. The second point: what we reached with the brothers in "ICNA" is considered a step in the right direction, the beginning of good and the first drop that requires growing and guidance.

9- **Re-examining our organizational and administrative bodies, the type of leadership and the method of selecting it with what suits the challenges of the settlement mission:**

The memorandum will be silent about details regarding this item even though it is logical and there is a lot to be said about it,

10- **Growing and developing our resources and capabilities, our financial and human resources with what suits the magnitude of the grand mission:**

If we examined the human and the financial resources the Ikhwan alone own in this country, we and others would feel proud and glorious. And if we add to them the resources of our friends and allies, those who circle in our orbit and those waiting on our banner, we would realize that we are able to open the door to settlement and walk through it seeking to make Almighty God's word the highest.

11- **Utilizing the scientific method in planning, thinking and preparation of studies needed for the process of settlement:**

Yes, we need this method, and we need many studies which aid in this civilization Jihadist operation. We will mention some of them briefly:

- The history of the Islamic presence in America.
- The history of the Islamic Ikhwani presence in America.
- Islamic movements, organizations and organizations: analysis and criticism.
- The phenomenon of the Islamic centers and schools: challenges, needs and statistics.

- Islamic minorities.

- Muslim and Arab communities.

- The U.S. society: make-up and politics.

- The U.S. society's view of Islam and Muslims ... And many other studies which we can direct our brothers and allies to prepare, either through their academic studies or through their educational centers or organizational tasking. What is important is that we start.

12- **Agreeing on a flexible, balanced and a clear "mechanism" to implement the process of settlement within a specific, gradual and balanced "time frame" that is in-line with the demands and challenges of the process of settlement.**

13- **Understanding the U.S. society from its different aspects and understanding that "qualifies" us to perform the mission of settling our Dawa' in its country "and growing it" on its land.**

14- **Adopting a written "jurisprudence" that includes legal and movement bases, principles, policies and interpretations which are suitable for the needs and challenges of the process of settlement.**

15- **Agreeing on "criteria" and balances to be a sort of "antennas" or "the watch tower" in order to make sure that all of our priorities, plans, programs, bodies, leadership, monies and activities march towards the process of the settlement.**

16- **Adopting a practical, flexible formula through which our central work complements our domestic work.** [Items 12 through 16 will be detailed later].

17- **Understanding the role and the nature of work of "The Islamic Center" in every city with what achieves the goal of the process of settlement:**

The center we seek is the one which constitutes the "axis" of our Movement, the "perimeter" of the circle of our work, our "balance center," the "base" for our rise and our "Dar al-Arqam" to educate us, prepare us and supply our battalions in addition to being the "niche" of our prayers.

This is in order for the Islamic center to turn - in action not in words - into a seed "for a small Islamic society" which is a reflection and a mirror to our central organizations. The center ought to turn into a "beehive" which produces sweet honey. Thus, the Islamic center would turn into a place for study, family, battalion, course, seminar, visit, sport, school, social club, women gathering, kindergarten for male and female youngsters, the office of the domestic political resolution, and the center for distributing our newspapers, magazines, books and our audio and visual tapes.

In brief we say: we would like for the Islamic center to become "The House of Dawa'" and "the general center" in deeds first before name. As much as we own and direct these centers at the continent level, we can say we are marching successfully towards the settlement of Dawa' in this country. Meaning that the "center's" role should be the same as the "mosque's" role during the time of God's prophet, God's prayers and peace be upon him, when he marched to "settle" the Dawa' in its first generation in Medina. From the mosque, he drew the Islamic life and provided to the world the most magnificent and fabulous civilization humanity knew. This mandates that, eventually, the region, the branch and the Usra turn into "operations rooms" for planning, direction, monitoring and leadership for the Islamic center in order to be a role model to be followed.

18- **Adopting a system that is based on "selecting" workers, "role distribution" and "assigning" positions and responsibilities is based on specialization, desire and need with what achieves the process of settlement and contributes to its success.**

19- **Turning the principle of dedication for the Masuls of main positions within the Group into a rule, a basis and a policy in work. Without it, the process of settlement might be stalled**

[Talking about this point requires more details and discussion].

20- **Understanding the importance of the "Organizational" shift in our Movement work, and doing Jihad in order to achieve it in the real world with what serves the process of settlement and expedites its results, God Almighty's willing:**

The reason this paragraph was delayed is to stress its utmost importance as it constitutes the heart and the core of this memorandum. It also constitutes the practical aspect and the true measure of our success or failure in our march towards settlement. The talk about the organizations and the "organizational" mentality or phenomenon does not require much detail. It suffices to say that the first pioneer of this phenomenon was our prophet Mohamed, God's peace, mercy and blessings be upon him, as he placed the foundation for the first civilized organization which is the mosque, which truly became "the comprehensive organization". And this was done by the pioneer of the contemporary Islamic Dawa', Imam martyr Hasan al-Banna, may God have mercy on him, when he and his brothers felt the need to "re-establish" Islam and its movement anew, leading him to establish organizations with all their kinds: economic, social, media, scouting, professional and even the military ones. We must say that we are in a country which understands no language other than the language of the organizations, and one which does not respect or give weight to any group without effective, functional and strong organizations.

It is good fortune that there are brothers among us who have this "trend," mentality or inclination to build the organizations who have beat us by action and words which leads us to dare say honestly what Sadat in Egypt once said, "We want to build a country of organizations"—a word of right he meant wrong with. I say to my brothers, let us raise the banner of truth to establish right "We want to establish the Group of organizations", as without it we will not able to put our feet on the true path.

- And in order for the process of settlement to be completed, we must plan and work from now to equip and prepare ourselves, our brothers, our apparatuses, our sections and our committees in order to turn into comprehensive organizations in a gradual and balanced way that is suitable with the need and the reality. What encourages us to do that—in addition to the aforementioned—is that we possess "seeds" for each organization from the organization we call for

- All we need is to tweak them, coordinate their work, collect their elements and merge their efforts with others and then connect them with the comprehensive plan we seek.

For instance, We have a seed for a "comprehensive media and art" organization: we own a print + advanced typesetting machine -t audio and visual center + art production office + magazines in Arabic and English [The Horizons, The Hope, The Politicians, Ila Falastine, Press Clips, al-Zaytouna, Palestine Monitor, Social Sciences Magazines.,.] + art band + photographers + producers + programs anchors +journalists + in addition to other media and art experiences".

Another example: We have a seed for a "comprehensive Dawa' educational" organization: We have the Daw'a section in ISNA + Dr. Jamal Badawi Foundation + the center run by brother Harned al-Ghazali + the Dawa' center the Dawa' Committee and brother Shaker al-Sayyed are seeking to establish now + in addition to other Daw'a efforts here and there...".

And this applies to all the organizations we call on establishing.

- The big challenge that is ahead of us is how to turn these seeds or "scattered" elements into comprehensive, stable, "settled" organizations that are connected with our Movement and which fly in our orbit and take orders from our guidance. This does not prevent - but calls for - each central organization to have its local branches but its connection with the Islamic center in the city is a must.

- What is needed is to seek to prepare the atmosphere and the means to achieve "the merger" so that the sections, the committees, the regions, the branches and the Usras are eventually the heart and the core of these organizations.

Or, for the shift and the change to occur as follows:

1 - The Movement Department + The Secretariat Department

2- Education Department + Dawa'a Com.

3- Sisters Department

4- The Financial Department + Investment Committee + The Endowment

5- Youth Department + Youths Organizations Department

6- The Social Committee + Matrimony Committee + Mercy Foundation

7- The Security Committee

8- The Political Depart. + Palestine Com.

9- The Group's Court + The Legal Com.

10- Domestic Work Department

11 - Our magazines + the print + our art band

12- The Studies Association + The Publication House + Dar al-Kitab

13- Scientific and Medial societies

14- The Organizational Conference

15- The Shura Council + Planning Corn.

16- The Executive Office

17- The General Masul

18- The regions, branches & Usras

- The Organizational & Administrative Organization - The General Center

- Dawa' and Educational Organization

- The Women's Organization

- The Economic Organization

- Youth Organizations

- The Social Organization

- The Security Organization

- The Political Organization

- The Judicial Organization

- Its work is to be distributed to the rest of the organizations

- The Media and Art Organization

- The Intellectual & Cultural Organization

- Scientific, Educational & Professional Organization

- The Islamic-American Founding Conference

- The Shura Council for the Islamic-American Movement

- The Executive Office of the Islamic-American Movement

- Chairman of the Islamic Movement and its official Spokesman

- Field leaders of organizations & Islamic centers

Five: **Comprehensive Settlement Organization:**

- We would then seek and struggle in order to make each one of these above-mentioned organizations a "comprehensive organization" throughout the days and the years, and as long as we are destined to be in this country. What is important is that we put the foundation and we will be followed by peoples and generations that would finish the march and the road but with a clearly-defined guidance. And, in order for us to clarify what we mean with the comprehensive, specialized organization, we mention here the characteristics and traits of each organization of the "promising" organizations.

1- **From the Dawa' and educational aspect [The Dawa' and Educational Organizational: to include:**

- The Organization to spread the Dawa' (Central and local branches).
- An institute to graduate Callers and Educators.
- Scholars, Callers, Educators, Preachers and Program Anchors,
- Art and communication technology, Conveyance and Dawa'.
- A television station.
- A specialized Dawa' magazine.
- A radio station.
- The Higher Islamic Council for Callers and Educators.
- The Higher Council for Mosques and Islamic Centers.
- Friendship Societies with the other religions ... and things like that.

2- **Politically (The Political Organization) to include:**

- A central political party.
- Local political offices.
- Political symbols.
- Relationships and alliances.
- The American Organization for Islamic Political Action
- Advanced Information Centers.. .and things like that.

3- **Media (The Media and Art Organization) to include:**

- A daily newspaper.
- Weekly, monthly and seasonal magazines.
- Radio stations.

- Television programs.
- Audio and visual centers.
- A magazine for the Muslim child.
- A magazine for the Muslim woman.
- Print and typesetting machines.
- A production office.
- A photography and recording studio
- Art bands for acting, chanting and theater.
- A marketing and art production office ... and things like that,

4- **Economically (The Economic Organization) to include:**

- An Islamic Central bank.
- Islamic endowments.
- Investment projects.
- An organization for interest-free loans .... and things like that.

5- **Scientifically and Professionally [The Scientific, Educational and Professional)**

Organizationı to include:

- Scientific research centers.
- Technical organizations and vocational training.
- An Islamic university.
- Islamic schools.
- A council for education and scientific research.
- Centers to train teachers.
- Scientific societies in schools.
- An office for academic guidance.
- A body for authorship and Islamic curricula.. . .and things like that.

6- **Culturally and Intellectually [The Cultural and Intellectual Organization) to include:**

- A center for studies and research.
- Cultural and intellectual foundations such as The Social Scientists, Society – Scientists, and Engineers Society.

- An organization for Islamic thought and culture.

- A publication, translation and distribution house for Islamic books.

- An office for archiving, history and authentication.

- The project to translate the Noble Quran, the Noble Sayings .... and things like that.

7- **Socially (The Social-Charitable Organization)-to include:**

- Social clubs for the youths and the community's sons and daughters.

- Local societies for social welfare and the services are tied to the Islamic centers.

- The Islamic Organization to Combat the Social Ills of the US Society.

- Islamic houses project.

- - Matrimony and family cases office .... and things like that.

8- **Youths (The Youth Organization) to include:**

- Central and local youths foundations.

- Sports teams and clubs.

- Scouting teams .... and things like that.

9- **Women (The Women Organization) to include:**

- Central and local women societies.

- Organizations of training, vocational and housekeeping.

- An organization to train female preachers.

- Islamic kindergartens ... and things like that.

10- **Organizationally and Administratively (The Administrative and Organizational**

Organization) to include:

- An institute for training, growth, development and planning

- Prominent experts in this field.

- Work systems, bylaws and charters fit for running the most complicated bodies and organizations.

- A periodic magazine in Islamic development and administration.

- Owning camps and halls for the various activities.

- A data, polling and census bank.

- An advanced communication network.

- An advanced archive for our heritage and production ... and things like that.

11- **Securitv (The Securitv Organization) to include:**

- Clubs for training and learning self-defense techniques.

- A center which is concerned with the security issues (Technical, intellectual, technological and Human)...and things like that.

12- **Legallv (The Legal Organization) to include:**

- A Central Jurisprudence Council.

- A Central Islamic Court.

- Muslim Attorneys Society.

- The Islamic Foundation for Defense of Muslims' Rights...and things like that.

And success is by God.

A list of our organizations and the organizations of our friends.

(Imagine if they all march according to one plan!)

1- ISNA = ISLAMIC SOCIETY OF NORTH AMERICA

2- MSA = MUSLIM STUDENTS' ASSOCIATION

3- MCA = THE MUSLIM COMMUNITIES ASSOCIATION

4- AMSS = THE ASSOCIATION OF MUSLIM SOCIAL SCIENTISTS

5- AMSE = THE ASSOCIATION OF MUSLIM SCIENTISTS AND ENGINEERS

6- IMA = ISLAMIC MEDICAL ASSOCIATION

7- ITC = ISLAMIC TEACHING CENTER

8- NAIT = NORTH AMERICAN ISLAMIC TRUST

9- FID = FOUNDATION FOR INTERNATIONAL DEVELOPMENT

10- IHC = ISLAMIC HOUSING COOPERATIVE

11- ICD = ISLAMIC CENTERS DIVISION

12- ATP = AMERICAN TRUST PUBLICATIONS

13- AVC = AUDIO VISUAL CENTER

14- IBS = ISLAMIC BOOK SERVICE

15- MBA = MUSLIM BUSINESSMEN ASSOCIAATION

16- MYNA = MUSLIM YOUTH OF NORTH AMERICA

17- IFC = ISNA FIQH COMMITTEE
18- IPAC = ISNA POLITICAL AWARENESS COMMITTEE
19- IED = ISLAMIC EDUCATION DEPARTMENT
20- MAYA = MUSLIM ARAB YOUTH ASSOCIATION
21- MISG = MALASIAN [sic] ISLAMIC STUDY GROUP
22- IAP = ISLAMIC ASSOCIATION FOR PALESTINE
23- UASR = UNITED ASSOCIATION FOR STUDIES AND RESEARCH
24- OLF = OCCUPIED LAND FUND
25- MIA = MERCY INTERNATIONAL ASSOCIATION
26- ISNA = ISLAMIC CIRCLE OF NORTH AMERICA
27- BMI = BAITUL MAL INC
28- IIIT = INTERNATIONAL INSTITUTE FOR ISLAMIC THOUGHT
29- IIC = ISLAMIC INFORMATION CENTER

A full text of the Explanatory Memorandum document is easily accessed at various sites on line, in Arabic and in English.

Included among them:

http://www.investigativeproject.org/documents/20-an-explanatory-memorandum-on-the-general.pdf

ADDENDUM 2

The Muslim Brotherhood "Project"

This document was recovered in a raid by Swiss authorities in November 2001, two months after the horror of 9/11. Since that time information about this document, known in counterterrorism circles as "The Project", and discussion regarding its content has been limited to the top-secret world of Western intelligence communities. Only through the work of an intrepid Swiss journalist, Sylvain Besson of *Le Temps*, and his book published in October 2005 in France, *La conquête de l'Occident: Le projet secret des Islamistes* (*The Conquest of the West: The Islamists' Secret Project*), has information regarding "The Project" been made public

Discovery of "The Project" occurred during the raid of a luxurious villa in Campione, Switzerland on November 7, 2001. The target of the raid was Youssef Nada, director of the Al-Taqwa Bank of Lugano, who has had active association with the Muslim Brotherhood for more than 50 years and who admitted to being one of the organization's international leaders

Included in the documents seized during the raid of Nada's Swiss villa was a 14-page plan written in Arabic and dated December 1, 1982, which outlines a 12-point strategy to *"establish an Islamic government on earth"*—identified as "The Project." According to testimony given to Swiss authorities by Nada, the unsigned document was prepared by "Islamic researchers" associated with the Muslim Brotherhood.

The following tactics and techniques are among the many recommendations made in *The Project*:

- Networking and coordinating actions between likeminded Islamist organizations;

- Avoiding *open* alliances with known terrorist organizations and individuals to maintain the appearance of "moderation";
- Infiltrating and taking over existing Muslim organizations to realign them towards the Muslim Brotherhood's collective goals;
- Using deception to mask the intended goals of Islamist actions, as long as it doesn't conflict with *Sharia* law;
- Avoiding social conflicts with Westerners locally, nationally or globally, that might damage the long-term ability to expand the Islamist powerbase in the West or provoke a lash back against Muslims;
- Establishing financial networks to fund the work of conversion of the West, including the support of full-time administrators and workers;
- Conducting surveillance, obtaining data, and establishing collection and data storage capabilities;
- Putting into place a watchdog system for monitoring Western media to warn Muslims of "international plots fomented against them";
- Cultivating an Islamist intellectual community, including the establishment of think-tanks and advocacy groups, and publishing "academic" studies, to legitimize Islamist positions and to chronicle the history of Islamist movements;
- Developing a comprehensive 100-year plan to advance Islamist ideology throughout the world;
- Balancing international objectives with local flexibility;
- Building extensive social networks of schools, hospitals and charitable organizations dedicated to Islamist ideals so that contact with the movement for Muslims in the West is constant;
- Involving ideologically committed Muslims in democratically-elected institutions on all levels in the West, including government, NGOs, private organizations and labor unions;
- Instrumentally using existing Western institutions until they can be converted and put into service of Islam;

- Drafting Islamic constitutions, laws and policies for eventual implementation;
- Avoiding conflict within the Islamist movements on all levels, including the development of processes for conflict resolution;
- Instituting alliances with Western "progressive" organizations that share similar goals;
- Creating autonomous "security forces" to protect Muslims in the West;
- Inflaming violence and keeping Muslims living in the West "in a *jihad* frame of mind";
- Supporting *jihad* movements across the Muslim world through preaching, propaganda, personnel, funding, and technical and operational support;
- Making the Palestinian cause a global wedge issue for Muslims;
- Adopting the total liberation of Palestine from Israel and the creation of an Islamic state as a keystone in the plan for global Islamic domination;
- Instigating a constant campaign to incite hatred by Muslims against Jews and rejecting any discussions of conciliation or coexistence with them;
- Actively creating *jihad* terror cells within Palestine;
- Linking the terrorist activities in Palestine with the global terror movement;
- Collecting sufficient funds to indefinitely perpetuate and support jihad around the world;

"The Project" was drafted in 1982 when current tensions and terrorist activities in the Middle East were still in early stages.

Access to the text of this document is available on line at several sites, including: http://www.investigativeproject.org/documents/misc/687.pdf

ABOUT THE AUTHOR

Marshall Frank is a retired police captain/homicide detective from Miami-Dade, Florida where he spent thirty years in various capacities of law enforcement, including sixteen years in Homicide and another five years in charge of CSI. He was also called to testify before the U.S. Congress regarding the problems of violent crime in America.

He is now the author of fourteen published books, including six suspense novels, one book of short stories, five books of non-fiction essays, one memoir and a how-to publication for beginning authors.

More than one thousand of his essays and editorials have been published in numerous magazines and newspapers, including a thousand articles in his blog site which span the spectrum from politics to music to movie reviews.

He is also a former symphony violinist and head of a non-profit organization that advocates for musical prodigies Frank holds a Bachelor's Degree in Criminal Justice from Florida International University.
His wife, Suzanne, is a sculpture artist.

For more information please visit:

www.marshallfrank.com
www.EverlyBooks.com
www.everlybookspublishing.com

Made in the USA
Columbia, SC
02 June 2017